Service Management

Service Management

Strategy and Leadership in Service Business

Third Edition

Richard Normann

JOHN WILEY & SONS, LTD

Chichester · New York · Weinheim · Brisbane · Singapore · Toronto

Other Wiley Editorial Offices

John Wiley & Sons, Inc., 605 Third Avenue,
New York, NY 10158-0012, USA

WILEY-VCH Verlag GmbH, Pappelallee 3
D-69469 Weinheim, Germany

Jacaranda Wiley Ltd, 33 Park Road, Milton,
Queensland 4064, Australia
a
John Wiley & Sons (Asia) Pte Ltd, 2 Clementi Loop #02-01,
Jin Xing Distripark, Singapore 129809

John Wiley & Sons (Canada) Ltd, 22 Worcester Road,
Rexdale, Ontario M9W 1L1, Canada

British Library Cataloguing in Publication Data

A catalogue record for this book is available from the British Library

ISBN 0–471–49439–9

Typeset in 11/13pt Times by Dorwyn Ltd, Rowlands Castle, Hants.
Printed and bound in Great Britain by Biddles Ltd, Guildford and King's Lynn
This book is printed on acid-free paper responsibly manufactured from sustainable forestry, in which at least two trees are planted for each one used for paper production.

Contents

About the Author   ix
Acknowledgements to the second edition   xi
Preface to the second edition   xv
Preface to the third edition   xvii

1 The myth and reality of a service society   1
Are we moving towards a service society?—An
interpretation of the macro trends—New ideas
about manufacturing companies—The
industrialization of services—The positioning of
this book—The status problem of the service
industries—Internationalization—Is the
management of services different from
manufacturing management?—The moment of
truth—Personality intensity

2 The new economic equation   24
The substance of innovation—The driving forces
for innovation—Results come from customer
relationships—The knowledge explosion—
Service loading—Relationing—Broadening—
Unbundling and re-bundling—Enabling and
relieving

3 Service management systems   46
Introduction—Product, production and
production system—Service systems as innovative

linkages between human capacities—Client
management and client participation—
Management, structure and culture—Effective
service systems are reproducible—Service
management systems

4 Dynamic diagnosis: virtuous circles and vicious circles 61
Mechanisms behind the circles—The ecology of
microcircles and macrocircles—The moment of
truth: the microcircle—The macrocircle—The
'internal service' circle—Relationships between
three levels—Circle or spiral—A comment on
concepts

5 The service concept 75
The service package: core and peripherals—The
composition of the package—Four important
ingredients of a service package—The service
concept and the service delivery system

6 Why strategic human resource development? 89
The personnel idea: the key to the service delivery
system—Definition of the idea—Blocked social
mobility—Blocked professional career ladders—
The energy of a life-stage transition—People who
have 'fallen between two stools'—Complements
to basic careers—Emancipation from unrewarding
environments—Ideas of temporary personnel: a
common phenomenon—Business problems solved
by focused ideas of personnel—Personnel ideas
may need to change—The personnel idea as a
tool for business improvement—The moral
dilemma

7 Getting people to grow 106
Training—The goals of training—Tailored
training programs—Follow-up and
reinforcement—Job design and role design—
Career design—Personnel: summary

8 The client as customer—the client as coproducer   115
Client participation in service operations—
Relieving logics and enabling logics—Making the
client productive—Creating customers—Market
segmentation—Individualising services

9 Technology, tools and setting   135
The power of information technology—Cost
rationalization—More effective quality control—
Making higher quality possible—Closer link-up
with the customer—Technology and design as a
factor affecting behaviour—The Internet and the
future—Introducing new technology

10 Image   149
Image as a management tool—What makes the
image?—Functions and target groups—Internal
marketing

11 The art and science of pricing   161
Why is pricing difficult?—The philosophy behind
pricing as a management tool—Typical elements
in pricing strategies—Pricing strategy and pricing
tactics

12 Creating, reproducing and refining business ideas   169
The business lifecycle—Reproduction—
Redefinition and continuous development

13 Diversification and internationalization   181
The delicate balance of the service management
system—Some diversification strategies—
Internationalization of services in a macro
perspective

14 Quality   197
Two basic philosophies—A systems view—
Starting from the moment of truth—Designing
quality into the service management system—
Quality, cost and profitability—Common reasons

for failure in quality management—Some points
to consider in setting up a quality program

15   Culture and dominating ideas as management tools   214
The origins and functions of culture—'New
culture' companies

16   Change and leadership   221
Diagnosis and overall intervention strategy—
Boosting efficiency and the quality of operations
(the 'industrial model')—Culture shock and
'lift'—Development of the service management
system: a structural approach—Strategic growth—
Leaders and leadership styles—Transforming the
vicious circle into a virtuous one: the role of
management

References   229

Index   231

About the author

Richard Normann is Group Chairman of SMG. He received his PhD from the University of Lund where he held a temporary professorship in parallel with his work as a consultant. He was President of the Scandinavian Institutes for Administrative Research (SIAR) before founding the Service Management Group (SMG) in 1980. He lives in Paris.

Richard Normann works as a management consultant on corporate and strategic business development mainly in Europe and the United States. Recently Richard Normann has also worked on national competitiveness at the country and regional level. Another important current emphasis is on health care systems.

Through his consultancy work he has been involved in major consulting assignments in the United States, Japan, Australia, the Arab world and Europe, as well as acting as a visiting researcher to the Harvard Business School.

In 1983 Richard Normann published the world's first book presenting an integrated framework on the management of service producing companies.

SMG reflects Dr Normann's interests in strategic change and business development in service- and knowledge-oriented organizations.

Acknowledgements to the Second Edition

The first impulse to write this book came in 1977 when I had the opportunity to conduct a multiclient study for about 20 Scandinavian service businesses on the specific management issues in services. The project, which was reported in 1979, clearly demonstrated that there were a number of important commonalities to the seemingly wide variety of participants (from cleaning via insurance to project management and venture capital services, to name just a few) which the participants felt were lacking in existing publications and courses on management. The project also gave me the opportunity to scan the emerging academic knowledge across the world, as well as to identify those companies which seemed to be most advanced in conceiving of principles of managing a service business and putting them into practice.

Apart from the group that I represented, which had a basically organization theory and business strategy background (if labels are necessary) there were two major centres of knowledge development at the time. One was the Harvard Business School, represented particularly by Earl Sasser and Daryl Wyckoff, the background of which was manufacturing strategy and which had been led into investigating the management of services more closely by the default of traditional manufacturing strategy models for producing intangible 'goods'. I want to thank them for their inspiration in the form of many articles and good discussions.

The second major group, unexpectedly, was French. At the Université d'Aix Marseille, Pierre Eiglier and Eric Langeard had come to approach services from a marketing background.

Together with them and some other colleagues, all curious about services and all ready for a career shift, we formed the Service Management Group (SMG) in 1980.

Many of the ideas of this book therefore are a result of teamwork in our Group. One of the basic models of the book, the Service Management System, results from an amalgamation of two frameworks. One is from an earlier book of mine, *Management for Growth* (1977) in which the themes of 'the business idea' (consisting of the market segment, the product, the production system and inner organizational arrangements) and the concept of organizational culture (dominating ideas) were prominent. The second is the service system, or 'magic formula', as described by Eiglier and Langeard in several publications, combining the ideas of market segment, service concept, delivery system, and image. Adding the concept of image to my earlier framework, and the concept of culture to that of Eiglier and Langeard, creates the synthesis of the Service Management System.

The second major impact on my thinking about services comes from Michel Crozier, whose own research into innovation reinforced many of my initial ideas about the nature of effective service systems and creative human capacity management. Together we have had many discussions about social innovation, and yet I feel we have only begun to scratch the surface.

A third crucial influence—much of it inspiring the changes in the second edition—comes from internal development work in SMG during the last few years. In a project where Bengt Haikola was my closest collaborator we developed a number of ideas about offering (service and product) design and strategies in the financial service sector. Another international multiclient project, 'Business Logics for Innovators', attempted to develop a new strategic framework for the 1990s, and strong influences from this work (reported in a book with Rafael Ramirez) can be found in the substantially reworked first two chapters of the second edition. I am deeply indebted to Rafael Ramirez for these contributions and for his partnership.

But many others inside or associated with the SMG sphere have helped substantially in elaborating the framework: Henrik Fock, Anders Brogren, Kaj Storbacka, Denis Boyle, Sigurd Lilienfeldt, Frank af Petersens, Gianfranco Piantoni, and Uffe B. Johansen, to name but a few. Many of the ideas from the second chapter were developed in *The Dance of the Invaders*, which I wrote with Johan Cederwall, Lars Edgren, and Anders Holst in 1989. And without the help and encouragement of my secretary and assistant Lillemor Fagerberg-Ask the second edition would not have materialized.

My general views of management, business development and change have also been influenced by working together with (in some cases several years ago) Chris Argyris, Erik Johnsen, Manfred Kets de Vries, Eric Rhenman and Lena Sonkin.

The most inspiring influence, though, has come from a number of ambitious and demanding clients of insight with whom my colleagues and I have been fighting on the barricades—to solve acute problems and even achieve more or less drastic turn-arounds, and to develop new ideas and innovative business strategies. They will remain unnamed. Throughout I have chosen to illustrate principles with real examples, sometimes rather elaborate ones. In some cases I have used generally known companies, some of which represent clients and others not. In other cases I have chosen to anonymize examples from client companies.

Figures 3.1 and 12.1 were originally prepared at the Scandinavian Institutes for Administrative Research in a project under my leadership on 'Development Strategies for Swedish Service Knowledge, (1978) before being published in Arndt and Friman's (1981) anthology of services. Table 1. 1 also draws on the same report.

Nancy Adler reviewed my English and provided invaluable comments for the first edition of the book.

In the final editing of the second edition Wayne Tebb has been an invaluable partner. He has reviewed the whole manuscript, particularly in view of the North American audience, and he has made innumerable inputs. He has also substantially influenced the largely rewritten chapter on technology. My deepest thanks go to him for his involvement and contributions.

My warm thanks to all of the above. And I also want to extend my deep gratitude to my wife Astrid and my children, Anja and Torvald, all of them wonderful partners, and who have put up with the severe international travelling schedule, which has made it possible for me to gather the experiences necessary to write this book.

La Celle Saint Cloud, France, November 1990

Preface to the Second Edition

This book brings together experiences from several years of research and consultation at top management level with service producing businesses.

The idea that the management of service businesses, and the design of effective service systems, is in many ways unique and must apply principles which are not covered by established management know-how began to be generally recognized in the late 1970s. In 1980 I was able to bring together a number of people of different nationalities to form a consulting company, the Service Management Group (now SIFO Management Group), with the aim of being in the front line in developing a cohesive framework as well as concrete techniques for management, business development and design of effective service systems. This book, which is only a beginning, reports some of our preliminary ideas.

The framework that is presented is fairly comprehensive and therefore, of necessity, superficial in many areas. Knowledge about service management moves ahead rapidly, and writing this book represents a step in that process. However, we have found that the overall framework as such, as well as a number of the individual concepts, have often been extremely powerful in influencing the mode of thinking of business managers and the course of events in their companies.

The main target group for the book is high-level executives in organizations whose 'products' have a high service and knowledge content.

Although of course every industry has its own specific characteristics and logic we have found that the ideas presented tend to be relevant to all service—and knowledge—intensive organizations, independently of their particular business. Maintenance services, hospitality services, financial services, professional services, airlines, and research organizations are only a few of the industries where we have worked and applied the framework with success.

There is increasing evidence that manufacturing organizations turn to service companies and service management know-how for new ideas. We have seen examples of product businesses finding quite new perspectives on their own situation by beginning to think of themselves as service organizations with, so far, a high degree of tangible elements to their services.

This second edition has been thoroughly reviewed and reworked. The basic ideas and models are the same—such as the 'moment of truth', the 'positive and vicious circles', and the 'service management system', which seem to have become household concepts in business and academic circles around the world.

The changes to the second edition are substantial and numerous, however. Sections on the role of information technology have been enlarged (and the corresponding chapter has been much developed), as has the case of McKesson. Sections on pricing have been amplified and collected in a separate chapter. The first and second chapters have been substantially rewritten and many new ideas have been added. This reflects the broader perspective of the 'service economy' (as opposed to the more narrow idea of the 'production of intangibles') emerging out of the work that our group has been involved in during the last few years.

The book has been written primarily with business organizations in mind but we find an increasing level of interest from public organizations, political organizations, and other non-profit-making organizations. This is encouraging, since particularly in most Western European countries so much of the service sector is presently being taken care of by such organizations and since in our opinion they will need to rethink both their management principles and service system design principles if we are to solve the imminent quality and cost crisis. Out of necessity this will be an area of deep change in the next 10 years.

Finishing this book feels like something of a liberation—we can now move straight on to the next stage of development of service management knowledge.

Preface to the Third Edition

Service Management—Strategy and Leadership in Service Business was first published in 1983. A second, updated edition appeared in 1991. The basic framework and concepts remained, but the book was updated particularly in view of the increasing role of information technology in services.

The book is still read by many managers in its 10 or so different language editions. Likewise, it continues to be standard fare for students at a number of universities and business schools. Several people have asked me for another slight brushing up of the book, still without compromising the fundamental framework. Here it is.

There were two purposes with this revision. One was to—again—stay in touch with new technological developments including the Internet era. So the chapter on technology has been revised with a number of new examples. On the other hand I have abstained from trying to make these revisions very deep and from trying to stay on top of all these developments. Frankly, one reason is that however much I would try, there would still be more modern and flashy examples before the book came off the printing presses. Those interested in the impact of new technology have a multitude of other sources; I cannot and do not intend to try to compete with those.

The other purpose has been to use a few more modern examples and take out some oldish ones. Again, this has been done with some caution. If there is an original example or story which is as relevant today—which, in fact, could just as well have happened today—I have not seen any reason to change it. And even if the superb restaurant Troigros (which maintains its three stars in the *Guide Michelin*) has changed its physical layout to some extent I have kept the old text, since the same basic mechanisms are at work today as 15 years ago.

In fact, the most important change probably is a reconfiguration of the content of the book.

Early on I introduce the metaphor of 'the moment of truth' which I wrote about extensively in other contexts in the late 1970s. I then introduce the notion of the service management system with its five components—the targeted customers, the service concept, the delivery system, the image, and the culture and dominating ideas. It is recognized that there has to be a fit between these various elements. But instead of then going on to describe each of these elements, as in previous editions, I have moved forward the section on the dynamic interrelationship between them, expressed as the existence of 'virtuous' versus 'vicious' circles.

I think the book has gained considerably in readability as a result of this. Introducing this mode of dynamic analysis and diagnosis of how things can go right or wrong first gives a better backdrop to the analysis of the various elements of the service management system than the original sequence which left the dynamic analysis to the end.

There are plenty of small adjustments here and there, and even the correction of a logical inconsistency that I discovered upon rereading the book. (I realized that I had confused, to some extent, the two ideas of peripheral services and of quality standards, in describing the service concept.)

But having said this the book remains essentially the same. I actually do not think that it would be possible for me to make a really deep revision; that would be another book (which at this moment I am close to finishing).

Whereas a process of recognizing and focusing on the particularities of managing services—as opposed to industry and manufacturing—was at the roots of *Service Management* at its birth, the macro context of business is different today. At that time I think there was a real need to emphasize the distinction—indeed, to over-emphasize it for pedagogical reasons. And for those who run certain types of businesses the special characteristics of companies we used to think of as being in the 'service sector' are still very relevant.

But it is now well over 10 years since I discarded the notion of distinguishing services as a particular *sector* in society, producing intangibles. Rather, we may talk about a service *logic*, the basic premise of which is that it is not the delivery of a product (tangible or not) but rather the support of customers' value-creating processes that is the battlefield for companies. And in this sense what we used to think of as manufacturing industry must adapt to this service logic. So the sector classification is no longer meaningful; what is meaningful is to understand the new logic. This was already a theme in the foreword of the second edition of this book. A really thorough rewriting of the present book would clearly force me to take this intellectual position and would therefore constitute a totally different book.

But, again, within its slightly more limited scope *Service Management* is about as relevant as ever.

I want to thank many people, including Professor Birgitta Wadell at the University of Stockholm, for valuable inputs and comments. Peter Nõu and Eskil Ullberg have helped me with the section on new technology. Svante Leijon has read the old book and suggested many editing points for this edition. Kristina Boman, who has assisted me for many years, has worked through the manuscript and done the final editing, supplying many helpful suggestions in that process.

Deep thanks to them all, and to many of my friends and colleagues whom I have not mentioned but who have directly and indirectly influenced this book.

La Celle Saint Cloud, France, September 2000

1

The myth and reality of service society

ARE WE MOVING TOWARDS A SERVICE SOCIETY?

The trends are suggestive. The most highly developed nations, such as the United States and the Scandinavian countries, have experienced a change in the basic structure of their economic activities, and some two-thirds of their gross national product already derives from non-agricultural and non-industrial operations. Regardless of how we define these terms, the trend seems clear.

But trends and figures can be deceptive, both in their historical interpretation and in their implications for the future. Looking back, several considerations should be taken into account. First, to some extent we are simply looking at illusory tricks of the art of accounting. When a housewife sends her children to nursery school so that she can take a job with a big cleaning company (one of whose clients may be the nursery school), the accountant can point proudly at an increase in economic activity; but what has really happened is that certain activities which were previously performed outside the marketplace have now come into the market and have therefore appeared in the books. So to some extent what we are now experiencing is a reorganization of existing services rather than the emergence of new ones.

Secondly, the rise of the service sector has become possible largely as a result of increasing effectiveness in the goods-producing sector. There is a close parallel here with an earlier historical 'wave': the shift from agriculture to industrial manufacture became possible because of the enormous increase in agricultural productivity, which left people free to do other things. But there is a complex mutual interrelationship here; the increase in agricultural productivity was in large measure a result of progress in industry, with the development of more efficient farming machinery. And now, unless productivity in the manufacturing sector continues to grow, we cannot afford an increase in the service sector.

Looking forward, we know of course that trends cannot continue indefinitely. Development goes on, but in other combinations among economic sectors. Campaigns for 'reindustrialization' are gaining ground, and engineering and the natural sciences have been proclaimed as professions of the future. In the European economies there is a growing recognition of the problems with the welfare state. Lack of resources in the public sector has led to the private production of services in health care and education, for example. Another contributing cause has been the desire of certain groups of citizens for greater freedom of choice.

This should serve as a memento for us to be cautious in relating official figures of GNP per capita to the real standard of living. It is by no means certain that transferring childcare from families to institutions, or substituting institutional health care for self-care activities in the family, represents a real rather than a formal increase in the value production of society. Similarly, in those countries where the informal economy performs a large share of the value-producing activities (it is not uncommon to encounter estimates of 25% of GNP for a country like Italy), the GNP per capita figures typically underestimate the standard of living of such societies.

Thirdly, what is accounted for as 'services' rather than, say, 'manufacturing' may vary substantially. For example, from one year to another, companies like the RCA Corporation were moved from the Fortune Industry 500 to the Fortune Service 500 because it had been acquired by what had previously been considered a service company. But a company like IBM, where a very small proportion of the jobs are in 'manufacturing', remained in the Industry 500. Recognizing that the boundary was becoming increasingly unclear, Fortune—which in 1984 (at last!) had acknowledged the existence of the service society by establishing a separate 'Service 500'—merged the two lists some 10 years later.

In the following pages we will make a brief analysis of what is happening—and this at two different levels. First we will look at things from a macro point of view, and then we will interpret the macro data and tentatively explain them in terms of a distinctive shift that is now taking place in the nature of value production in society.

AN INTERPRETATION OF THE MACRO TRENDS

According to a study by FA-Rådet in Sweden (the Swedish Council for Management and Work Life Issues) the evolution of employment in society is the following:

Active labour force in Sweden (%)			
	Agriculture	Manufacturing	Services
1870	73	12	5
1900	61	24	9
1950	21	34	42
1980	6	23	71
1990	5	21	75
2000	4	17	79

Source: I framtidens kölvatten (In the Wake of the Future), H. de Geer *et al.*, Liber 1985

Likewise, proponents of the arrival of a service society will get support for their ideas by looking at other statistics. For example, out of the 100 largest companies in the world which were started in the 1960s and 1970s, 56 were in pure services, another eight were in services where some tangible product was part of the service (and this includes hamburger chains!). The remaining third was dominated by high tech companies particularly in the information industry, such as Apple, Compaq, and so forth (ESIF data). The 'service wave' as a phenomenon becomes even more persuasive when we consider that between 80% and 85% of information technology products are sold to the service sector and the remainder to the manufacturing sector.

To better illustrate the dynamics of change we will introduce the following framework (Figure 1.1). A matrix with the inherent

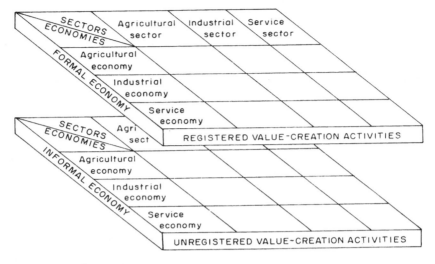

Figure 1.1 Sectoral matrix

natural agricultural, industrial and service economies along one
dimension is compared with the classical economic sectors of agriculture, industry and services. All activities which contribute to
productive value are by definition in one of the three economies.

- The 'agricultural economy' is all those 'agricultural activities'
  related to the basic production of foodstuffs from the soil and
  similar activities.
- The 'industrial economy' comprises the 'industrial activities' in
  which the main focus is on transforming physical materials into
  tangible products.
- The 'service economy' consists of 'service activities' which are
  brought to bear on physical objects, human subjects, information or institutional entities in such a way that these are somehow influenced without being physically transformed; or where
  the focus is on the *use* and *functioning* of the objects which are
  subject to the activities rather than on the physical transformation of them.

Sectors are an arbitrary convention used to record activities
within an economy, and the transactions between economies. Accountants and economists assign a value to such transactions and

make determinations as to the sectors in which they should be credited. As subsequent examples will show, the sector record is often an imperfect representation of real economic activity. The 'sector' convention, of course, was once introduced as a reflection of what was then—probably usefully and appropriately—perceived as an inherent difference between types of activities. What we suggest is that the nature of economic activities has now changed to the extent that the sector convention is superfluous.

In order to understand more fully the impact of services we have to add another dimension, a second plane, to our framework which differentiates between the formal and the informal economy. The matrix in Figure 1.1 allows us to examine the 'official' or formal economy, that which officially is deemed to be a part of the GNP. However, a significant contribution to the process of 'production of value' is made by activities outside the official economy which are not recorded or assigned value. These contributions of the informal economy include unpaid work in the home, barter, and volunteer effort, be it helping friends or organized group efforts.

Let us now look at some of the dynamics within this three-dimensional matrix.

The 'formal–informal' dimension does not necessarily relate to some imagined 'real value' for society and for citizens. If a parent places his/her young child in a daycare facility, the service activity has moved from the informal economy to the formal economy. Similarly, if a family which is caring for an elderly relative in the home places him or her in a care facility for the elderly, the service has merely been transferred to the 'formal' economy.

Traditionally the agricultural economy was constructed of a multitude of largely self-sufficient economic units operating within the informal economy; i.e. most transactions from production to consumption occurred within a unit of production, the small family farm. Industrial society, with its physical, temporal, and functional separation and specialization of activities, created a profound shift. There was an explosion of transactions taking place between units of production rather than within units of production. The formal economy is largely a function of the differentiated and specialized economy in which different units fulfil different functions which are interdependent and require transactions. With the coming of industrial society, an increasing proportion of the production of value within the agricultural economy shifted from the informal to the formal dimension. And the increasing interdependencies between the industrial economy and the agricultural economy resulted in both an increase in the production of value, owing to mechanization, and an increase in transactions amongst the units of production within the agricultural and industrial economies.

It is clear that the agricultural sector moved into the industrial economy in the developed countries a long time ago.

My brother is a farmer, and looking at his farm I can hardly imagine a more rapid and decisive process of industrialization. Investments are enormous, specialization high, and the farm is totally dependent on specific, specialized external inputs on a continuous basis. Labour per unit of area has decreased drastically and electronics and other technology have taken over.

What I fear—for him—is the second move. Agriculture and the farm now operate in the industrial economy. Farming will surely move from the industrial economy to the service economy. Currently, the internal dynamics are those of an industrial economy. Output is still standardized and anonymous. Focus on customer contacts, and integration of the farm's processes with the customers' processes, are practically non-existent. Information flows are not with customers, and so forth.

I permit myself to think that the lack of recognition on the pressures on agriculture to move into the service economy lies at the root of many current problems of the agricultural sector. The individual farmers, agribusiness executives, government officials and politicians are trying to solve these problems using recipes belonging to an old era—continued industrialization and regulation. There are a growing number of exceptions, however. Quite a few agricultural businessmen establish direct contact with the consumer through farm-outlet stores and the like.

Within the formal economy, a comparison of the level of recorded activity of the industrial and service sectors of different countries reveals one of the problems with the arbitrary convention of economic sectors. For example, in West Germany sectoral economic statistics indicate that, comparatively, the service sector is considerably smaller relative to the industrial sector than in the United States or Sweden. Does this mean that the German service economy is relatively underdeveloped? Such a conclusion cannot be drawn without further analysis. German industrial sector companies tend to contain, within themselves, relatively more service functions; these functions are typically performed in specialized, separate legal entities in many other countries. In this example, the institutional settings differ substantially; however, the economies are not necessarily different.

There is no reason to believe that the specialization trend will stop. We can expect a further shift of activities from the informal to the formal realm. This specialization now increasingly is into service rather than industrial types of activities, however.

What we see today is a gigantic reshuffling of activities between different types of units in society, creating a new specialization pattern in which one type of specialization may create opportunities for other units to in fact despecialize and perform a broader range of activities than in the past.

This is amply illustrated by the present trend in consumer appliances and electronics. Many of the new products and services today permit the consumer to perform a broader range of activities and functions for himself: listen to and play music, bake his own bread, cook gourmet food, bring the world of cinema into his home, perform more health care in his home, get involved in 'Outward Bound' and similar types of adventures, and so forth.

We believe there is a fascinating change of logic in the reshuffling of functions taking place in the present-day ('service'-dominated) economy *vis-à-vis* the industrial economy. Whereas the industrial economy was characterized by 'specialization-relieving', thus in fact impoverishing consumers in terms of their range of activities, the present trend is towards 'specialization-enabling', enriching the individual's activity options. Present-day goods and services are designed in such a way that the individual can save time, become more and more independent of location restrictions, squeeze more accumulated knowledge into every time-location unit, and be better able to use his own knowledge and resources for things he could not do before. (Stanley M. Davis in *Future Perfect* (1987) suggests that with our new technologies we are transforming our concepts of time, space (or location) and matter. The new technology encourages and demands an increasing knowledge component in goods and services. Inherent capacities of the technology and the presence of an increased knowledge component have a dramatic effect on time, space, matter, the nature of products/services and the producer/consumer relationship).

The movement of activities from the informal economy to the formal economy is by no means uni-directional. Now, as we encounter growth in the service economy we see a rapid reverse movement from the formal to the informal economy as many value-production service activities move back into the informal domain. With the advent of relatively cheap and efficient communications equipment, forwarding by mail and the traditional means of payment become superfluous. The human service component moves to the informal economy.

The *trend towards self-service* has been extensively analysed (Toffler, 1980; Naisbitt, 1982). We cannot afford to buy time from others, but we have an increasing amount of discretionary time which we can use to service ourselves. We become both producers and consumers of the service—or, to use a new and telling expression, 'prosumers'. The 'prosumer' or self-service trend is really about a reciprocal plus-sum game between the formal and the informal economy.

A steady shift is taking place in the structure of the service sector. The basic way in which services are conceived—as regards content and the process of production—is changing radically. Companies have to look at consumers in different ways. The new creative service company must consider the consumer as part of its workforce. The innovative service company sells not only services—it also sells knowledge, organization and management. All this presents us with a tremendous challenge and, above all, with new opportunities, which will be examined in subsequent chapters.

NEW IDEAS ABOUT MANUFACTURING COMPANIES

Taking the 'industrial sector' as the point of departure, it is obvious that much of it already functions according to the service economy, or is quickly moving there.

The distinction between manufacturing companies and service companies is, at best, hazy. In 1980, 85% of the profits of General Electric derived from the sale of products; now three-fourths of the profits come from the sale of services (*The Economist*, 1999). Is IBM selling goods or services? Is Volvo becoming a service company insofar as a good deal of its production is being leased out (in package deals including insurance and maintenance) rather than sold? How should one interpret the fact that manufacturing is being increasingly automated, while a growing proportion of the jobs in manufacturing companies are now concerned with information processing and internal services rather than with manufacturing as such? Statistics about the relative number of manufacturing and service *companies* might give us one picture, statistics about manufacturing and service *jobs* quite another.

One thing is certain; many organizations which used to think of themselves as manufacturing companies will have to learn (or are already starting to learn) to see themselves more as service organizations and to accept the consequences of this new view. Many such manufacturing companies have been fighting a tough battle as they have shifted from a traditional production to a marketing orientation; for several, the next step will involve a shift towards a service orientation.

This is a logical and not necessarily a dramatic development. The capacity to manufacture a good product that fulfils genuine needs, and a strong market orientation, provide a good basis for becoming service-oriented. And I predict that many good market-oriented and customer-oriented manufacturing organizations will be taking a keen interest in the new insights and the new management concepts that are now being developed to promote more effective service performance.

A simple analysis of the cost structure of goods today reveals that service activities account for a substantial portion of the value and the price of manufactured goods. If we define manufacturing functions as activities that:

- physically change materials,

and service functions as activities that:

- relate to the transactions of intangibles,

- influence access to and availability of physical objects, and
- influence the utilization of other tangibles or intangibles,

we can easily infer that there can be no such thing as a pure industrial economy. Service activities—internally or externally produced—are a necessary, and an ever-increasing portion of the cost structure of manufacturing companies. These functions generally add value by increasing the accessibility and utilization of goods. They tend to be in closer proximity to the consumer than the manufacturing functions. It is rather typical that service activities account for half or more of the price of goods.

We expect the service functions to be important in the consumer goods industries; however, many tend to underestimate their importance in other industries. (An internal study in SMG revalued that nearly two-thirds of the cost of a North Sea oil rig was attributable to service activities.)

There is a new logic of value-adding in industry. Its affinity to the service economy rather than the industrial economy is revealed by the increasing importance of service functions in the cost structure. In addition, the very nature of service functions is changing. An example is provided by the change that has taken place in means of export transportation in the Swedish economy (Table 1.1).

Table 1.1 Swedish exports (except iron ore): evolution of means of transportation towards 'time/location flexibility and precision intensive' methods

	Ship and railway	Truck and air
1967	76%	24%
1970	69%	31%
1975	64%	36%
1980	54%	46%
1986	45%	55%

Source: Andersson and Strömquist (1988)

Why is there a trend towards relatively more expensive means of transportation? Our interpretation is that this is a sign of the shift of focus from the process of physical production to the process of utilization of what is produced. The market tells us that it is now more important to have the goods (the same could be demonstrated to apply to services) available in the right place, at the right time, than it is to minimize the cost of each unit of bulk or weight. The buyer is becoming time-sensitive, not just price-sensitive. Part of the value attributed to a purchase is the impact that the purchasing activity and subsequent use of the good or service have on the buyer's time. As we will see, in the service economy the management of time becomes a primary focus of attention. The essence of the service economy is the precise matching of complex activity sets between different units.[1] Matching is partly about being able to build, develop, and cultivate *relationships*, a central concept in service management.

THE INDUSTRIALIZATION OF SERVICES

One more shift within our matrix deserves to be pointed out, namely the 'industrialization of services'.

To the extent that services deal with intangibles many techniques that we associate with 'industrialization' have typically been applied to the provision of services in the last decades, in many cases with an explosion of productivity as a consequence.[2]

The critical importance of 'intangibles' in the service equation has contributed to services being seen more as art than science. There has been a tendency to regard service and service production as not basically susceptible to the benefits of Big Management and Big Organization—that is, to the advantages of scale. This also may have been due in part to a misconception that advantages of scale were only possible in the mass production of

---

[1] Time sensitivity as a service attribute and the precise matching of activity sets is explored in greater depth in *Designing Interactive Strategy* by Normann and Ramirez (1994).

[2] However, in our view the notion of productivity in services—or, more appropriately, in the service economy—has not yet been sufficiently studied or even conceptually understood. The reason for the latter is that 'productivity' must be related to the objective function of 'value production'; and the logic of value production is different in the agricultural, industrial, and service economics. In this book I will only hint at some of the points of departure for a new notion of value production; for an in-depth exploration of that, see *Designing Interactive Strategy*, by Normann and Ramirez (1994). A key proposition is that it is not only futile but also illogical to try to isolate productivity in the service sector from productivity in the total economy. Another is that productivity improvements increasingly take place through what the authors call reconfiguration and restructuring of activities across traditional boundaries.

physical products. But the last couple of decades have witnessed a change in this fundamental view.

Some services have long been thriving in certain large business organizations. In the transportation industry there is a need to develop geographical networks and to invest significantly in the equipment and infrastructure to service that network. 'Bigness', in this instance, is a form of market coverage. Similarly, the banking and insurance industries are fundamentally based on the laws of big numbers and statistical averages. As these examples illustrate, there is a size threshold which is a prerequisite to participation in certain industries.

Traditionally, 'bigness' in some services—particularly those with low entry barriers (limited capital required, no sophisticated skills required)—was seen as unnecessary or even counterproductive. However, recent developments include the rise of giant corporations in what used to be considered simple, traditional service industries such as food and lodging, cleaning, industrial food services, security, etc. The large-scale advantages are not immediately apparent. Unlike a motor car manufacturer, the cleaning firm cannot jam 50 000 cleaners together in one place and obtain scale effects. The cleaners have to go out into the field singly to manufacture their 'product'. So where is the scale effect?

The answer is not a simple one; it will have to be formulated in several dimensions. The new innovative views about what the service company produces and how it produces it are part of the answer. Scale effects can apply to marketing, purchasing, management, organization, knowledge and even to esoteric factors like 'culture', and it is the recognition and the creative implementation of these dimensions which have made possible the emergence of vast enterprises like McDonald's, the Club Méditerranée, and McKinsey & Co.

Another factor furthering the development of large-scale enterprise is the importance accorded to image and 'brands' in today's world of business. Your customers are surrounded by 'information static'; once you have penetrated the static and successfully implanted yourself in their minds, it is essential to capitalize on your success. Consider Coca Cola, which has now begun to define itself as a 'brand management' company. One of many other examples is the Disney movie, *The Lion King*. At the time of the premiere, almost 200 *Lion King* products, from T-shirts to

CDs, were put on the market. A year later, *The Lion King* opened as a play on Broadway; when leaving the theatre the audience had to pass through a shop that sold all the products associated with *The Lion King* brand that had been built up. Another interesting case is that of Bernard Loiseau, the French chef. In December, 1998, his three-star French gourmet restaurant became the first establishment of its kind to list its shares on the stock market as a business that would exploit the powerful image which it had built up.

THE POSITIONING OF THIS BOOK

As we now leave the three-dimensional matrix we will take the opportunity to use it for framing the content of this book.

First, this book is about management of companies and similar production/provision organizations, not about society or macro-economics. It has business management focus. It attempts to provide managers with insights into enhancing the profitability and growth potentials of their companies.

Secondly, the major focus of this book is in the front right-hand corner of the upper or 'formal economy' plane of our matrix: companies providing mainly intangibles functioning according to the service economy logic. I have chosen this limitation because I felt it was the most practical way to transfer, in a 'pure' sense, a set of ideas about *the engineering of the intangible.* These ideas, I believe, will drive the development of the service economy across all sectors.

Our whole culture, tradition, and language, is much more comfortable in dealing with the physical, the concrete, the tangible, than with the abstract and intangible. (Compare the problems that areas like psychology, sociology, economics, etc. have had in becoming accepted as 'sciences'. Western thinking is highly oriented towards 'rationality', positivism, quantification, and measurability. Oddly enough, the concept of 'measuring' has the same roots as the Sanskrit word 'maya', but in Sanskrit 'maya' means 'illusion'! Systematic reflection on the world of the intangible has been reserved for priests and philosophers. *But value creation in today's economy is increasingly related to intangibles, and*

*managers who do not have even a systematic language for looking
at those processes will inevitably lag behind.*

We will refer to other examples and 'boxes' in our matrix, but
our focus and our point of departure is the service sector, within
the formal service economy. Much of the value-creating process
for the customer is an interplay between that which takes place
within the formal economy and that which takes place within its
substantial shadow component in the informal economy. Therefore, we will make frequent reference to this depth relationship.
Examples from and reference to other parts of the matrix will
serve to illustrate the movement of economic activity to the service economy, and to differentiate the strategic and management
implications of the service economy.

THE STATUS PROBLEM OF THE SERVICE INDUSTRIES

It is sometimes claimed that service businesses lack the status
associated with manufacturing, and that this is the reason for
many of their problems. It is true that some service businesses are
low status; however, there are many others which have relatively
high status. Problems are not unique to those with low status,
although some problems are more acute for such businesses.

Those service businesses with the reputed low status tend to be
those which perform functions:

1. that were traditionally performed by individuals granted lesser
   status when they were part of the informal economy;
2. that everybody claims expertise in and knowledge of (albeit
   not always correctly);
3. that require employees with lesser formal education; and,
4. that are considered 'dirty' work or necessary evils.

Cleaning, cooking and to some extent care of younger children
are services, traditionally performed by women in the home, and
about which we tend to claim knowledge. As the feminist movement has correctly pointed out, these services and the people who
perform them have been and continue to be undervalued. Other
services such as security, sanitation and waste disposal we

consider 'dirty' or evil necessities. As consumers we are inclined to despise what these service suppliers do, and often only notice them at all when they fail!

These image-generating factors tend to reflect on the whole company, a sort of anti-halo effect. We tend to think that working in companies concerned with such activities, even perhaps as managing director, is not particularly prestigious. This is unfortunate, for not only are the services performed inherently valuable, the sophistication required to manage such service business well is high.

In fact, no other businesses are perceived as covering such a wide range on the status scale as the service industries. Some service organizations cater for our most esoteric requirements (the church, the arts, and so on). Others cater for needs and deal in resources which are extremely precious to us all (money: banking; health: health care). Both these types tend to enjoy very high status, although we do not always think of them as advanced 'businesses'. Many types of service are represented by companies of the lowest as well as the highest status: a modest barber's shop is not ascribed much status by anyone, while 'Monsieur Alexandre' can expect invitations to the most glamorous of parties.

Why these reflections on status? Because they have implications for the management of services, for the possibilities of recruiting people who are both motivated and skilled, for the methods of developing and maintaining a 'culture'. The problem of recruiting bright, motivated and skilful managers to businesses which are sometimes regarded as enjoying little status and yet which are extremely sensitive to the quality of their management is certainly a serious one. In fact, it seems to me that these businesses must be among the most difficult and the most professionally challenging to manage.

Since the first edition of this book was written, a number of works have been published that seek to distinguish between 'service companies' and 'knowledge companies'. Strictly speaking, I find the concept of 'knowledge companies' as ordinarily used to be highly misleading. The difference between BMW, McDonald's and McKinsey is not that one is more or less knowledge-intensive than the other; all of them are based on knowledge. The difference lies in the degree to which the knowledge has been successfully built into what the firm offers to its customers. When people speak of knowledge companies, they usually mean those whose structural capital is relatively limited by comparison with a manufacturing enterprise, and where knowledge must be transmitted to customers through people who are expert at solving the specific problems of each situation.

At the extreme, one might even say that the concept of a knowledge company often refers to a firm which has failed—or not yet succeeded—in effectively incorporating knowledge into its structure, or into its products and services. Actually, many companies formally based on problem-solving by individuals are destined to evolve into ones that with increasing effectiveness 'package' the knowledge of individual professionals. Thus, many professional groups today—such as consultants, accountants, physicians—are finding that numerous tasks which previously required the problem-solving ability of the individual professional can now be accomplished with information technology. Thus, setting premiums at insurance companies is now done largely by computer programs, to take one example. And there are many others.

The concept of a knowledge company is thus misleading, although I myself employ it at times, since it has become so well established. In this book I use 'service' as a concept that also refers to companies which offer problem-solving by highly trained individuals. But the distinction between companies that supply standardized service (usually based on extensive structural capital), and those that provide service in the form of professional problem-solving, is, of course, valuable nonetheless, since the management and structural issues facing the two types of companies may differ sharply.

INTERNATIONALIZATION

There is also another perspective. In most advanced and industrialized economies there should logically be greater dependence on international trade in services for the maintenance of equilibrium in the international balance of trade. However, most authorities and industry associations have so far failed to realize that service industries can be a resource in this context. The facts tell us though, that the service sector is an important one and is becoming more so. In the foreign trade of the United States, a massive surplus in the service sector offset an equally large deficit in manufactured goods.

Economies such as those of the Scandinavian countries, which have organized their societies so that as many of the necessary services as possible are being produced in the public sector, are now having tremendous balance of payments problems, and one of the main causes has not even been recognized. The task of producing services (the growth industry) and of investing, for major segments of the service economy, has been handed over to the public sector. In a time when the export of services could have a significant impact on the economy, a major portion of the resources invested in service capacity is in the hands of organizations which are not designed for operating in open markets and which have no incentive to exploit their knowledge internationally. In most instances their current mandate precludes such activity. The American experience illustrates the potential value of service economy exports. In Sweden both the public sector and business circles have long considered 'industry' more prestigious than services. Moreover, establishing various forms of 'welfare services' has come to be viewed as a matter for the public sector and basically not an area in which private business should get involved (Normann, 1980). As a consequence, precisely this sector of society—which is a very large one as well as a growing international 'industry'—has been deprived of the competition that brings innovation and improved quality. And in the same sector little or no international business has been developed by Swedish enterprise. It would be appropriate to speak of a knowledge capital in captivity, a national investment which has been severely deprived of opportunities to earn a good return. I would term this phenomenon 'the Swedish captivity' (Figure 1.2).

The Treaty of Rome which provides for free movement of people and free establishment of a service operation in any style once it has been accepted in one state, should considerably promote the internationalization of services within the European Community. To facilitate this process, however, a set of concepts appropriate to the service sector is required.

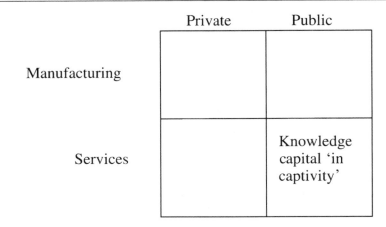

Figure 1.2 'The Swedish captivity'

IS THE MANAGEMENT OF SERVICES DIFFERENT FROM MANUFACTURING MANAGEMENT?

The answer to the question in the heading is yes and no, depending on how clearcut we want our definitions to be. My aim here is not to argue one way or the other, but to single out what is of primary importance in the management of service activities.

Much of what we already know about good management in general naturally also applies to service activities, but when my colleagues and I began to work more systematically with service companies we soon identified several factors that distinguished the best from the less successful, and a pattern began to emerge. It is interesting to note that a few other professionals in the field in other parts of the world were beginning to tackle these problems at roughly the same time, but from different angles.

At the Harvard Business School, for example, one group started to attack the problem from the point of view of manufacturing strategy, discovering that traditional approaches were inadequate when it came to the production of intangibles which could not be stocked (Sasser, Olsen and Wyckoff, 1978). At the same time, marketing people such as Eiglier and Langeard (1975, 1977) were approaching service organizations from their own particular angle, while the group with which I am associated was starting out from the point of view of strategy and organization as well as the role of management and leadership.

What are the characteristics of service organizations? At this stage let us just consider some of the most obvious features (see Table 1.2 below).

Table 1.2 Some typical differences between manufacturing and service industries

Manufacturing	Service
The product is generally concrete	The service is intangible
Ownership is transferred when a purchase is made	Ownership is not generally transferred
The product can be resold	The product cannot be resold
The product can be demonstrated	The product cannot usually be effectively demonstrated (it does not exist before purchase)
The product can be stored by sellers and buyers	The product cannot be stored
Consumption is preceded by production	Production and consumption generally coincide
Production, selling and consumption are locally differentiated	Production, consumption and often even selling are spatially united
The product can be transported	The product cannot be transported (though 'producers' often can)
The seller produces	The buyer/client takes part directly in the production
Indirect contact is possible between company and client	In most cases direct contact is necessary
Can be exported	The service cannot normally be exported, but the service delivery system can

One is the basic *intangibility* of services (as opposed to the concreteness of manufactured goods). This immediately suggests several related properties: services cannot be stocked; they cannot easily be demonstrated; and while they can be sold, there is not necessarily any transfer of ownership. Some of the consequences of a 'production' approach to logistics and marketing will be immediately apparent to the reader.

Secondly, most services actually consist of *acts,* and *interactions* are typically social events. The control and management of social events calls for certain special skills and techniques.

Thirdly, the production and consumption of a service cannot always be clearly kept apart, since they generally occur simultaneously and at the same place. The 'manufacturing' takes place in the field, as Levitt (1972) has pointed out. One consequence of this is that the structure of service operations is generally much more dispersed and local than the structure of manufacturing operations. And functional differentiation, between producing and selling for example, tends to become vague or disappear altogether.

Moreover, as has been suggested above, the customer is often more than just a customer—he is also a participant in the production of the service. A haircut, the cashing of a cheque, education—none of these can conceivably be produced without the participation of the consumer. Thus the service company not only has to get in contact with the consumers and to interact with them socially; it is also necessary to 'manage' them as part of the production force (Normann, 1982).

This list could be extended, and obviously some of the characteristics mentioned may apply to some manufacturing activities too; certainly there are a number of borderline cases. It is an old trick among some manufacturers, for example, to increase the element of intangibility in their product (General Motors, IBM and Christian Dior have all done this in different ways). Again, my point is not to try to exaggerate the differences but to try to identify what is intrinsic to services.

Table 1.2 can be seen as a typical 'first generation of service knowledge' statement of established truths, and thus serves a pedagogical purpose. However, it must be stated that those truths today are being challenged in many ways which will be highlighted later on in this book. For example, new communication and information technology clearly increase the possibilities to 'store services', and to make person-to-person interaction in their provision unnecessary.

THE MOMENT OF TRUTH

Most services are the result of social acts which take place in direct contact between the customer and representatives of the service company. To take a metaphor from bullfighting, we could say that the perceived quality is realized at the moment of truth, when the service provider and the service customer confront one another in the arena (Figure 1.3). At that moment they are very much on their own. What happens then can no longer be directly influenced by the company. It is the skill, the motivation and the tools employed by the firm's representative and the expectations and behaviour of the client which together will create the *service delivery process*. A large service company may well experience tens of thousands of 'moments of truth' every day.

THE MOMENT OF TRUTH

Figure 1.3 The moment of truth: where the quality of a service operation is created

This particular attribute of services also underlies many other typical features that have to be taken into account when effective service delivery systems are being designed. We shall refer to the concept frequently in the following pages.

PERSONALITY INTENSITY

It is often argued that service operations tend to be more labour-intensive than manufacturing, the implication being that personnel management is critical to success in a service business. However, I would maintain that while this is true in some cases, the idea that services are more labour-intensive or personnel-intensive is basically mistaken—or rather, it is not the important point.

In fact, many services are extremely capital-intensive and are becoming more so. In addition to traditionally equipment-based services such as airlines, services such as security or banking are becoming increasingly based on equipment and advanced technology. Nonetheless, those services still retain an important element of person-to-person contact, and will continue to do so. And in many other services, too, the logic of the moment of truth holds, even though customers may not have face-to-face contact with the people providing the service. When we eat at a famous restaurant or fly in a jumbo jet we are certainly very much aware of the presence of the chef or the pilot, although we may never actually see them.

Instead of classifying businesses as capital-intensive or personnel-intensive, we have found it more useful in our group to classify them in terms of *'personality intensity'*. Most services, and many other business, are personality-intensive in the sense that the quality supplied to the customer is essentially a result of the way people perform in the specific situation (regardless of whether or not they are backed up by a large amount of capital and equipment).

When the performance of individuals or small groups, who may have a high degree of discretion to influence the specific situation, are a key factor in determining quality and economic performance, then there are important implications for the way in which a company is run. Even services which appear to be very standardized—such as the McDonald's hamburger restaurants—in fact depend a great deal on the performance of individual people. If you buy a car, it never occurs to you to wonder whether or not the production-line worker was smiling or showing pride in what he was doing, or to be interested in how he was dressed or whether he was a nice person; when you buy from the McDonald's 'production line', you are affected by all these things.

Service companies tend to be personality-intensive in this particular sense—in the day-to-day production of quality. Negative or positive performance by individuals may have a tremendous and immediate impact on how individual customers perceive the quality of what they have been given. There are relatively few ways of covering up lack of enthusiasm or the absence of a decent performance on the part of the individual. The effects and the feedback are immediate and striking.

This is part of the basis for another observation that my colleagues and I have made, namely that *effective service companies are often based on social innovation.* Inventing the appropriate roles and role constellations, diagnosing and finding ways to use human capacity and energy, designing ways to make people and groups of people learn skills quickly and to maintain the skills while keeping alive the enthusiasm and the thrill of personal development—all these are typical examples of social innovation.

Social innovation is thus a means whereby quality and cost efficiency can both be achieved. In the following chapters we shall see many examples of such innovative approaches to the mobilization and focusing of human energy.

2

The new economic equation

The logic of value creation in society and in service industries is changing at a rapid rate. In the first part of this chapter we will look at some of the driving forces and innovation patterns.

The concept of 'assets' is also changing. Profitability and growth today come from the skilful management of many assets, a great many of which are not reflected in the accountant's view of the balance sheet, and are intangible. Customer relationships are the most crucial of these assets. The competition for customers and customer bases is becoming fierce. Management focus must shift towards management of this critical asset. In the second part of this chapter we will examine the underlying value-creation dynamics and their impact on the customer relationships.

Together these forces are forging the new economic equation for business.

THE SUBSTANCE OF INNOVATION

Innovation in service industries could be the subject of a lengthy book on its own. We shall therefore have to limit ourselves here to a few observations and pointers. The ideas put forward will be based on observations from our own 'clinical' work.

We have often come across the notion that service business ideas and new services are less 'sophisticated' or less 'advanced' than the latest innovations in manufacturing, or even that they are 'really just common-sense'. As ordinary consumers we tend to be more impressed by advanced technology than by simple things like hamburgers or clean offices. But we should not take it for granted that a Boeing 747 is a more advanced innovation than the system required to provide effective catering for the tens of thousands of people who work at the Boeing headquarters in Seattle.

If we examine the substance of innovation in the service and know-how sector a number of trends are evident. There is a movement towards *more complex service concepts* (see also Chapter 5). Along with an increase in 'manpower substitutes' there is an increasing element of know-how and management transfer. The insurance industry will later be used as a dramatic and recent example of such an evolution. A related trend can be seen in the development of client-oriented multiservice companies, in which the various needs of the clients form a basis for broadening the range of the services provided by the service company.

These developments in service concepts lead to *innovation in the service delivery systems* as well. For example, in the health care sector there has been a long period, particularly in the European welfare states, during which therapeutic services only have been supplied to the clients, while all the related knowledge and skill has been retained within the system providing the service. There is growing recognition that the failure to transfer knowledge to clients and to stimulate their potential self-care capabilities is plunging the health care systems into catastrophe both in terms of quality and cost. New alternative systems in which knowledge and self-help capability are transferred to clients will offer a great challenge in the future (and will no doubt be violently opposed by the present establishments). Another example of a delivery system innovation concerns a greater ability to 'reproduce' service delivery systems. We could call this the art of 'McDonaldization', and we shall be returning to it later.

As society evolves and consumers enjoy greater freedom, they manifest more varied expectations. Citizens are already rebelling against the captivity policy of the huge, dominating, often government-run institutions. The segmenting and differentiating mass markets are leading to *more specialized services displacing the one-kind-only dominating service response.* 'Dominating' institutions are being challenged by new services responding to the marketplace demand for greater variety in services. The previously unchallenged health care services are encountering competition from new services based on ideas of health promotion and health-inducing lifestyle activities. Airlines have generally become more attuned to the needs of passengers and stopped treating them like prisoners, though not without continued severe relapses into their previous attitude.

Explicitly recognized technical and social innovations are being used to formulate the redefinition of services. It could be argued that the whole art of service management both as a discipline and as a management practice is largely based on the recognition and conscious application of social innovation.

THE DRIVING FORCES FOR INNOVATION

To better illustrate service innovation, let us make a simple preliminary systematization of the different types of driving forces. As illustrated in Table 2.1, we can characterize them in two

Table 2.1 Driving forces behind innovation in service management systems and some illustrative examples. (Note that in practice most examples cover more than one dimension.)

Internal basis for service management innovation system	External driving forces		
	Fossilized institutions	New values—and lifestyles	Need for greater efficiency
Social innovation		Club Méditerranée EF Education	
Client participation	Health maintenance organizations		
Role sets			
New linkages		Internet services	J-C Decaux
New sources of human energy		Weight Watchers	
Technical innovation	Gambro	Sony Walkman	Mobile phones
Network effects	Federal Express	Hard Rock Café	
Reproduction innovation or scale advantage in management	Nursing-home chains	McDonald's	Risk management services Cleaning/building maintenance McKesson

dimensions. First, 'internal' driving forces for service, and management system design, serve as a basis for innovation; and secondly, 'external' driving forces open up opportunities for innovation.

Internal driving forces providing a basis for innovation include:

- four types of social innovation (client participation, role sets, new linkages, new sources of human energy)
- technical innovation
- network effects, and
- reproduction innovation or scale advantage in management.

External driving forces creating opportunities for innovation include:

- fossilized institutional contexts
- new values and lifestyles, and
- the need for greater efficiency.

New technology is a borderline case between the two dimensions. The development of new technology tends to be a general process in society as a whole, shaping the context, shaping the marketplace, and shaping the service provider. However, the application of new technology to specific contexts and problems can be influenced by the individual company or even a single person. Information technology, for example, represents a broad, general development process the fruits of which are being applied and refined by thousands of service (and other) organizations in connection with different problems and different areas of use. Technologies that are widely accessible, connected for example with architecture or with food preservation, are being picked up and adapted by service organizations of all kinds, from banks to hamburger chains, as an integrated and sometimes even a key part of their businesses. For convenience we have treated 'new technology' as an internal driving force.

One reason why service innovations often fail to appear spectacular is that many of them are actually based on *social innovation,* on innovations that create new types of social behaviour, that use social or human energy more efficiently, that link social contexts to each other in new ways.

One type of social innovation consists of *client participation,* of inducing the client to take over more of the process of 'production' or of providing the service. The most obvious examples are the self-help and self-service concepts evident in abundance. There are also many more sophisticated manifestations of this phenomenon. For example, the current trend of large business corporations taking over risk services (in captive insurance companies) and financial services in 'in-house' banks, are drastically changing the structure of the financial services industry world-wide.

The case of J-C Decaux illustrates another type of social innovation which involves creatively *linking different contexts,* in this case municipal authorities, bus passengers, the general public and advertisers.

The case of J-C Decaux

J-C Decaux is a successful French service company. It puts up and maintains bus shelters in French towns free of change. The shelters are financed by providing advertising space.

Bus shelters used to cause the towns a lot of trouble—they were ugly, they invited vandalism, they were costly to maintain, and their design varied and was not generally very functional. When J-C Decaux recognized this problem and proposed a solution, hardly anybody believed in his ideas. But he managed to gain the confidence of some important *maires* and was allowed to experiment. He then quickly proved his point.

A very important part of the concept was the care that went into the physical design of the shelters. They are pleasing to look at, they are easy to spot, they are secure, and the lighting system and the arrangements for setting up and changing the posters are highly ingenious. The posters also require very special production arrangements in order to fit into the system, and the company provides the necessary facilities which were not otherwise easily available on the market.

The pleasing design, the visibility, the functionalism and the neatness of the shelters, which make a generally favourable impression on the public, are naturally important in attracting advertisers and preventing objections on the part of local political opportunists that a private company has taken over what could be considered a municipal function.

However, there is no way of escaping vandalism and the need for maintenance altogether, and the way J-C Decaux has solved this problem is a crucial part of his service system. Maintenance has to be frequent and perfect. At first the towns tried to maintain the shelters on their own, using low-paid, unmotivated personnel, and there were great problems with high absenteeism and labour turnover. Experiments in subcontracting to maintenance companies also proved disappointing, and it was decided that the company would have to set up its own maintenance service.

Every shelter is visited regularly three times a week. There is also an emergency service. The maintenance people are well paid and have their 'own' cars (i.e. they use the same car all the time and do not have to bring it back to the company garage overnight). The cars are equipped with radios and a set of sophisticated tools for effective cleaning. If anybody from the company notices signs of vandalism or anything else wrong with the appearance of a shelter, he reports it at once to the relevant member of the maintenance staff and the emergency service goes into action.

Thus the maintenance crews are highly motivated. Every member has a sense of proprietorship towards his equipment and his own particular shelters; he takes pride in maintaining them well. His feeling of being independent and yet part of a team is reinforced by the wide latitude he is given as regards working hours, etc.

The company's organization stresses the importance of the key relationships—with the towns, with the advertisers, and with the maintenance crews themselves (Mr Decaux points out that the maintenance people always have direct access to him should they need it). Another detail which aptly illustrates the company culture is that every employee keeps a scraper in his car—and if he sees something wrong with a shelter, he will use it!

J-C Decaux also illustrates a third type of social innovation, that of *creating new roles or new role-sets*. The maintenance people in this organization clearly represent a role innovation; people with that kind of responsibility, and that kind of equipment and function, had obviously not appeared before. Another very innovative French service company, Club Méditerranée, has made the concept of the *gentil organisateur* famous. Career and job rotation systems then also helped to establish unique role relationships in this company between the *gentils organisateurs,* the clients and the managers of the vacation villages, providing another example of *new role-sets.*

Today J-C Decaux has developed into a large international company which has broadened its product range to include related services, such as electronic billboards that announce events and happenings in a city, provide information on the traffic situation, etc. The company is growing and has established itself with contracts in major cities in Scandinavia, Central Europe and the United States.

A fourth type of social innovation is that of discovering and employing *underutilized and hitherto unfocused human energies*. EF Education, for instance, is a master of the art of finding and organizing such energy, whether it be the specially recruited sales office managers or the families who receive the children in their homes.

The case of EF Education

The main business of EF Education is to arrange language courses for schoolchildren during the summer or other school vacation periods. The company has its head office in Stockholm, but its operations are completely international. During the mid-1960s the company was a pioneer in this field, and it is still the world leader. It has over 100 main sales offices in about 60 countries, sending children to England, the United States, Germany and France.

Over 500 000 children travel with the company each year, and with such wide-ranging operations the system is obviously rather sensitive: parents and school authorities would see to it that scandals or bad service were quickly and widely advertised, and this would certainly affect the volume of business.

Basically the system works as follows. Personal marketing is directed towards pupils in the relevant areas, age groups and schools. Those who enrol are transported generally by air to London, let us say, and from there to the centre of their choice—usually somewhere by the sea. There they receive food and lodging during their stay and attend language courses led by professional teachers who are aware of the children's individual levels of knowledge. The teachers also understand the special difficulties which each language group can experience in learning (in this case) English. During their stay they also have opportunities to meet local residents and take part in excursions.

There does not seem to be anything very unusual or striking about all this, although the skill and care that goes into the development of teaching methods and materials should not be underestimated. Sending children abroad to learn new languages while also learning about new cultures is an old tradition. What made EF Education so successful was the new way of constructing the service, which brought costs down far below previous levels, suddenly making the service accessible to the typical middle-class family. Furthermore, EF Education has achieved considerable success in maintaining and reproducing both their service delivery and the necessary internal climate and management system. Although the original system could theoretically be imitated by others locally and temporarily, EF Education has in fact been able to grow consistently and to take over ailing imitators, permeating them with its own viable culture and management system.

How is the service actually achieved? A great deal of the personal marketing is done by other pupils, generally those who have taken part in earlier visits. They have well-designed brochures to help them and they are paid on a piece-rate system based on the number of enrolments they achieve. The financial reward would certainly seem low to a professional salesman, but these pupils are not professional salesmen and the pay makes a substantial addition to their total income.

The young 'salesmen' are supported by representatives from the sales offices, who also try to keep schoolteachers informed about EF Education and the opportunities they provide for improving the performance of pupils and school classes. The sales offices also handle the practical details of registration, the distribution of brochures, and so on.

The company soon discovered that the charter airlines had adapted their capacity to weekend needs—most people stop and start their vacations at weekends. Thus on Saturdays and Sundays the planes were busy going to Majorca and the Canary Islands, but in the middle of the week they were underutilized. School children, it was argued, don't mind travelling midweek, and so it was possible to bargain with the airlines and to buy their midweek capacity at low cost.

The professional teachers in charge of the courses were ordinary teachers (of the relevant language) from the children's home countries. They were being paid during the summer by their regular employers; they had long vacations; and it was good for them professionally to go to, say, England to brush up their English. They were thus quite happy to go along for very reasonable fees.

Food and lodging were provided by carefully selected families in the host countries. These families were quite happy to receive foreign guests. Admittedly the financial gain was nominal (in some countries or regions host families refused to be paid at all), but the arrangement meant company for their own children, a break in their regular routine, and perhaps even a chance to act as ambassadors of their country's culture.

Naturally, EF Education set up its own organization in the host countries, to deal with the logistics and with the important task of finding suitable families and teaching premises (not difficult in the summer, when the local children are also on holiday and schools are empty and available at reasonable cost).

Other cases—examples of internal driving forces

Service innovation may result from synergistic combinations of several types of social innovation. F International, a UK based company, is a large systems consultancy which develops, maintains and supports complex computer applications. It has combined *new role sets,* with *underutilized and unfocused human energy;* these, tied together with superb marketing and linked decentralized work sites (made possible with information technology), result in a highly successful information technology support service. In a time when there is a severe shortage of top-flight computer and information technology professionals, F International has built a dispersed but highly skilled workforce, some home-based and part-time, The new role set, a key feature of which has the customer's work move to the provider's employee rather than the reverse, provides customers with access to expertise which would otherwise be unavailable to them.

Another internal driving force that leads to innovation consists of *scale advantages in knowledge.* Such innovations often assume their most concrete expression in effective reproduction formulas and innovative organizational arrangements reflecting the idea that 'small is beautiful on a large scale'.

While the McDonald's of this world have been the prototypes of this type of innovation, similar ideas are now spreading into many other contexts, including health care and nursing homes. Particularly in the European welfare states, health care systems were created during the 1950s and 1960s, and even since, which were based on the idea of scale advantages in logistics, technology and production resources. Some hospital management organizations, nursing home chains and home and self care support organizations are now demonstrating that effective production is often better if it is restricted to a small or limited scale, and that the real scale advantages are to be found in knowledge and management and the effective utilization of existing resources, including the client.

Yet another type of driving force in the design of a service system originates in *network effects.* Here we should make a distinction: on the one hand we have scale effects and lower costs caused directly by the network organization, as in the case of McDonald's for instance; and on the other we have situations in which some value accrues to the other members of the network each time a new member is added.

Examples of network value accrual include hotel reservation systems (where each new hotel makes it easier for the others to keep clients within the chain), goods transportation companies (where each new local unit represents the addition of a new and perhaps attractive service to all the other units) or consulting firms (where a new international office may make it easier for other offices to acquire large international companies as clients, perhaps creating a more exciting and rewarding internal context and putting the company in a more favourable position in the vitally important recruitment market).

As major manufacturing companies become truly international they look for services which match their international coverage. This accounts, in no small part, for recent waves of mergers and buyouts in the advertising and public relations services, and among consulting and auditing firms.

External driving forces

Let us now look at some of the external driving forces that provide openings for service innovations. Numerous classifications are conceivable here, but I will limit myself to three.

One obvious driving force is provided by the appearance of *new values, new problems and new lifestyles.* Services connected with travel, entertainment and education are obvious examples. New problems such as crime pave the way for security companies.

Another very strong driving force behind the development of new services is the *greater need for efficiency* in (business) organizations and, to some extent, among individuals. When companies assess the return on their investments and their scarce management resources, they often decide to hive off certain management problems that are unrelated to their core business; this paves the way for many specialist subcontracting services.

A company engaged in oil exploration in the North Sea may hire an industrial food service catering company from Texas to provide the food services on a drilling platform. Faced with the problem of a low return on insurance investment and inefficient traditional banking services, many large industrial companies now prefer to employ firms specializing in the transfer of knowledge and management skills such as risk management and cash management. If a technologically advanced company finds that 80 per cent of the problems of its personnel department stem from dealing with cleaners, it may prefer to ask another company which specializes in dealing with this personnel category to take over its cleaning operations.

A third driving force behind the emergence of new services is the *lack of sufficient innovative capacity in many established organizations*. It is striking to see how many service innovations thus owe their success to the inability of others.

Federal Express became possible because of the inefficiency of the US Mail. Similarly, City Mail and a number of local postal service companies have grown up because the Swedish Postal Service could not respond to the wishes of various customer groups. EF Education to some extent waged guerrilla warfare against a school system that failed to provide adequate language instruction. The furniture company IKEA, with its focus on lifestyle, flourished because the furniture manufacturing and distributing industries were inefficient, and it could successfully grow because the established companies chose to defend their traditional efficiency instead of challenging the newcomer with innovations of their own.

The dimensions that we have outlined here, together with a few examples, can be found in Table 2.1. The positioning of the examples in the matrix naturally represents an oversimplification, since in practice most of them combine several of the driving forces. For combinations of driving forces are also necessary if high efficiency is to be achieved.

RESULTS COME FROM CUSTOMER RELATIONSHIPS

In this section we examine the underlying value-creation dynamics and their impact on this most crucial asset, customer relationships. Because this asset does not appear directly on the balance sheet and is intangible, we often find ourselves without the terminology or framework to examine it. This discussion of the provider–customer role constellation begins to address that problem.

Consider the following minicases:

'The Know-How Room' literally is at the core of ServiceMaster which is rapidly expanding its multiservice business to hospitals internationally. This room—situated at the centre of the headquarters and with a glass wall to the corridor—contains all the physical products, all the operations and management manuals, visualizations of career paths, and other symbols for key knowledge essential to the business. From this room, the rest of the company can be seen as a big apparatus to bring the knowledge to the marketplace and to find price carriers for it.

Volvo has managed to make what is in other countries considered a luxury vehicle the most sold car in its domestic market. It has done so by drastically changing the offering to the customers, including several financial services, privileged access to auxiliary components such as gas stations; and by introducing measures to change the way in which the used-car market operates.

In working with an industrial insurance company one SMG consulting team found a distinct lack of profitability in spite of what seemed like quite successful acquisitions of new interesting customers. In taking a sample of customer relationships the team found the following: serving a customer to his satisfaction and with good profitability for the insurance company typically cost a certain fixed amount plus a certain sum of the premium income (index 100). Acquiring a new customer from the competition and serving him to his satisfaction cost considerably more (index about 130) for the first couple of years. Bringing back a dissatisfied customer who had left and gone to the competition similarly cost much more—index over 150. The case team's analysis showed that the insurance company put too few resources in maintaining its existing customer base and therefore had to put too many resources into chasing new customers, which explained the lack of profitability.

Another SMG client team worked with a big, multibranch advertising agency. Comparing the performance of the branches over time, they discovered some startling facts which had escaped management. For example, one year two branches had the same sales, result level, and cost structure (and, consequently, had been paid the same bonuses). Next year one of those branches had fallen back very seriously. A deeper analysis showed that during the first year this particular branch had reached its profits by creating considerably less satisfaction (and even bad will) among customers, and local management had created a feeling of frustration and alienation among several of the key people—several of whom then left. But in comparing the various agencies management had had no tools to assess the assets consisting of motivation of the personnel and of the degree of satisfaction of customers.

A large security guard company had problems year after year in one of its regions. As an experiment it then installed a system of 'round table' joint quality reviews together with the customers in that region, on a systematic basis. It only took one year for that region to become the company's most profitable one.

In an article in *Business Week* (1987) on the Coca-Cola Corporation, some of the lessons then recently learned by the company are described. The first major lesson was 'to move fast when it makes a mistake'. The second was to find new ways of using Coca-Cola's powerful brand names. 'We are making the trademark work harder.' Now, on the threshold of a new century, Coca-Cola for all practical purposes has defined itself as a 'brand-management company'.

All these mini-stories serve as variations on and illustrations of the changing concept of 'assets', particularly the customer relationship. We will give ample illustrations later in this book of the importance of intangible assets such as company image, company culture and employee motivation and loyalty. In the remainder of this chapter we will focus on changes in the provider–customer relationship. (Yet another level of analysis of the emerging role of the customer will be found in Chapter 8.)

THE KNOWLEDGE EXPLOSION

Customers today—whether they be institutional customers or end consumers—take a more active interest in what their providers provide and how they function.

One reason for this certainly is the increase in the level of knowledge of typical customers. In many areas, access to information and knowledge today is more or less general. When the finance department of an industrial company can monitor the money and capital markets on its own—why would it need to go to the bank? When knowledge about health and lifestyle can be more and more efficiently packaged and made available to everybody—surely this will influence the relationship between the public and their physicians.

What we see today in the world is a gigantic increase in the amount of information, with a corresponding redistribution of knowledge as a consequence. This does not necessarily mean that the world is becoming wiser, but it does influence customer–provider relationships. Customers are more knowledgeable, they can shop around, they can influence what their providers do, they can take more free and informed choice as to what to do for themselves and what to leave to their providers.

Private customers, today, are moving away from the consumption patterns of mass production society. Their activities and consumption patterns are highly focused on the reinforcement of their own identity and this probably leads to a higher differentiation of lifestyles. Customers need to be handled in a more individualized way. Institutional customers show variations on the same theme. Each and every such customer today is busy becoming successful in its particular activity—but every company becomes unique as traditional industry boundaries and descriptions no longer apply.

We should not conclude, however, that there is no market for mass-produced goods and services. For instance, a customer with culinary interests may cultivate a lifestyle that includes preparing gourmet meals outside of work, while opting for the standard menu of the employee cafeteria on working days. Being unique is a matter of unique combinations—not of being unique in all respects all the time.

Since private customers as well as institutions are involved in an increasingly individualized and unique process of value creation, it is not strange that they are interested in the roles they play in these value-creating processes. Therefore they get more and more involved in what their providers do with them. These demands for a differentiated and unique input to produce a differentiated and unique output (largely made possible by new technological developments) is at the foundation of what is possibly the most important management problem today, namely handling the relationship with customers. We have less and less of a traditional producer–consumer relationship and more and more of an integrated relationship which is characterized by coproduction of value.

Thus, the increasing knowledge of customers today coincides with an almost explosive increase in their needs for advanced knowledge. As the consumption patterns and business problems of customers become unique and more and more complex, they must find more effective ways of using their own resources and knowledge. In effect, they need to complement themselves with knowledge from the outside.

Without advanced knowledge of how we effectively communicate with customers—both ways—we underutilize the assets that we have built in our customer relationships. Without advanced knowledge about flexible manufacturing systems our return on the available time between an external change and a reaction in the form of a new product or service is too low. Without knowledge of logistics we use our capital in-efficiently. Without state-of-the-art knowledge on 'strategic human resources management' the return we get on the payroll costs and our investments in recruitment and education will be too low. Without creative ideas about how to repackage our knowledge into new products and services which can reach customers in new and more effective ways, we underutilize the investments in our production system.

The interdependencies and the integration between functions and resources are increasing rapidly. Knowledge and resources, even if of very high quality, will remain less than optimally productive unless they are complemented with and balanced by other knowledge and other resources. The rapid changes and the increasing competition require companies both to increase the knowledge within themselves and to increase the inflow of knowledge from the outside. Therefore we experience the paradoxical situation that advanced companies have more knowledge than other companies, but that they still buy relatively more advanced knowledge from the outside.

Practically all economic theory and most of the literature on management—including the literature on business strategy—seems to be based on the assumption that value of some form is created by one actor (the producer) and then sold to another actor (the consumer, or the user). An example is the theory of Michael Porter, which is symbolized by the most central concept of that theory—'the value chain'. But we believe that in today's reality the metaphor of 'the value chain' is off the mark, since it misses the often synchronous and mutual interplay between providers and customers. Both contribute to the creation of value—the transfer of value functions poorly when it flows in only one direction. Strictly speaking, therefore, concepts like 'producers' and 'consumers' are misleading in today's economy.

In order to understand the logic of the service economy and some of its management consequences, we must develop a set of concepts for viewing different dimensions to the creation of value. The nature of the transactions taking place between providers and customers is changing along at least five important dimensions.

SERVICE LOADING

Transactions rarely comprise only pure goods. In addition to the necessary auxiliary services, like physical distribution, the amount of service function which is a part of the offerings to customers tends to increase.

We must distinguish between what the offering is like and what the provider puts the price on. For many goods it is typical that the price is on the tangible items and that a number of associated services are provided 'for free'. But this is only a matter of convention, and it means that the company has chosen—perhaps by convention or perhaps for reasons of competitive tactics—to add the price of the services to the price of the tangibles and to 'bundle' them. Plus, the fact that many tangible goods serve as 'price carriers' for intangible services sometimes tends to blind us to the importance of the service content of the offering, and therefore makes us underestimate the importance of the service economy.

RELATIONING

Not only customer relationships but also the time dimension of each transaction tends to become longer. Sometimes this is natural since part of the services associated with, say, a product may be essential to the function and value of that product over a long time—servicing a car or maintenance of production or information technology equipment. But we also see many more instances of the offering taking the form of a kind of 'contract' which gives the customer a stream of services over time, availability of services on an 'on call' basis, etc. Very often such relationship offerings have a self-reinforcing character since the provider and customer tend to learn more about each other and increase their degree of mutual adjustment and interdependency.

We will call this trend of transactions and value creation, from the 'ships meeting in the ocean' character to more of a long-term character, *relationing*. It is clear that with increased *relationing* the customer contact and the maintenance of the customer relationship will become the strategic focus of the company. More than anything else it will be the ability to maintain a solid and profitable customer contact that determines growth and profit potential of the provider. As a result, the focus of investments and management solutions in such situations is moved closer to the contact systems with the customers: the access channels, the communication systems, the customer-interactive parts of the organization.

BROADENING

The content of the transactions tends to involve more functions or aspects of what the customers do. Thus, banks and insurance companies are moving towards becoming multiservice financial companies. Car producers provide cars and financing and insurance and maintenance contracts and fuel and around-the-clock emergency services. In this sense offerings tend to be increasingly 'system'-like.

We call this process *broadening*. Broadening is a natural consequence of the importance of the customer contact and actually represents a strategy for the provider to capitalize on this contact—just as it represents a strategy for the customer to capitalize on the investments that he has made in his provider relationships.

(Let us make it clear that broadening is not a universal process, even though the driving force towards it is universal. Markets and technologies are changing so fast that there will be ample opportunities for more 'narrow' providers who fulfil few but specialized functions for their customers. Their window of opportunity comes from their capacity to quickly exploit an emerging market or the advantages of a new technology early in its lifecycle. As the market expands or the technology matures, the service provided will tend to become integrated into the offerings of the 'broader' providers. At this stage these more specialized providers often have to choose to continue with their 'prospecting' approach and find new service opportunities, merge with or engage in co-operative ventures with a broader provider, or go out of business.)

Broadening redefines the competitive systems of today. It requires that providers master many more skills, develop a broader base of assets, and adapt their organization and management methods. In the 'broad' company, knowledge management in its widest sense becomes a critical success factor. (This is one of the major explanations for the explosion of co-operation strategies in today's business world.)

UN-BUNDLING AND RE-BUNDLING

Very large parts of society, especially those related to the provision of services (banking, insurance, telecommunications, media, airline and railroad transportation, health care, basic and much of continued education, etc.) have been highly regulated. Regulation tends to protect established actors, who tend to standardize and to bundle together their offerings on a take-it-or-leave-it basis for the customers.

Bundling—a term which we found when we started to work with insurance companies—means either that a company forces the customer to buy a whole range of items as a package (or to buy nothing at all), or that some items serve as price carriers for other 'free' items, the former therefore subsidizing the latter.

With deregulation and other competitive pressures we see a tendency towards *un-bundling,* and then a tendency towards quicker and more market-driven (rather than monopoly) *re-bundling* (Normann *et al.,* 1989). Again, this means that the interrelationships between providers and customers will be much more driven by need-oriented matching between the activities of the parties than on the monopoly-based and provider-oriented conventions of the regulated era.

Un-bundling and re-bundling reinforce the competitive pressures associated with all the other aspects of the provider–customer interrelationship in that it will accelerate the process of broadening (or the opposite, in terms of un-bundling) and open up the arena for new players. There are numerous examples of the explosion of new competitors and new types of offerings. (One is the US health care market after the regulatory changes of 1983. Another is in media like TV and radio, where technological development made deregulation possible and to a certain extent unavoidable.)

The example of the US airlines following deregulation is interesting. In 1978 there were 36 large and medium-sized carriers which, following deregulation, grew to 123 by 1984. By 1986 mergers, acquisitions and bankruptcies had reduced the number of carriers to 78 (source: Duggan, 1988). In addition, in 1985, the five major carriers had 69% of the market, in 1986 they had 77% and by 1988, six major carriers had 95% of the market. This clearly illustrates the network-effect advantage and the fact that the broadening process accelerated too rapidly for the weaker providers of transportation to respond. Ten years later, the same tendencies could be found in European air transportation. The area of telecommunications, once strictly regulated, today appears to be a fight between traditional 'broad-based' players, specialized new operators who are trying to 'un-bundle', and others who in a new and creative fashion are seeking to 'bundle' and 'broaden'.

ENABLING AND RELIEVING

A clearly interesting dimension along which there is a universal change process in the provider–customer relationships is one which we will call *enabling versus relieving.* As we mentioned in the first chapter, and as will be discussed more in depth in Chapter 8, the service economy implies a reshuffling of tasks between providers and customers. Whereas industrial society essentially 'relieved' customers of the need for performing certain functions (because they could profitably be performed with scale advantages in specialized units), the service economy tends to give back opportunities to customers and make it possible for them to do things which they could not do before. Does this mean that we are going back to the state that existed before the industrial economy? No, it means that many more providers will provide offerings which help the customer do things for himself, rather than have the provider do things for the customer. This is what we call an 'enabling logic'.

Complex, broad, relational offerings tend to be characterized by a mixture of *relieving and enabling* elements on the part of the provider. And in many industries we see competition between 'relievers', and 'enablers' who pursue different roads towards largely the same goals. Home health care and preventive health care and self-health care business both competes with and complements more traditional relieving (institutional) health care methods. Relievers such as ad agencies compete with computer manufacturers and their desktop publishing systems who function as enablers for clients to do the work on their own. Microwave oven manufacturers and pre-prepared gourmet food manufacturers compete with gourmet restaurants. A key feature of enabling is that it increases the knowledge transfer component in the service provider's offering. The enabler must master both the technology and the customer's work processes.

Again, the strategic consequence for companies is that they have to find a nuanced mix of relieving and enabling elements in their relationships with customers, in order to find a balance and a formula for total resource utilization which creates the highest net value.

SUMMARY

We need a new conceptual language that allows us to capture the essence of the new economy. Whatever label we want to put on this economy we have to admit that the nature of value production is changing and that the relationship between the players is becoming more complex. It becomes more interdependent and reciprocal rather than sequential. It takes on the nature of coproduction rather than a simple producer versus consumer/user logic. It does not take the form of value chains but of networks.

New technological changes greatly help in exploring and exploiting the opportunities provided by this new logic. Complex interaction is now possible over long distances. On the one hand there are increasing requirements for simultaneity of action between the coproducers (and 'just in time' management and 'flexible manufacturing systems' are examples of technologies and management solutions to allow for more precise such time matching). But on the other hand coordination is easier as 'remote control' opportunities provide independence of location and of time relationships (more intangibles can now be stored, such as in expert systems).

Table 2.2 shows some trends in the innovation content for service and know-how-based industries.

Table 2.2 Some trends in the innovation content for service and know-how-based industries

Transfer of 'manpower and product'	— Transfer of —customer-oriented systems —knowledge —management
Innovation in 'products' and 'service packages'	— Innovation in delivery systems and distribution —reproduction ('McDonaldization') —packaging of knowledge
The dominating 'product'	— The active, dominating customer (tools for self-help)
Technical innovation	— Social innovation and 'hi-tech'–'hi-touch' (organizing behaviour and social interaction)

The industrial economy and the transactions of physical products led to a 'time and location' liberation from earlier restrictions about interaction between production resources. There is no reason why we should not continue to move in the same direction. Today, the options for change and the pressures for more resource-effective value production (and the pressure for more effective use of all available resources, tangible and intangible) impede this movement as we learn how to master the complexity and make the new forces facilitate this movement. In summary, the service economy provision logic has two main aspects:

- Because of the increased complexity of interaction between productive resources there is a competitive pressure to squeeze more out of each resource, and to better match resources with each other for mutual leverage. The result of this is a new interactive logic between providers and customers. This, in turn, means that the relationships and the investments in the provider–customer relationships become assets in themselves, the management of and return on which becomes a critical issue in the service economy.
- In addition we experience a fast relative growth of transactions of intangible elements. This requires us to develop a language of 'the engineering of the intangible'.

This book attempts to provide an answer to these two needs.

3
Service management systems

INTRODUCTION

In discussing the nature of effective service systems, and how to manage them, we will refer to four examples which will illustrate some of our main points. The first two examples were presented in Chapter 2. You will recall J-C Decaux, the French company that erects and maintains bus shelters at no charge to the towns. Its service was founded on creatively linking new contexts; its effectiveness bolstered by its innovative personnel policies. The other example, EF Education offering vacation language learning opportunities, is based on creating new role-sets. McKesson and Troisgros, two additional examples, are presented here to enrich the perspective of effective service systems.

The case of McKesson

McKesson is a very big distributor of pharmaceutical products to independent pharmacies, the largest distributor of wines and spirits, and the largest distributor of chemicals in the USA. In addition it is also a large food distributor. This case focuses on the distribution of drug and healthcare products, which represents roughly 60% of McKesson's revenues and slightly less than 50% of its profits.

In the late 1970s, McKesson came very close to selling its pharmaceutical wholesale and distribution businesses, for it saw that chains were buying up independent pharmacies everywhere, effectively making its clientele disappear.

Instead of selling the business, however, McKesson decided that it would offer pharmacies things other than what it up to then provided to them so as to enable its clientele to survive. 'Your success is our success' was the slogan it adopted. This change, (which involved broadening the offering), was based on an excellent understanding of the strategic potential which its economies of scale and economies of scope provided. It is upon these economies that it based its comparative advantage.

McKesson's 'core' strategy was to enable its clients to survive by providing the individual pharmacy with elements not previously available to them at reasonable cost. While prior to the chain buyout wave such offerings would have been, at best, interesting, McKesson understood that the chain buyout wave converted such offering elements into necessary ones. McKesson continued to believe that the provision of pharmaceutical products to the pharmacies remained its core business. It also realized that the new business situation transformed what its customers required to competitively serve *their* customers.

McKesson exploited the economies of scale and scope it enjoyed in things like efficient ordering and processing of insurance-based billings. Its offering came to include many more enabling elements. McKesson understood the fundamental transformation in the business logic of its clients caused by the chain buyout phenomenon. It, however, made available this broadened offering in an un-bundled form: the pharmacy retained its independence to buy pharmaceuticals without buying the other components.

McKesson's 'survival package' consists of many parts which can be bought as one system (bundled) or in separate chunks (un-bundled). However, owing to the 'business logic' which underlies the whole strategy, when a pharmacy signs up for the one-month renewable 'survival' package their purchases of the (core) pharmaceutical products typically increases by an average of some 30%.

The 'flagship' element of the new offering was called *'Economost'*. Economost allows the individual pharmacy to know how well it is selling each product. It suggests the optimal placement for the different products on self-serve pharmacy shelves and prints out tailor-made pricing labels. This last element is called *'Econoprice'*, and—true to form—is available un-bundled.

Pharmacies that are new customers find the un-bundled offering particularly attractive. The mass-produced individualization aspect allows pharmacists using Economost ordering to correlate their order and the way it is packed at McKesson's to the specific layout of the ordering store. Unpacking the order and stocking the shelves is one process. It reduces inventory storage space and stocking delays, and it increases inventory turnover. It not only saves time but also it makes money.

'Econotone' is a similar competitiveness enhancer for smaller pharmacies. It offers the ordering element but does not include the price sticker element.

'Econocharge' provides pharmacists with credit control and accounts receivable management.

'Econoplan' helps pharmacists with their marketing activities.

'Econoclaim' helps pharmacies handle insurance and government claims, improving their cash flow.

With this broadened and un-bundled offering, McKesson leveraged its customer's overall costing. The individual pharmacies that utilize McKesson's options are now able to match the advantages which the 'chaining' of pharmacies brought to their competitors the big chains.

McKesson is in essence marketing knowledge. Technology allowed McKesson to embody the knowledge transfer to pharmacies in a physical form (computer terminals with access to the knowledge base). By ensuring that its customers started well along the experience curve before anyone else realized of what that curve consisted, it effectively discouraged customers from switching to alternative suppliers.

Simultaneously, it made its customers co-produce some of the value-adding. The customer tailors his business to fit the competitiveness-enhancing tools that McKesson has designed. This takes both training time and a way of operating that increase customer loyalty.

Interestingly, McKesson does not work on long-term contracts. The monthly contract is renewable, and paid in advance. This probably allows the independent pharmacists their independence in ways that matter to them. This very short feedback loop informs McKesson very quickly of their customers' satisfaction with the products and the service.

McKesson has applied the same strategic understanding that it used *vis-à-vis* its customers to itself. In so doing it has been able to improve business not only for itself and for its customers but also for its providers. McKesson's electronic ordering systems, for instance, give pharmaceutical suppliers a better indication of demand, enabling them to better manage inventories.

McKesson took some of the high-cost activities that its clients used to do, broke them down into components or elements, and through relieving some elements and enabling others, transformed the 'business logic'.

With the advent of pharmacy 'chain' logics, McKesson realized that its customers (the independent pharmacies) effectively became the scarcest resource in its business. Recognizing the strategically critical nature of this asset, McKesson swiftly made keeping customers (or keeping customers 'alive'!) the highest investment priority.

This is a superb example of how, knowing that the customer base could not itself be managed, a firm (McKesson) can decide to manage the inputs which the customer base requires (to survive).[1]

The case of Troisgros[2]

Troisgros is one of the great French three-star restaurants—if connoisseurs were to vote for the best, Troisgros would stand a good chance of winning.

But we do not have to penetrate the subtleties of *l'art de la cuisine* in order to find Troisgros a fascinating subject of study: the company is interesting simply as an example of a service system. Let us see what it is like to pay it a visit.

Troisgros is situated in Roanne, more than 300 kilometres from Paris and quite remote, it seems, from anything that could be considered worthwhile or interesting. The only reason to go to Roanne appears to be to visit Troisgros, and people from all corners of the world have realized this.

You are most likely to arrive by car and to have ordered a room to stay overnight. Suppose you arrive between five and six in the afternoon, prepared to spend a couple of hours relaxing in anticipation of the expected experience at table.

Knowing that this is an old railway restaurant you will look for the railway station, and you may have to search a little before you find anything that looks promising. Eventually, however, you drive through a gateway and find yourself in a closed courtyard, neat and clean and surrounded by parking places under the jutting-out first floor of the building. Somebody will come and help you, and you will be checked in and shown your room—all in a friendly, family atmosphere. You have entered the world of Troisgros.

You will be very pleased with your room, with its elegant modern design evocative of a railway carriage. Troisgros is not going to deny its origins. On the contrary it emphasizes them: you are in the old railway restaurant in Roanne, far away from everything. You open the shutters

---

[1] In 1999 McKeson may have made a strategic error in purchasing a computer-services company; this move caused the price of McKessons stock to drop. However, it does not affect the above analysis of the core operation, which continues to prosper.

[2] Since I wrote the above the first time there have been some changes at Troisgros, such as a suspended garden above the parking place. The quality is the same, and I have essentially retained the original text.

and find yourself looking out over the courtyard. Across the yard to the right you see a huge almost floor-to-ceiling window; inside, white-clad figures are beginning to gather, arranging things with great efficiency but apparently without flurry. You are looking into the kitchen, which seems open to you in every detail.

A small Citroën comes into the courtyard, driving up to what must be the entrance to the kitchen. Somebody—you might recognize him as one of the Troisgros family—goes down to the driver, who lifts out a box of large, beautiful salmon. The fish are turned over, touched, and investigated from every angle. A few are selected and taken up to the kitchen, where you see them being rinsed immediately and stored in a cool place.

Another person turns up. The procedure is repeated; this time it is ducks, or vegetables. You realize that the people working in the kitchen have just been having their dinner, sitting together round a table and somehow giving the impression of a wonderfully pleasant atmosphere. But now they are getting organized, scattering to the different parts of the kitchen. Nothing is being cooked yet; everything is being prepared— professionally, efficiently, and with great care to detail. The whole process exudes superb, total control.

You realize that you have changed your plans—you had meant to have taken a shower by this time. But you notice that others windows are also open, and that the other guests are watching too. Now and then some of the white-clad young men in the kitchen glance in your direction—they know they are being watched; it is obvious that they are working 'on stage' and that they are aware of it; they are putting on a good show. You suddenly realize that every single one of them knows he is part of a unique team putting on a unique performance, and he is proud of it.

After taking yet another look and admiring the spacious, functional, impeccable layout of the kitchen, you realize that hunger is setting in; you take the shower you had postponed because of the unexpected performance, and soon you wander along in the direction of the restaurant.

But it is not quite time; the restaurant has not opened yet. So you go to the bar, and here you are in for the next surprise. Again you find the friendly atmosphere which you now realize pervades the place but you are surprised to find that the people sitting in the bar are not only travelling gourmets like yourself, from Paris, London or New York; instead most of them seem to be local people and few of them are going to eat in the restaurant. They sip their drinks and have a few snails or petits fours to eat; and going from table to table, chatting relaxedly, is one of the Troisgros family who seems to be everybody's friend. Somebody hands you the menu; after a while the doors to the restaurant are open, and a new performance begins. But we can leave our description here; the reader is advised to learn about the rest for himself.

In both of the examples above, we can clearly see the importance of skilfully designed systems, both within the company and in its relationships not only with the customers, but with suppliers as well. Furthermore, the social dimension, the human-relations aspect, is extremely important, particularly at Troisgros.

PRODUCT, PRODUCTION AND PRODUCTION SYSTEM

It is a striking feature of many successful services that the service itself seems simple and uncomplicated. It is the ability to create a system which can produce and reproduce the service while maintaining its quality which often constitutes a major problem in any attempt at innovation in service organizations. We will discuss the design of such systems in considerable detail in the following chapters.

In practice it is difficult in a service operation to distinguish clearly between the service, the process of providing the service and the system for delivering it. Since the service itself almost always consists of an act involving the customer, quality will also be perceived by the customer in items of this interaction. Similarly, the system producing the service will be judged from the behaviour and style of the contact personnel and the physical tools and facilities on display. The very intangibility of a service automatically forces the customer to look for additional clues for evaluation.

Consulting services, barbers' shops and banks all clearly illustrate the close identity between service, service delivery process and service delivery system from the customer's point of view. The case of Troisgros shows us how the whole service delivery system can unexpectedly become part of the customer's experience. The J-C Decaux case—where rather less of the service is provided in direct customer contact, although it is highly visible to the customer—demonstrates the need for holistic thinking in designing service systems. The service could not have been realistically conceived without concrete and innovative ideas about how to create it. Briefly: the ability to think in terms of wholes and of the integration of structure and process is indispensable to the creation of effective service systems.

SERVICE SYSTEMS AS INNOVATIVE LINKAGES BETWEEN HUMAN CAPACITIES

What is the product of J-C Decaux? The business can usefully be described as creating a new linkage between towns and advertisers, in which the role of the company involves the careful organization of this linkage to enable the participants to reap the benefits of a high-quality relationship. The company is an organizer of people not employed by itself; it provides an infrastructure consisting of its own structure and systems to make the new organizational linkage viable.

A typical feature of service companies is that one of their outputs is new *social relationships* and that they have to extend their organizing capability well outside their own company. An analysis of the principles involved will appear in later chapters, and we will then look particularly at the way the service company has to 'organize' its client.

It is also worth noting that many of the linkages representing the crucial outputs of service companies are unconventional or unexpected. People or groups or sectors normally regarded as separate are linked together (cf. Crozier, 1982). To return to J-C Decaux: the company brings together elements from the public sector (towns), the private sector (advertisers) and individual households (bus travellers and poster watchers). And the company creates this complex picture partly as a result of individual pride and entrepreneurship among its maintenance staff.

EF Education provides an excellent illustration of a feature which characterizes many successful service organizations, and which we could call *human capacity management.* Their accomplishment was to design a service delivery system which could produce a relatively complex service at a much lower cost than had been possible before. The example makes it clear that the guiding principle was to identify and exploit existing over-capacities and unused sources of energy. This applied to physical facilities (overcapacity in the airlines, unused school premises), but it also applied with particular force to the use of human energy.

EF Education is also a supreme example of a company extending its organization into domains outside its own borders. The 'salesmen', the teachers and the host families are crucial parts of the service delivery system—and yet none of them belong to the EF organization. But they are organized, and they are rendered productive. The first step in this organizing process is to identify the particular needs, energies and life situations of the outside participants. It is interesting to note that all these categories were paid relatively little by the company—and yet they were quite happy to perform. The explanation is that EF Education had designed tasks based on such a clear understanding of the particular needs of the groups concerned that the participants thought *they* were being rendered a service! The 'salesmen' received a tremendous boost to their incomes; the schoolteachers who also helped to promote the service were interested in raising the standard of their classes; the teachers who went to the host countries had a paid holiday and acquired some useful experience; the host families were chosen because they were likely to appreciate the experience offered them. Without this consistent sensitivity to human situations and needs, and without a task system designed to meet these needs, the provision of the service would not have been possible.

McKesson's system also extended far beyond the boundaries of their own organization. They created new patterns of behaviour both with their suppliers and with their customers that greatly deviated from the established norms but which made much more effective use of resources in the total system. This new pattern creation even extended to their customers' customers. McKesson used information technology innovations as their leading tool to achieve these new role constellations.

Many of the most interesting service ideas exhibit similar cross-boundary organizing characteristics: for instance, health maintenance organizations and cooperative housing administration companies. On the basis of our experience, we find it fairly obvious that a societal organization with a highly bureaucratic separation of different sectors, and other hindrances to the creation of new linkages, would not be beneficial. This is probably the main reason why so many of the new, interesting complex service systems seem to originate in the United States. And we have noticed that in France, a highly regulated country, several of the most interesting new services have popped up under the legal mantle of the 'association', a kind of intermediate structure between business company and a voluntary club, which facilitates and legitimizes new linkages and unconventional forms.

But the question of how we could design societies of a more organizable—or rather reorganizable—kind will have to be the subject of another book.

The EF Education example also illustrates those instances in which absolute control is necessary because nothing must go wrong. This is why the company formed its own tightly-knit organization for selecting families and why it developed its own teaching materials.

CLIENT MANAGEMENT AND CLIENT PARTICIPATION

All our four cases show how the client can be made into an active participant in the service system. The schoolchildren studying at EF Education were certainly very much part of each other's environment during excursions and classes and other events. The clients' changed behaviours were both a result of, and a prerequisite for, the McKesson service system. Equally striking is the way the client is drawn into the service delivery system at Troisgros—and I don't mean that he chooses his food and transfers it from the plate to his mouth. The design of the system is such that clients and employees are unexpectedly linked (there is hardly a kitchen in the world, even in the greatest restaurants, that is not carefully concealed from the client's view, even if the trend is towards greater openness in this regard).

The customer is not just an onlooker; his presence in this particular context creates a social dynamic which makes the employees conscious of their roles and their prestige, which in turn helps to create a genuine new experience and a sense of participation in the customer. In a well-designed service delivery system we will find that the employee, the client and any other organized but not employed participants all emerge from the process of service delivery and/or service consumption with an enhanced sense of self-esteem.

It could even be argued—although it seems thoroughly out of place in the case of Troisgros!—that a degree of quality control is incorporated into the service delivery system. Some of the production process takes place before the eyes of the customer instead of being hidden from him. I imagine that most French three-star restaurants have to give more thought to supervising and controlling quality than is necessary at Troisgros.

The Troisgros case amply demonstrates yet another principle: the importance of harmony and mutual support between the main parts of the service delivery system—staff, client and physical setting. Everything seems to be reinforcing everything else in a rising spiral of quality and atmosphere. It was the special layout—the courtyard, the huge kitchen window and the impeccable kitchen—which made possible the linkage, which in turn created the social dynamic. In this setting the client is almost compelled to receive impressions, to be aware of an experience, while the self-respect, the motivation and the excellence of the employees are almost certain to be enhanced. To achieve the same effects without this complementary physical setting would have required other, probably more expensive, means, if indeed it were possible at all. Again, the service on offer (the experience which the customer undergoes) is uniquely linked with the service delivery system.

MANAGEMENT, STRUCTURE AND CULTURE

Service is a social process, and management is the ability to direct social processes. And service organizations are more sensitive to the quality of their management than probably any other kind of organization. An important part of management consists of identifying the critical factors which make the particular service system function and designing powerful ways of controlling and maintaining these attributes in a very concrete manner. If the details do not function properly, no grand design will ever succeed. But again, since service is a social process, there is a need for individual motivation and freedom, and for freedom at the local level, which management must also cater for. Because of these seemingly contradictory demands the management and structure of the effective service system will exhibit certain special and characteristic properties.

One such feature concerns the importance ascribed to values and culture and ethos—the guiding principles. On making contact with any really successful service companies, one is aware almost immediately of a special kind of ethos emanating from every employee and infecting the client as well. Infusing an organization with values directly related to the success of the business is an effective (and sometimes the only) way of controlling a decentralized operation which is probably heavily dependent on individual contributions. Many service companies enjoy tens of thousands of client contacts or moments of truth every day, most of them probably involving employees working in the field. There is no other way of achieving high quality in every single contact by maintaining a pervasive culture and making sure that every employee not only possesses the appropriate skills but is also guided by the appropriate ethos.

In the case of J-C Decaux we mentioned a couple of very simple and concrete ways in which key values and the necessary ethos are consistently maintained: the principle of direct access to the leader for the maintenance staff, and the principle whereby every employee carries a scraper in his car. In no way can these messages be wrongly interpreted, and they serve to focus everyone's minds on the critical points and on those important things which create quality. The other companies in our cases are equally infused with a unique behaviour-oriented culture.

This kind of unique behaviour-oriented culture may be partly maintained—and indeed created—by a special type of relationship between the centre and the periphery (or local level) in the service organization. The power relationships are often quite different here, and more unusual, than those which evolve in production companies. Sometimes the local units actually own the central unit. There is an interesting Swedish company, Praktikertjanst, whose key employees are a thousand or so doctors and dentists, which not only employs its 'employees' but is also owned by them. Syndicate or federation type structures, where members retain a high degree of autonomy, are fairly common.

McKesson, through information technology, has created a system in which major redistributions of tasks and mutual role changes are achieved without central ownership, franchising contracts, or other formal attributes of a cooperative or federative structure. These and similar arrangements tend to emphasize and to embody in concrete form one of the key characteristics of effective service systems, which can be summarized succinctly as 'Small is beautiful on a large scale'.

EFFECTIVE SERVICE SYSTEMS ARE REPRODUCIBLE

One of the reasons for the industrialization of service operations, and the emergence of large service companies in sectors which used to be regarded as local or belonging to the cottage industry class, lies in the improvement of methods for reproducing services. The reproducibility of a service system is based first on *identifying its absolutely essential elements* and secondly on *designing effective ways of controlling and recreating these elements*. The prototype which immediately comes to mind here is McDonald's, where control of the physical layout, of personnel policy, of the assortment of services and the purchasing of raw materials is given concrete form in the franchising agreement, the basic ingredient in the reproduction formula.

Service systems that are too complex, or rather those that are too unclear, cannot be reproduced. And service systems that are heavily dependent on particular cultural or other environmental features are also difficult to reproduce. It is no coincidence that health care organizations originating in California have found great difficulty in breaking into Sweden, for example. The really effective service system may in fact be quite complex; but it must be possible to analyse it down to its very bone structure. Otherwise it will remain a local phenomenon.

SERVICE MANAGEMENT SYSTEMS

The four cases and the ensuing analysis of some of their salient characteristics have so far been used mainly to alert the reader to the characteristic features of service systems. They will also serve as a point of reference in the following chapters.

We have stressed the importance of adopting a holistic approach to the construction—or indeed the study—of service systems. It is necessary to identify the key determinants of success in a service business and to reflect them in the management and culture of the organization, so that a system can first be reproduced and subsequently maintained systematically over a long period of time. Thus we need to define a number of concepts which will help us to study the structure of service systems. I shall describe below what we in our group call *service management systems*. The basic conceptual framework is illustrated in Figure 3.1 and its five main components will be studied in detail in the following chapters. These components are:

1. *The market segment.* This refers to the particular types of client for which the whole service system was designed.

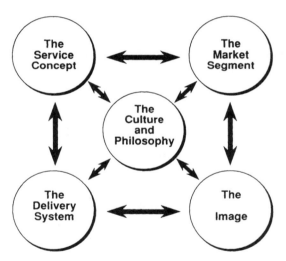

Figure 3.1   The service management system

2. *The service concept.* This constitutes the benefits offered to the client. As we shall see, the service concept often consists of a very complex set of values which are frequently difficult to analyse. Some of the benefits are physical and some are psychological or emotional; further, some are more important and may be called *core* services, while others are more *peripheral* in character; some characteristics can be measured and specified, while others may

be of the utmost importance but are almost impossible to specify in concrete form.

3. *The service delivery system.* This is the equivalent of the production and distribution systems in manufacturing organizations, but it is often very different in character. We shall deal at great length with the service delivery system, since it is often here rather than in the design of the service concept that we find the most unique and innovative ideas of a service company. In analysing the service delivery system we shall look at three subcomponents:

(a) *Personnel.* As was pointed out in the first chapter, service organizations are generally *personality-intensive,* and the most successful of them have conceived extremely creative and rigorous ways of finding and developing and focusing human resources. Similarly, they have discovered ways of mobilizing people other than their own employees. We shall devote two chapters to the staff component of the service delivery system.

(b) *Client.* Our four preliminary cases served to illustrate that the client plays an interestingly complex role in the service organization, since he not only receives and consumes the service but also serves as a component in its production and delivery. Thus, in a service business, clients must be selected and managed as carefully as employees.

(c) *Technology and physical support.* It has already been pointed out that while most services are *personality-intensive,* they often require a great deal of capital or equipment as well. We shall be dwelling less on technology and physical support than on the other parts of the service delivery system, since the role of this factor here does not differ significantly from its role in manufacturing companies. However, it should be remembered that the impact of new technology—particularly information technology—on services is going to be enormous. In our analysis we shall look at technology and physical components mainly in the light of one special characteristic: that services almost always involve social interactions, and that physical tools—from computerized airline reservation systems to the design of restaurant tables—are critical to the functioning of such interactive systems.

4. *The image.* This is regarded here as an information tool whereby management can influence staff, clients and other resource-holders whose actions and perceptions of the company—what it is and where it is going—are important to market positioning and cost efficiency. In the long run, of course, the image depends mainly on what the company actually provides and who the customers actually are; but in the short run the image, although deviating from current reality, can be used as a tool for the creation of a new reality.

5. *The culture and philosophy.* This embraces the overall principles by which the social process leading to the delivery of services and benefits to clients is controlled, maintained and developed. Once a superior service delivery system and an appropriate service concept have been created, no other component is more crucial to the long-term efficiency of the service organization than its culture and philosophy, which shape and rejuvenate the very values and ethos on which the company thrives.

These five components, then, comprise the service management system. The idea of the service management system has gradually evolved in the course of a long period working with all kinds of service organizations. In its theoretical contents it to some extent integrates but also transcends two other models: that of the 'service system' or 'magic formula' as developed by Eiglier and Langeard (e.g. Langeard, 1981a,b) and that of the 'business idea' as developed in Normann (1977). The two models have also been augmented; in particular, the idea of constitution and philosophy as dynamic elements has been more clearly expressed.

The model has the character of a system consisting of components and emphasizing the relationship among them. While the model may be perceived as static, we would underscore that working with it must be a process of a cultural nature. We use the term 'process' to stress the importance of developing the system; we say that the process is 'cultural' because it concerns something created by human beings. Therefore, service management should not be viewed as engineering leadership in the operation of complex machinery, but as social leadership in the creation of development, and cultivation of dynamic, living human culture. In this book we shall devote considerable attention to the process and the dynamics which both create, and are created by, the service management system.

4

Dynamic diagnosis: virtuous circles and vicious circles

MECHANISMS BEHIND THE CIRCLES

Why is it that some restaurants in a district always seem to be crowded whilst others are half empty or have to close down? Why do good service businesses sometimes suddenly go bad? Why do some successful service companies grow so rapidly? Why can we nearly always tell at once whether a service company is successful or not?

Service organizations are extremely sensitive to the quality of management. The intangibility of their output and the generally high 'personality intensity' of their production apparatus tend to make their input/output ratio extremely sensitive and variable. A few motivation problems, a few transactions that fall down on quality or a little general sloppiness—any of these can plunge the service organization into a 'vicious circle'.

Because of this great sensitivity to good or bad management, we cannot often attach an 'average' tag to a service organization's performance. Either it tends to have problems or it tends to do pretty well. The symptoms of success are many: profit, growth (or possibly a strong tendency to grow which is consciously resisted in order to maintain equilibrium and service quality), good staff morale, no problem in finding eager potential recruits, low customer turnover and a queue of potential customers knocking on the door. The problem organization, on the other hand, tends towards poor economic performance, unsatisfactory growth, sloppiness, low morale, high customer and staff turnover, and a log of management effort spent on trying to win back dissatisfied customers.

Once again it must be stressed that a service organization is a complex and sensitive system in which a variety of functions and elements are closely interrelated. Thus, in a diagnosis of the difficulties of a service organization *only rarely will a single symptom or a single problem* prove to lie at the root of the trouble. It is therefore generally more fruitful to diagnose the problems in terms of 'vicious circles', in which many different factors reinforce one another. This type of description reflects the systemic character of the organization, and helps to identify the key strategic areas in which a change could turn the vicious circle into a 'virtuous' or benevolent one.

How do vicious circles arise? Let us look at some common mechanisms, brought together in Figure 4.1.

○ Complicating the service management systems
○ Growth without control
○ An inappropriate power structure
○ Mismatch between service package and customer expectations
○ Bad or sloppy operations management
○ Inappropriate economic control systems
○ Inability to attract staff

Figure 4.1   At the eye of the vicious circle: causal factors

Complicating the service management system. A bank invested in a number of new peripheral services, leading customers to expect ready accessibility and a high level of service at a low price. But these expectations were more than the bank's service delivery system could live up to; the internal and external images became blurred and the company was well into a vicious spiral before the necessary changes (in this case resimplification and refocusing) were made.

Growth without control. A frequent phenomenon, as we shall illustrate in several examples later on. Many have tried to reproduce a service management system without sufficient simplification of the 'magic formula' and without sufficient support systems to ensure an appropriate reproduction formula. One should also beware of mixing and diluting service management systems.

An inappropriate power structure. A particular example of this, which appears to be rather common, is a power structure that lacks balance between central and local units. The following case of a large Swedish retail chain illustrates a deeply entrenched vicious circle:

The chain was created in the 1930s, when it was based on the idea of central purchasing, simple outlets and low prices. Although the shops were regarded as 'low status', the basic formula which permitted low prices gave it a good following and it grew rapidly. It was also among the first to adopt and implement important new ideas such as self-service in all its stores. When the chain of stores first started, it was difficult to recruit store managers from within the industry, since 'retail people' were not attracted by the low-status image. However, the company developed a personnel idea that was very well adapted to its situation at that time: it recruited as store managers officers who had retired early from the army. The ex-officers were able to keep order and exercise discipline in the stores, and since all crucial decisions were anyway made centrally, their lack of knowledge of the industry was not important.

As the years passed, other organizations gradually attained the same advantages (e.g. of large-scale purchasing) but sometimes using quite different organizational concepts. There were voluntary chains, federative organizations and various other arrangements. The price advantages disappeared, and success in this industry gradually became more a question of local adaptation and highly energetic local management. While the low-status image of the retail chain had largely disappeared from the public's mind, it had persisted inside the company. The central purchasing people and the system-development people had all the power, and all the problems were seen as an expression of the need for more central control. The idea that the store managers were not really very professional and could not therefore be given more freedom of action was reinforced. But at the new stage in the development of the industry this whole idea was wrong. It was supported and reinforced by the traditional power system, however, until, finally, the company collapsed and had to be reconstructed financially.

Mismatch between service package and customer expectations. When we use the service of an airline, we think primarily about being transported from one place to another. And yet the service we receive also contains a great many other components, such as seat reservation, check-in and baggage handling—what we have here termed peripheral services. This whole system must work well if we are to feel that we have been given good service. Many companies make the mistake of thinking it is enough if the primary service is good.

When a service company experiences some form of economic pressure, it often gets itself into a vicious circle as described on the left-hand side of Figure 4.2. It starts to cut down a little on its service, especially its peripheral services. An airline, for example, may allow longer check-in queues or reduce the amount or the quality of the food it serves.

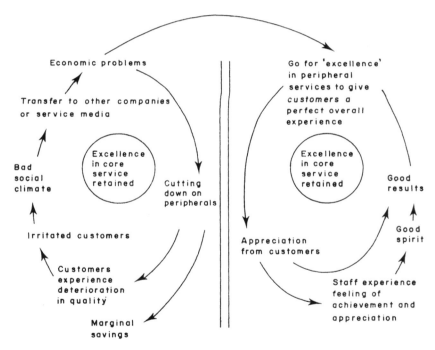

Figure 4.2   Quality: a vicious or a virtuous circle

This can lead to some slight marginal savings, but the customer's perception of the quality he is getting can change dramatically as a result of such apparently small adjustments. Customers are no longer as happy as they might have been, which affects the social climate at the check-in desk or in the aircraft, which in turn reduces the enthusiasm and motivation of the service personnel. The customer's negative experience is then reinforced, which in turn reduces his own contribution to the overall quality. And so, as the negative effects reinforce one another, the vicious circle continues in an ever accelerating downward spiral.

Under the same conditions another airline might come to quite different conclusions, even succeeding in raising the quality of the peripheral service instead, perhaps at very little cost. The result will be customers who are pleasantly surprised and pleased, a positive social climate and a good atmosphere, and a stronger positive experience of quality. The staff feel that they have achieved something and that they are appreciated.

Thus the best way of handling the original problems might have been to support genuine 'excellence' in both the core service and the various peripheral services. And certainly any adjustment in a service package has to be based on a profound understanding (often difficult to achieve) of the delicate composition of the package and what constitutes quality to the clients. Very small measures, strategically applied, often produce big effects as a result of various reinforcement mechanisms. But the connection between small measures and big effects works in both directions: it can lead to a vicious or a virtuous circle.

Our experience has taught us that '12 pluses are needed to cancel out a single minus', and this explains why service companies often seem to go into vicious circles, for instance when important people leave or other radical administrative changes are made. In such situations the detailed knowledge which has been acquired in the course of a long pragmatic learning process, which makes it possible to allot to each section of a service package its particular value, is easily lost. Thus, minuses can readily arise, and the company must go to considerable trouble to achieve the 12 offsetting pluses that are required.

Bad or sloppy operations management. In the retailing industry there is an old saying: 'retailing is detailing'. This could be taken as a motto for all service industries. Attention to detail, making the small things function, and the daily maintenance of the system's performance—all these are crucial to success. Profit margins are often small, and results are greatly dependent on efficient cost control and the ability of supervisors and local managers to stimulate motivation and focus the human energy available in the company.

There are many symptoms of inadequate operations management, and Table 4.1 provides a striking illustration of some of them. Analysis of staff and customer turnover can be quite revealing. Statements to the effect that 'I don't know what my superiors really expect of me' are clear indications of weak operations management. Sloppy cost control and general symptoms of low morale are others.

Table 4.1 Typical quotations from a local office in a large service organization where operations management and results have begun to deteriorate

I don't know what my boss thinks I'm good at.

Some people escape from their responsibilities. Others have to do the hard work, which means a lot of overtime.

Most things in this place are really very unclear.

Management often say 'yes' or 'no' without fully realizing what it's all about.

Our internal problems are often discussed, but nobody really does anything about them.

Under the present circumstances there doesn't seem much point in really betting on the job.

My boss doesn't seem very interested in what I'm doing.

We're very bad at helping each other.

It's difficult to do a good job when you only get sporadic information about what goes on in the office.

Inappropriate management control systems. A high level of people orientation tends to be a feature of effective operations management in service organizations. Management must consider people as individuals while also promoting the kind of general social climate which is necessary to the good performance of these individuals. But it is also important that the *'hard' control systems,* particularly the managerial accounting systems, are *clearly defined and appropriate.* In the following example a company had unnecessary problems, and failed to achieve its potential, because its economic systems were inappropriate:

The company in question was a major international engineering and technical consulting company. Its traditional home base was the building and construction industry of a European country, where the industry was subjected to strict regulation by way of government norms. One norm gave the maximum hourly rate that could be charged by the individual consultant. The company had adopted these official norms for its external pricing on the home market. In a highly flexible project or matrix type organization of this kind, there were naturally a great many internal deliveries between various resource and specialist units.

In dealing with the market, any particular unit was naturally interested in making a profit. When using its own resources, or buying resources internally, it had to pay the real cost. Since there was a ceiling, the contribution margin tended to be lower for the highest paid and generally the most skilled people. There was consequently a tendency wherever possible to use people whose contribution margins would be higher.

The effect of this internal costing system was a curious one: many of the best and most experienced people, who would really have been in a position to supply more value to the client, tended to find it difficult to 'get jobs' internally. As a result, the company failed to use its best resources to its own best advantage, and it was quite obvious that a better utilization of resources would have produced higher quality in individual projects, more growth and better financial results.

It would be beyond our present scope to examine this question in further detail here, since our purpose is not to discuss the technicalities of operations management. But the more we have worked with service organizations the more we have found that inappropriate operations management plays an important part in creating problems and vicious circles. And 'inappropriate' here includes hard control systems which fail to focus attention and to direct behaviour towards those aspects of the business formula which are crucial to success.

Inability to attract staff. Unless a company's image and its performance are such that it will automatically attract the kind of high-quality, highly motivated people who are in themselves a necessary condition of further excellence and growth, there is almost no way of preventing the company from plunging into a vicious circle.

THE ECOLOGY OF MICROCIRCLES AND MACROCIRCLES

The various examples of circles, most of them vicious, in the previous section differ somewhat in their character. Some of them apply to situations of short duration and to isolated parts of a service company's operations; others concern the longer run and the overall evolution and positioning of the organization's structure, strategy and problem-solving abilities. We shall now try to show that close linkages exist between circles (virtuous as well as vicious) at different levels, and to indicate the nature of these linkages.

THE MOMENT OF TRUTH: THE MICROCIRCLE

Once again it should be stressed that any analysis of service operations must begin at the moment of truth, at the company–client interface where quality as perceived by the client is created. A major aim of any service organization in which there is any kind of person-to-person interaction must be to achieve a positive social dynamic in confrontation with the client, so that the service supplied and the client together form a mutually reinforcing system. In fact, a good indicator that a 'virtuous circle' exists at the moment of truth is that both the service supplied (the company's contact person, who may or may not be a company employee) and the client should feel 'uplifted' by the interaction in some way (strengthened, excited or just generally aware of a positive experience). Such feelings will reinforce the efforts of both participants to produce a good service (see Figure 4.3).

The importance of this virtuous circle is obvious, especially if we bear in mind that the client is also a producer, a participator in the service delivery process. The dynamics of this circle are beautifully illustrated by the following quotations from a passenger and a stewardess of an airline which experienced a dramatic reversal in its fortunes following extensive efforts to focus on value to the customer while also paying attention to (and expecting more of) its personnel. A representative statement from a customer about six months after the reform program was launched was:

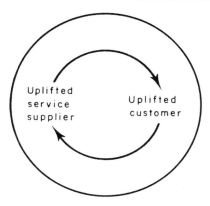

Figure 4.3 The virtuous microcircle at the moment of truth

The attitude of the personnel and the value you get for your money have changed dramatically. You would hardly believe it's the same people in those aircraft any longer.

And when we asked a stewardess how it came about that the behaviour of personnel had changed so much in such a short time, she pondered the question for a few seconds and then in a flash of insight said:

No, we have not changed. But our customers have! Somehow they are quite different now, and that makes everything a lot more fun and you feel you get something from them, and so you also want to give.

THE MACROCIRCLE

The 'virtuous macrocircle' seems an apt way of describing the stable circumstances that lead to long-term success in a company: a strong market position, good economic results and the constant maintenance and evolution of one or more well-functioning service management systems (see Figure 4.4).

We shall return later to the very direct links between the microcircle and the macrocircle. First, however, pursuing our analysis, one more 'virtuous circle' should be mentioned, relating to the necessary accord between the internal climate of the company

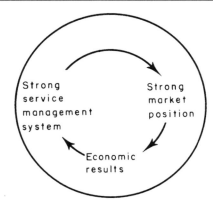

Figure 4.4   The virtuous macrocircle

and the climate and standards of excellence necessary to a good service operation.

THE 'INTERNAL SERVICE' CIRCLE

In analysing the key principles of successful service organizations (see Chapter 3), we noted frequently that the borderline between employee and client, and between employee and other representatives of the service company, is a complex and often also a hazy one. Companies like EF Education have to be very imaginative about organizing and motivating a variety of external human resources in order to achieve efficient service operations, and quite often these external resources even feel that the company is doing them a service rather than the other way round.

Experience clearly shows that this attitude of good service on the company's part must apply to all those who work for it, including its formal employees. If the contact person is an important means whereby the company can give the customer value for money, then the company must also give value to those who work for it.

It is very important in this context that *the attitudes and norms prevailing inside the company and the attitudes and norms required at the moment of truth with the customer should accord with one another.* Research has shown (Schneider, 1980) that a contact person who is expected to apply one set of norms and one type of behaviour in his customer relationships but who is exposed to a different and conflicting type of behaviour on the part of management and supervisors is being placed in an ambivalent and contradictory situation which soon becomes untenable. In the end, the employee cannot cope with several incongruent sets of behaviour stemming from several different cultures or norm systems, and gradually the behaviour displayed to the client will begin to approach the behaviour of the supervisor towards the contact person. In order to reduce dissonance the employee will tend to change his own behaviour to be more in line with dominant norms he encounters.

My interpretation of the theoretical findings and my own experience thus suggest that, to be successful, a service company must strive to see that a *single set of basic principles* pervades the whole organization, from top management, through all levels and right up to the moment of truth. Double signals will create double binds and schizophrenic situations for the people on the barricades. A common, pervasive set of principles, effectively communicated and consistently implemented at all levels, is vital.

Thus we can depict a third type of virtuous circle, which must be actively implemented at all levels of the organizational hierarchy. To stress the idea of creating an all-pervading organizational climate consistent with the climate essential to the moment of truth, we can call this circle the 'internal service' circle (Figure 4.5). The internal life of the organization also consists of moments of truth, when people and groups from different hierarchical levels and different functional sectors help each other to operate (i.e. provide 'services' for one another), with the ultimate aim of bringing all resources to bear on the customer.

RELATIONSHIPS BETWEEN THREE LEVELS

The difference between being in a 'virtuous circle', where positive action reinforces positive action, and being in a vicious circle at any of the levels we have discussed, is in itself important. However, the fact that the circles at the different levels are often closely and directly interrelated explains why it is often possible,

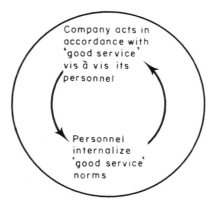

Figure 4.5   The virtuous 'internal service' circle

even in a fairly short time, to achieve a major 'lift' or reversal in a service organization with dramatic results.

An understanding of the nature of these 'circles' also tells us something about how to reverse unfavourable situations and how to undertake change processes in service organizations. We shall return to the question of intervention and change strategies later.

In Figure 4.6, the various circles have been combined. The links between the macrocircle and microcircle are often quite direct: a precise, consistent and efficient provision of service at the moment of truth leads to satisfied customers, which in turn makes for easier repeat selling and a better market position. Success and an image on the recruitment market reinforced by satisfied customers and by a reputation for good 'internal service' means that the company can be selective in its recruiting and that it can maintain a staff characterized by pride, self-esteem and high motivation, all of which will in turn reinforce its ability to handle the moment of truth.

A profound understanding of the dynamics of the virtuous circles and their interrelationships is at the root of creative, result-oriented management and of effective intervention in service companies.

CIRCLE OR SPIRAL—A COMMENT ON CONCEPTS

In conclusion, a comment on the use of the two concepts of circle and spiral: vicious and virtuous circles are the concepts generally

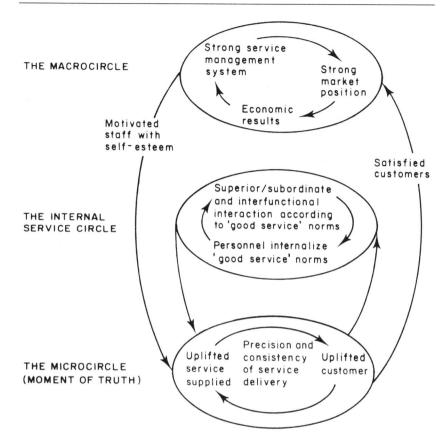

Figure 4.6   The virtuous circles of the service company

used by practitioners. In certain respects, however, they may be misleading, since spiral movements are often involved in both cases; there is no return to the exact starting point, but to a state which is either somewhat better or somewhat worse.

Nevertheless, we have hesitated to replace the circle concept with that of a spiral consistently throughout our discussion. The word spiral has a connotation of a relatively dramatic upward or downward movement. Such dramatic developments may indeed occur in the short run. But in our experience, a good service company will more often be typified by virtuous circles and will seek to preserve this situation in various ways. A more pronounced upward spiral movement is considered hazardous, with hyperactivity and burn-out among the risks. As customers we like to be given a 'lift'—up to a certain limit. Beyond that limit, we may temporarily feel that we are experiencing a complete success, but in the long run we would prefer something more 'normally' good, more reliable, and longer-lasting. As for service companies that are not so well managed, they may be able to struggle onward for a relatively long time, but they have to spend a lot of energy trying to keep vicious circles from degenerating into downward spirals.

5

The service concept

THE SERVICE PACKAGE: CORE AND PERIPHERALS

A physical product can be clearly and unequivocally described in terms of its attributes (if not its functions): size, parts, materials, and so on. A service cannot be as easily specified nor can it really be demonstrated before purchase. One way of conceiving a service on offer—the benefits offered to the client in a service system—is to use a physical product as a metaphor and to list as clearly as possible exactly what is being offered or what is going to be achieved as a result of rendering the service. A good rule of thumb here is to start by listing all the areas or points of contact with the client. In the case of airline transportation, we could start with making the reservation; we could then proceed to arrival at the airport, finding the check-in desk, checking in, and so on.

After establishing what the client is going to receive and experience at all these contact points, we can then work backwards and consider the processes necessary to the achievement of the desired point-of-contact effect.

By looking at the service on offer in this way we can arrive at a description of a 'service package'—a set of related items offered to the client. Sometimes one of the items is clearly predominant. In an airline service, the actual transport of the client from Paris to London is probably more important than the cleanliness of the airport (the reason we are there is to be transported, not to look at a clean airport, however much we may appreciate it). To the client of a consulting company, the quality of the consultant's recommendations should be more important than the physical appearance of his report. In such cases we can distinguish between a *core service* and other ancillary or *peripheral services,* which are all part of the package (Figure 5.1).

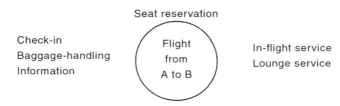

Figure 5.1   Core service and secondary (or peripheral) services

However, the distinction between core and peripheral services is not always clear cut. Especially where there is little difference between the core services of competing companies, the client's choice may be determined by what we could tend to regard as peripherals. In our group we have seen examples of this in many businesses, including insurance, consulting and airlines. This type of situation often leads to competition in terms of peripherals, with a kind of tacit agreement between competitors that the quality and further development of what is supposedly the core service may not be all that important or costly considering that competitors may respond with a similar counter-move. Gasoline (petrol) suppliers do not compete on the price of fuel but by offering better opening and closing hours, various bonus gifts etc.

The customers' experience and evaluation of the total service they get is determined by two factors:

- whether the service package includes all the elements (core and peripherals) that he expects, and
- the extent to which each of these elements meets the various standards and quality criteria that he expects.

Thus, a customer may be dissatisfied with respect to, say, airport bar service either because it is not there at all, or because it is there but functions slowly or otherwise does not meet his standards.

In evaluating a service the customer is greatly influenced by habit and by what he has been led to expect. Nobody expects a

Chateau Lafite and silver cutlery in a McDonald's restaurant, and yet the quality there can be perceived as superb. Nonetheless, a type of service and a level of quality suited to McDonald's would bring Troisgros to bankruptcy and the *Guide Michelin* inspectors to suicide within a few days. When he embarks on a charter flight with his family, the businessman accepts without protest the cramped space and longer waiting times that would be quite unacceptable on his business trips.

By contrast, a charter-flight passenger who never travels on business may expect first-class service on the charter flight. The advertisements may have given the impression that the service level would be the same as on regularly scheduled flights.

It is when the service package does *not* contain what we have been led to expect by previous experience or by promises that we complain. As consumers we are in fact so guided by habit or expectation that we hardly notice good efficient service. If we go to a good restaurant, we expect the food to be excellent and the service to be courteous, and we expect an airline to keep the waiting time at the check-in desk down to a reasonable level. When normal, good service is provided, we accept it without a second thought. We notice the lack of good service, or service which falls below what we have come to expect, much more than we notice normal, satisfactory service. (We may also notice *exceptional service.*) We accept being treated to higher standards than we had come to expect, but if the service falls short of our expectations in some respects, we immediately register the fact and react to it.

It can be very revealing to do a short mental experiment, assigning a plus to every aspect of a service package which is at or above the standard we expect and a minus to any peripheral service (or, of course, core service) in the package which falls below standard. Someone (I am not sure who) has said—hitting the nail exactly on the head—that, psychologically, 'it takes 12 pluses to make up for a single minus'. When a service is provided, it is always the minuses that we notice, while we tend to forget the pluses.

It should be emphasized, however, that we may also make note of *exceptional service.* Doing something extra and unexpected may be what the customer will remember. For example, arranging a trip for a group may mean including a pleasant surprise, something that the group feels no other competitor would have given them. We know by experience that these occasions are what many people remember and can make up for occasional blunders. After a trip which has been impeccably arranged from a logistic standpoint, few travellers will be enthusiastic customers, though they probably will be satisfied customers.

Thus, customer expectations are something which a service company should analyse. It is wrong to believe that 'the customer is always right'. In fact, customers often are unreasonable, or do not know what they expect. And we would go further: they often do not know what they need, and what would be best for them. It is not uncommon for customers to put demands and have expectations which are in reality inconsistent with their self-interest.

So the good service company has to find a way to steer through the dilemma that it has to make its customers satisfied to survive, but it cannot accept at face value what the customers say and think (although it certainly must *listen to, interpret* and *handle* the customers' expressed opinions).

However, since quality is subjectively perceived, service firms should think twice before adding peripherals or increasing the quality level in one or more dimensions of their service package. It is easy to raise expectations, but it is very difficult to reduce them again. Secondly, the firm must be absolutely certain that it can manage the additional peripheral service (or the enhanced level of quality) with the necessary consistency and cost efficiency before embarking on such a course. By the same token, it is exceedingly dangerous to create expectations which it then proves impossible to live up to. One of the most common mistakes that service companies make is to start image campaigns without ensuring that the organization can live up to the image and provide services according to the expectations created—the inevitable result is loss of credibility, customer frustration and cynicism among the staff.

Service companies quite often seem to fall into the trap of adding more and more peripherals. Apart from diverting attention from the development of the core service, this may complicate the service delivery process more than was intended and at the price of hidden costs.

A typical example of this is the familiar upgrading spiral, whereby a retailing company starts by offering very low prices, sacrificing peripherals to maintain a good core service (i.e. goods at low prices). If the company then successively adds various peripheral services, it may become impossible in the end to maintain the original low price which constituted the core service. This may or may not be an advantage, but one thing is certain: it is extremely difficult to discontinue peripheral services once the customer has become used to them.

In the late 1960s a large Swedish bank decided on a strategy of extending its peripheral services in order to compete for clients. With a view to attracting customers and drawing ahead of the competition, the bank began to offer all sorts of savings plans, competitions, travel arrangements and other attractions. The cost seemed low, since the network was already there. However, the benefits were also rather meagre, since the peripheral services offered were not particularly unusual or advantageous to the clients (nor in themselves were they profitable to the bank); creeping increases in administration costs soon made themselves felt, and it became difficult to redirect the attention of the staff to the real core of the banking services.

When these consequences of the new strategy began to have a negative effect on the bank's economic performance, a clear change was made in both strategy and focus: many peripherals were cut out and the bank relayed a new message to its customers and to its own staff—from now on it was going to operate as something very simple and very difficult, namely, an excellent bank. This strategy, supported by a variety of active measures, gradually proved to be extremely beneficial. Moreover, it was much more difficult for competitors to imitate 'being an excellent bank' than providing customers with a lot of peripherals.

We shall later do a more detailed analysis to this kind of defocusing mechanism which jeopardizes the core service when we discuss the question of diversification.

THE COMPOSITION OF THE PACKAGE

Different types of elements can constitute the service package. A useful classification has been proposed by Sasser, Olsen and Wyckoff (1978), who suggest that a service offering can include three types of element, namely:

1. facilitating goods (physical items such as the food in a restaurant or the hardware in a computer service operation);
2. explicit intangibles, or physical benefits;
3. implicit intangibles, or psychological benefits.

These elements may be combined with our concepts of core and peripheral services, as shown in Figure 5.2.

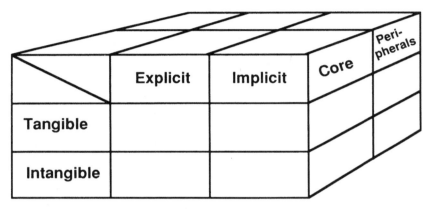

Figure 5.2   Features of the service package

The distinction between explicit and implicit intangibles is well known to anyone who has provided or purchased a service. Sometimes it is hard to say which is the more important. A company providing language vacation tours for schoolchildren is obviously offering better knowledge of a language as an explicit intangible; as a slightly less explicit intangible it is also offering the prospect of adventure and new experiences for the child; but in many cases the highly implicit intangible benefit to the parents, who can at last get rid of the child for a couple of weeks so as to live the good life themselves, may be an equally decisive factor in their purchase of the service.

The service offering can also be described in terms of the functions which it fulfils or the problems which it solves for the *client.* One function could be to provide extra *manpower* or *capacity,* perhaps to cope with peaks in the workload. For example, a large industrial company may have its own security force but may still want to bring in guards from a security company for special events or tasks. A general class of function can be subsumed under the designation *facilitating services.* Typical examples are cleaning, security services, computer services, consulting services, auditing and advertising. The logic behind this kind of function is that the buyers, be they individuals or organizations, would be better off concentrating their efforts on their own 'core process' rather than diverting their attention to specialized and perhaps difficult tasks which could better be obtained from outside. It should be noted that some of the services which are bought from outside may not necessarily be explicit; they may be more in the nature of implicit intangibles. An example could be industrial cleaning; officially the client company is acquiring access to specialized knowledge, but in fact it may particularly appreciate the ability of the service company to cope with certain 'difficult' personnel categories and thus to facilitate the work of the client's own personnel function.

The service company may be selling the *advantages of scale,* which could include knowledge advantages (experience effects). This can be exemplified by a transportation company which can pool several clients to fill the available capacity, or a security company with its experience of perhaps hundreds or even thousands of different situations which, if the company is well organized, can be brought quickly to bear on any particular case. Scale advantages may also mean the client gaining access to a network (a hotel owner may join a world wide hotel reservation network), or to specialized administrative systems. One type of service business idea in fact consists of taking a number of hitherto dispersed units and creating the right infrastructure to raise the quality of them all on a large-scale basis. The central organizations of several retailing chains or garage and car services represent a case in point.

Many of the most important offerings of the service companies are, as we have seen, implicit intangibles. It is not uncommon for consultants to provide a service which could more aptly be termed 'reassurance' than anything else; the client has really done his own problem-solving but feels uncertain and wants service of 'taking the blame'; the client realizes that unpleasant things have to be done but wants the recommendations to come officially from elsewhere. This same service might be called 'legitimation'. Service companies often help clients to do legitimately what they have or would like to do but would not do under normal circumstances or without external pressure. Tour operators who dispatch Scandinavians to Spain and other places to escape the drinking regulations of their home countries are very aware of this function!

Besides creating reassurance and absorbing uncertainty, the service company can also fulfil the function of supplying the client with variety and experience and even adventure.

FOUR IMPORTANT INGREDIENTS OF A SERVICE PACKAGE

Service offerings normally comprise a combination of the following four components:

- specialized capacity to deliver services
- linkages and social relationships
- transfer of know-how
- management and organization as a service product.

A service concept will generally include several of these, and sometimes all of them.

Specialized capacity to deliver services

It should be noted that service companies not only compete with each other: they also compete with their own customers. The restaurant competes with the housewife and with the company canteen; the cleaning company competes with the maintenance staff of its clients; the consulting company competes with its clients' staff experts and managers. That the service company can encroach on these fields at all depends on its ability to do things better and/or more cheaply, or on the client's temporary or permanent lack of capacity.

In providing services of this kind, the service company's task is theoretically quite simply to prove that it can add more value to the client's operations than the client could by performing the same operations himself.

Linkages and social relationships

As we saw in the previous chapter, another function of the service company is to link clients and other resources in new ways. It may be a question of new linkages or old linkages in new contexts. The discotheque, the bank and the insurance company all do this in different ways for individual customers. We have seen how J-C Decaux linked towns and industrial companies and the general public. Tour operators and transportation companies are other obvious examples.

Many potential service ideas of this kind are neglected in the public sector. A good childcare service would quite likely do far better by acting as a 'broker' between families, helping them to make the right linkages, than by building day care centres and employing expensive personnel. Our experience suggests that there will be many more openings for this type of service idea in the future.

Transfer of know-how

Companies which primarily supply specialization or service capacity can exist, as we have seen, because they possess some kind of relative advantage. This advantage is often in the nature of some special skill or know-how. A company may have more skilled resources, or it may have access to some large-scale administrative system or to some highly advanced technology which needs to operate on a larger scale than the individual client can afford. To some extent such companies operate because the client is at a disadvantage with regard to some skill or know-how. There is an inherent dilemma here (a problem or a possibility, whichever way one wants to look at it): should this gap be closed by supplying a service or by providing know-how?

We can illustrate this with the example of the bank. Basically, many banks have made money because their industrial clients possessed little awareness or knowledge of financial strategy or cash management. Their lack of knowledge made it easier for the banks to sell their own financial services. Alternatively the banks could have decided to sell know-how. Admittedly most banks do now try to provide 'cash management and education', but they are generally rather ambivalent about it since the result might be to reduce the calls on their more traditional financial services. Nevertheless it is becoming increasingly common for banks, insurance companies, security companies and others to include formal courses and other types of training in their service packages, at least as options.

Many service companies find themselves having to make the transition from providing services to supplying a good deal of know-how as part of their service package. We shall return to the question of the balance between these factors below.

Management and organization as a service product

An interesting trend is that many service companies are now actually selling *management systems* rather than services as such. Large insurance companies and brokers faced with industrial clients who form captive insurance companies may decide to provide the service of managing the captive companies rather than selling insurance themselves. Other companies offer to manage hotels, waste-handling systems, hospitals, cleaning services in hospitals, and so on. As consultants we have quite often found ourselves having to decide whether to sell consulting services or actually to take over part of the management (not the ownership) of a client company.

We are certain that this trend will continue. The development of service companies has been largely based on a greater awareness and knowledge of precisely what constitutes good management of service systems—'service management'. Obviously the capacity to implement this management knowledge is becoming a marketable commodity in itself.

This development has several interesting implications for services in the public sector. In many modern crisis-ridden welfare states, where it is still widely believed that the privatization of services is not the right remedy or where such a process would run counter to accepted ideology, it would be possible to maintain control of resources and services in the public sector while institutionalizing the competition for management services (between several private companies, between private and public companies, or even between domestic and international companies).

However, organization and management do not necessarily have to be part of the explicit or formal service package, although, without being officially recognized, they may still be a key part of the service offering. A company like Weight Watchers, for instance, links its clients together and helps them to organize their lives in new ways; it is actually performing a management service. A consultant working for a client company and expected to submit a diagnosis and recommendations for dealing with a particular problem may discover that the client is inadequately organized to do his own problem solving and that this is really the basic problem; the consultant may then prefer to help the client to manage his problem-solving better.

In Chapter 8 we shall examine some of these points in greater detail, as part of our discussion of the role of the client in the service management system.

Balancing the different aspects of the service offering

The insurance industry, and in particular the segment dealing with industrial insurance, provides a striking example of how the four aspects of the service offering have to be balanced and rebalanced against one another.

The traditional service used to be the provision of financial risk-absorption capacity. In this field, because of its financial strength and the law of numbers, the insurance company has a comparative advantage over the client. The original idea of the insurance company was in fact to link clients together, thereby pooling their risk absorption capacity. In a sense the insurance company acted as a broker between its own clients.

As the cost of capital increased and the very large industrial corporations emerged, the knowledge and awareness of many clients also increased. They were, in addition, more likely to possess the financial capacity to take and absorb risks. Many of the largest therefore created their own captive insurance companies, or got together and started captive association pools. The insurance companies no longer had the comparative advantage needed to support their basic service; many of their clients had achieved the same level of capability as themselves.

At first most insurance companies and brokers resisted these trends, but they soon realized that to survive they had to adapt. Several strategies have emerged. One line of action has consisted of selling management services—for example the management of captives or association pools; this was an area in which the insurance companies still have a comparative advantage over their clients. Another strategy was to increase the know-how content of the service, the most obvious way being the inclusion of what are known as 'risk management' services. Here the insurance companies also had an advantage over their clients because they had a much larger pool of experience (albeit until then not very well systematized or exploited) to draw on.

Many insurance companies now place considerable emphasis on selling risk management; others still hesitate, foreseeing that one result of increasing a client's knowledge may be his realization that he now has less need of traditional insurance services. However, the most progressive insurance companies look at it differently: by selling risk management skills they help their clients to discover hitherto hidden costs and risks; they then apply themselves to developing new types of insurance service to cover this kind of risk.

Yet another line of response has been to add specialized peripheral services such as improved statistics, on-line information systems, accident and damage prevention and control systems, and so on. To cater for the varied needs of different clients and market segments, many companies also sell these services 'un-bundled' and for separate fees, i.e. not necessarily linked with one another or with traditional insurance services at all.

This differentiation and extension of the service package to include more than the traditional services (including, in particular, management and know-how) has made insurance companies very much more aware of the problems of their clients and thus more generally client-oriented, a fact which is also reflected in the organizational forms and general strategies of those insurance companies which work with commercial customers. Individual attention to large customers and greater market segmentation, with streamlined service packages adapted to each segment, are developments which have accompanied the above-mentioned changes in the service offering.

THE SERVICE CONCEPT AND THE SERVICE DELIVERY SYSTEM

It should now be clear to the reader that many services are exceedingly complex phenomena which can he conceptualized in several different ways. As was stressed in the previous chapter, it may even be difficult to separate the service concept from other components of the service management system. Since the client generally participates actively in the service operation, he will evaluate everything that he experiences of the whole delivery system.

For this reason we shall be discussing issues in several of the remaining chapters which might well have been included in our present discussion of the service concept. The chapters immediately following will deal with the components of the service delivery system which 'produces' the service concept as depicted in Figure 5.3. The client generally regards such things as the nature

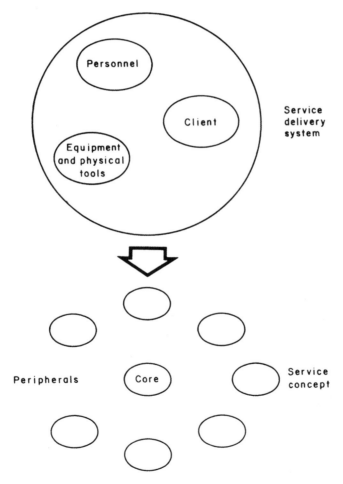

Figure 5.3 The service concept and the service delivery system

and quality of the contact staff, the physical facilities and equipment used by the service organization and how these are presented, and the identity of the other clients (what 'club' is the client joining?) as part of the benefits that he will receive, and thus in our terminology as part of the service concept.

In the chapter on the client and the market segment we shall investigate more closely the decision-making process of the client confronted by a service offering.

A crucial element which cannot be disregarded in any description of a service is its price. I have elected to discuss price separately in Chapter 11.

The subject of quality—necessarily a vital issue in any serious service organization, and one closely related to the service concept—will also be discussed in greater detail in Chapter 14.

6

Why strategic human resource development?

Services are often people- and personality-intensive businesses, and therefore one might expect human resource development to have been a strategic concern of management. Unfortunately, in both manufacturing and services, there are probably more businesses which paid inadequate attention to human resource development than recognized its strategic nature.

In Chapter 1 we illustrated the movement of functions and activities from other economic sectors and from the informal economy into the formal service sector. The ever-expanding service sector has been changing in a number of ways:

- Customers are more discriminating and demanding.
- There are more competitors with more product offerings with shorter lifecycles.
- The capital threshold for entry into service business is higher.
- Equipment and technology are increasingly important elements in producing the service offering.
- The knowledge component in product offerings is escalating dramatically.
- The 'quality of life' expectations of the service workforce are higher.

If today's service business wishes to continue earning an appropriate return on its resources, its significantly greater capital investment and its customer base, then it can no longer treat strategic human resource development as an option. A competent and dedicated workforce is a key resource. While technology and equipment are important new elements of many services, people continue to play often different but nevertheless pivotal roles. They are essential in analysing and interpreting what is happening in the marketplace, their creative capacities are required to design and refine the product offerings and the service delivery system, their discretionary capacities construct the 'fit' between the product offering and the customers needs, and they are the 'face' of the service organization at the 'moments of truth'.

In many companies expenditures on human resource development have been seen as costs rather than investments. Perhaps with the higher levels of capital expenditure in services, the investment on human resources will seem in better proportion. The potential benefits of expensive equipment will not be realized if there is no opportunity for employees to develop the necessary competence. Then all that costly equipment will be of little use.

Services require a greater knowledge-based workforce in order to respond effectively to the rapid change which the future offers. People who have developed their knowledge capacities have often in the process developed parallel reference groups and parallel loyalties to knowledge peers and mentors. This can be viewed as a threat to their loyalty to their employer or as a potential asset, providing the employer with an extended informal knowledge network and intelligence-gathering capacity. Changing gender relations and two-career families are altering the choices and the responsibilities for men and for women. This has implications, for employee transfers, travel, flexitime, part time careers, career development, etc.

Employees expect to remain personally in control of their knowledge and skill development. They expect to be treated as autonomous individuals, in a mutually beneficial partnership with their employers.

The combination of marketplace and work force factors are making it imperative that corporations build in flexibility, and the capacity for change and renewal from within. The very forces that make one's customers a most valuable intangible asset, are contributing to the need to treat human resource development strategically.

THE PERSONNEL IDEA: THE KEY TO THE SERVICE DELIVERY SYSTEM

The second component in the service management system, after the service concept, is the service delivery system. It is frequently difficult to distinguish between the service concept, the service delivery system, and the service product offering. Many successful services seem perfectly simple and logical. However, closer examination often reveals a complex design in which *some innovative arrangement or formula for mobilizing and focusing human energy* has been devised, creating both success and the illusion of simplicity. It is in the design of systems which can realize services consistently and with cost effectiveness that most of the innovation in this field is to be found.

In the first chapter we touched on the idea of 'invisible assets', including the loyalty and motivation of people. There is no doubt that people represent tremendous assets, and that the way these assets are managed can easily make or break the profitability and growth potential of a company. Consider the following:

An express delivery company calculated the value of assets which each of its drivers 'managed' each week on average. Counting the customer base, this came to $14 million per driver. Then the company started calculating how much it invested, per driver, to keep/develop this 'asset' . . .

A large life insurance company had a sales force of 100 000 people. Every year they lost 10 000 people (and, of course, many of the customer contacts of those sales people). They counted that, on the average, they had to scan 15 applicants to get one new sales person. Consequently, this company had to review 150 000 job applicants every year. And these resources were committed only to the sales force, and only to the recruitment phase . . .

In the pursuit of higher productivity and improved profit, many companies have invested significant resources in training, career planning, compensation strategies, only to find that, at best, they obtained marginal short-term gains. Often the strategy, the structure, the history and the norms within a company impede the potential and the productivity of employees. A great many service companies already face this dilemma; strategic human resource development may provide a way out.

No wonder that the concept of 'strategic human resources management' has been gaining ground. Without active human resources management, a service company cannot maintain its virtuous circles, for example—see Chapter 4. We may draw an analogy to sports and the performing arts. Without skilful management—coaching—no championship team or ensemble can stay on top.

DEFINITION OF THE IDEA

There are essentially two elements in the management of human energy in business organizations. One can be described in terms of training, indoctrination, career planning, organizational development, etc. These and similar methods, which will be discussed in the next chapter, are intended to promote better use of the potential motivation and skills inherent in the members of an organization.

The second and complementary element means ensuring that the right people are recruited to start with. It is not surprising that service-oriented companies tend to put the utmost effort and care into screening and selecting their staff. Nonetheless the general level of knowledge in this area appears to be underdeveloped. New concepts and more sophisticated management tools are both needed.

We can call the arrangement by which a company mobilizes and focuses human energy by selecting the 'right' people the company's *personnel idea*. This can be quite precisely defined:

The company's personnel idea refers to the degree and type of fit between *the particular life situation and life needs of a particular group of people* and the *setting or context* that the company can provide for that group *while pursuing its own business needs*.

People in different social situations, at different stages of their lives and with different lifestyles have different needs, motivations and ambitions. They will mobilize their energy for the company only if the tasks and activities required by its business needs somehow fit their needs as individuals. And—even more interesting—this is a plus-sum game: by providing a suitable setting or context for the individual the company performs a service for him and, in many cases, also an important social function.

This is part of the background to the common claim that service companies must market themselves not only to their clients but also to their employees. We would like to go further, and say that for long-term success the service company must fulfil a genuine function for the personal development of its employees.

The company which is consciously using the philosophy underlying the 'personnel idea' will identify segments in the market of potential employees and will subsequently concentrate on recruiting from those segments that specifically fit the tasks and growth needs of the business. This segmentation, of course, will operate in several dimensions, including education and skills. But the company must also concern itself with a deeper level of needs, particularly those which are not being fulfilled by the situation in which people in the target group are currently functioning, and which can therefore be seen as an important source of human energy.

Let us look at some such segment types, and see how they can be transformed into functioning personnel ideas for specific companies.

BLOCKED SOCIAL MOBILITY

Several companies in the cleaning and maintenance business, such as ServiceMaster or International Service System (ISS) of Denmark, intentionally recruit largely from the lower ranks of society, particularly among people who would otherwise have difficulty in finding employment. By offering its employees a place in a 'maintenance hierarchy', the company provides them with an opportunity for rising in rank rather than being condemned to unemployment or to remaining permanently at the lowest level in the hierarchy of the employed. In various other ways, too, these companies give their employees a status and dignity in society which would otherwise be denied them, thereby helping a particular social group while also mobilizing its motivation to promote a successful business. In many countries such companies employ a large proportion of immigrants or the wives of immigrants, who would otherwise have great difficulty in finding a job.

But problems of social mobility and mobility in working life are certainly not limited to the lower ranks of society:

An important ingredient in the business idea of EF Education concerns the local sales office managers. These are typically young women between 20 and 30 years old, often of 'good' family, with high personal ambitions but without the specialized education which would have enabled them to accede to professional careers as managers, lawyers or doctors like their brothers. The job of an EF office manager demands intelligence, hard work and a certain flair for leadership, rather than any of the specialized skills taught in professional schools. The job of running a successful office and managing a workforce of perhaps 10 people or more offers status and career opportunities for people who otherwise might have become housewives or executive secretaries.

BLOCKED PROFESSIONAL CAREER LADDERS

Many service companies take advantage of the fact that skilful people can fall into 'career traps' or 'blind alleys' in their workplaces. Thus, airlines often recruit air-force pilots facing premature retirement or a less glamorous career behind a desk.

The first low-price department-store chains built in Sweden in the 1930s were heavily controlled from the centre, and the job of being a local store manager was generally looked down on by people established in the trade. But these companies found another group to recruit from—middle-aged army officers who had realized they were never going to achieve top rank and who did not feel ready to retire. They were given another career opportunity and they fitted the job beautifully: what was needed in a store-manager job at that time was an ability to maintain order and discipline, while the lack of retail experience was no disadvantage since all crucial decisions were taken centrally.

THE ENERGY OF A LIFE-STAGE TRANSITION

The notion of 'life stages' or 'life passages' is popular today (Sheehy, 1974; Levinson, 1978). It is well known that life tends to follow a pattern of existential transitions or even crises—periods of life when individuals struggle to grasp and develop their identity in the light of their past development and their image of what the future may bring. There is evidence that significant personal growth occurs in people strong enough to genuinely face and fight these life-transition battles, while those who manage to avoid the inner struggles inherent in such transitions do not develop to the same degree.

In many ways the level of human energy is particularly high—and probably also particularly searching and unfocused—during transition phases of this kind. Divorces, career changes, new hobbies, new social linkages and the rupture of old ones—these are all tools that some people use to handle the transitions (or they may be symptoms of the transitions); some people, however, lack such tools. It is interesting to note that several service companies have understood the particular life needs and energies inherent in such transitional stages, and they have designed their organizations so as to constitute an arena in which people can fight their personal battles while also contributing to the business. The following is an example of a personnel idea based on this type of thinking:

Club Méditerranée, the successful French company in the organized vacation tour business, systematically employs young, unmarried and adventurous but responsible people to take care of their clients on location—the famous *gentils organisateurs* (GO). When they are taken on, the GOs know that their time in the company will be very limited. During this period the company can provide them with exactly the combination of variety, adventure and experience that helps them develop as individuals at that particular stage in their lives—a setting that would be quite inappropriate even a short time later when they will want to settle down and get married, having become saturated with the kind of experience offered by the company.

PEOPLE WHO HAVE 'FALLEN BETWEEN TWO STOOLS'

Many people prefer a lifestyle which does not fit with traditional types of job or career opportunities. Temporary help agencies, for example, provide opportunities for people who for some reason want to work part-time and who prefer variety to stability.

A research-oriented management consulting firm recruited its members from two main sources: among entrepreneurial academics who had become disillusioned with the bureaucracy of the business schools after a couple of years as professors there, and among people in large businesses or consulting firms whose excellent academic background and intellectual curiosity and agility were not finding fulfilment in their present situations. The consulting firm tried systematically to create a setting for both the 'entrepreneurial academics' and the 'intellectually adventurous managers' who did not seem to fit into academic life or into the business world.

In the same way it could be argued that 'super-speciality' retail stores base their personnel idea on the fact that many people find difficulty in choosing between their hobbies and the traditional unrewarding jobs. The best hi-fi stores and gourmet stores, for example, intentionally provide a context for the 'non-entrepreneurial hobbyist', who then contributes his love and affection and sometimes also surprising skill to the job in return for the chance of integrating work and hobby in his lifestyle. This 'integration' of life sectors for people who would otherwise have fallen between two stools also used to provide the foundation of well-functioning medical care, including hospital care. It is therefore interesting to see how attempts in Sweden and elsewhere to dissociate work from the sense of meaning and the personal identity that stem from a social vocation among nurses and doctors has led to a dramatic drop in the energy injected into the job (and consequently to lower productivity). By making people sit on one work chair and another 'hobby' chair rather than designing a context to satisfy both sides of their lives, the personnel idea has been shattered, the quality of the service reduced and the cost structure upset.

COMPLEMENTS TO BASIC CAREERS

It has struck my colleagues and myself that many service establishments, while operating as businesses of their own, are also fulfilling another function by catering for a specific step in the career ladder of some quite different career system. Many

Swissair cabin attendants are actually in the Swiss hotel and restaurant business, and they regard their work at Swissair as an agreeable and rewarding but temporary experience. At the same time they are bringing all the skills they have learnt in the hotel and restaurant business into their work as cabin attendants. A chain of restaurants which serves Japanese food sends young and not yet fully-fledged Japanese chefs to its restaurants in the United States. This gives the young people a chance to develop their skills while also receiving great appreciation from clients who are not in a position to recognize that the chefs are not yet true professionals. The great French restaurants are able to maintain staffs of highly motivated and able apprentices at very moderate cost, since young people queue up for the jobs; nothing could help their future careers more than having spent a couple of years *chez Bocuse* or *chez Troisgros*.

There is a further benefit to these restaurants with regard to staff competence. The desire of apprentices to learn under knowledgeable and proficient master chefs motivates the masters to take a more systematic look at their own skills. Tacit knowledge is thus forced to the surface. That is why you learn as long as you teach, and you learn even better if you have demanding students.

Studying personnel ideas in the building maintenance (cleaning) sector, we found that quite different personnel ideas could be equally successful provided they were well thought out and the appropriate adjustments were made in other parts of the service management system. Some companies are very concerned with 'professionalizing' the cleaner's job and giving it status; consequently they look for people likely to feel a degree of long-term and serious commitment to the job. Others evidently look for people whose families are always going to be their main concern; these companies design the job without any pretensions to status or professionalism, aiming instead to give what are basically home and family-oriented people a convenient opportunity and an agreeable context in which to make some extra money. This second kind of company clearly aims to complement the primary context of its employees' lives.

While both these strategies tended to work well in the cases we studied, we also found that companies which were unable to make up their minds about their stance, or which only paid lip-service to the 'professional' strategy, all had problems.

EMANCIPATION FROM UNREWARDING ENVIRONMENTS

We have seen that some service companies are able to position themselves as complements to other career systems, or to provide solutions for people whose career opportunities or social mobility are blocked or who are stuck in contexts that fail to use their inherent energy and skills. These observations can be further generalized: some service companies have shown great awareness and understanding of the blocked energy of people in generally dull, unrewarding or suffocating situations.

Thus a major explanation of the success of certain financial companies in areas such as leasing or factoring lies in very selective recruitment among banking personnel, whereby potentially entrepreneurial bank employees are offered a more exciting alternative. One British retailing company systematically aims at employing bright but unfulfilled women suffering from the constraints of their midlife, middle-class marriages. Carefully nurtured, such people can bring tremendous dedication and energy to even the simplest of jobs, which they see as a means to personal emancipation and growth.

IDEAS OF TEMPORARY PERSONNEL: A COMMON PHENOMENON

It is far from unusual in service industries that the employment provided is in some way 'limited', perhaps to a certain period in a person's life, a certain time of day or a certain season.

This pattern in understandable in view of the types of human energy that are tapped by the service companies in our examples. A life-phase transition is specific to a particular finite period. A person may need to enter another context to seek enrichment without necessarily wanting to abandon his or her previous context altogether. This temporary quality in fact appears natural in many cases, and there is no doubt that a similar line of thought could be successfully applied to manufacturing companies as well. However, since the need for sensitivity and skill in managing human energy is clearly more important in service industries, it is in this sector that we find the greatest innovativeness in connection with 'temporariness'.

A problem that has to be solved whenever temporary employment is involved concerns the *process of exit*. Here the degree of innovativeness varies very much. Some organizations continue to employ people long after the initial fit between the individual's life situation and the job has disappeared. In other companies there is little need to worry about the exit process, since the whole personnel idea is based on the availability of an exit, as in the case of the Swissair cabin attendants. But in many cases the necessity of inventing an exit solution is an important one: what should an EF office manager do at the age of 32, when most of her friends have married, when she is too good at her job to be readily replaceable, too bored with what she is doing, and too worried about her life to put as much energy into the job as she used to?

Thus innovative ways to provide systematically for 'beautiful exits' are an integral part of the total personnel idea of many successful service companies. An example of how this can be built into the total organizational system is provided by large management consulting firms such as McKinsey & Co.:

The company realizes that much of its success depends on the energy of young, skilful executives who want to grow in the hierarchy more quickly than is allowed for by the limited growth of the company as a whole. Part of the solution is to recruit more bright people than are needed and to offer them the chance of a very successful career, while also laying off a high proportion of staff. An integral part of this strategy is the effort that goes into guaranteeing 'beautiful exits'. Very great care is taken to see that those who leave the company find good positions elsewhere. Thus, such a management consultancy firm provides its young employees with a guarantee of success in an internal career or the opportunity of finding another excellent career somewhere else.

Those who leave the consultancy firm at the right time may remain valuable to it, but as clients rather than employees. For instance, they may join companies which require consulting services from time to time. What would then be more natural than to turn to former colleagues for assistance.

BUSINESS PROBLEMS SOLVED BY FOCUSED PERSONNEL IDEAS

Implementation of the personnel idea can help to achieve a fit between potential but blocked social energy and business needs. We have identified a number of sources of energy and we have indicated several kinds of specific business problems which they have helped to solve. In addition, there are a number of general management problems that can be handled by developing innovative personnel ideas.

One such area concerns counteracting the effects of fluctuations in workload with the help of a flexible supply of production capacity—an end to which ideas of temporary personnel can often provide the means. Fluctuations in demand are generally a more severe problem in companies which supply services than they are in companies manufacturing goods, since it is not generally possible to stockpile services. Companies supplying services therefore have to look for other types of buffers.

Another kind of problem common to many service businesses should also be mentioned. A great many service jobs suffer from a built-in dilemma: while perhaps not requiring a very high level of education or technical skill, they may nonetheless be very demanding; extremely tricky situations may well arise and have to be dealt with by the employee.

This observation perhaps calls for clarification and illustration. A characteristic common to many service companies is that a lot of employees at all levels in the hierarchy are in regular contact with customers. These contacts are often of a purely routine nature, but there is always the possibility of disturbances or crises which have to be handled not only with technical skill but also with a certain degree of personal tact and wisdom. While most of the hotel night clerk's job may seem to be rather dull, we can be certain that situations quite often occur calling for extraordinary personal judgement and diplomacy on his part—much more than will ever be demanded, for example, of a technically skilled worker in an automobile factory.

Many services are preventive in character. Most of the time—very often, all the time—the relationship between a specific customer and his insurance company (or the same customer and his security guard company) follows a routine path that calls for little skill or personal qualities on the part of the service company employee. While dullness, lack of challenge and boredom are the hallmarks of the everyday life of a patrolling security guard, what the client pays for is his ability to rise to the occasion when the once-in-a-lifetime emergency does occur.

This dilemma—the great gulf between the general dullness and the occasional need for extraordinary skill that occur in the same job—is a difficult one. The service company cannot afford to employ people who have all the potential and skill for the once-in-a-lifetime situation but who hardly ever have to use it; and such skilled people would be bored by the everyday routine of the job. On the other hand, the company cannot afford not to have the skill, the personal qualities and the motivation available to solve the problem when it does arise, because that is what their service is all about. Innovative personnel ideas, often of some temporary or transient kind, tend to be important ingredients in solving such dilemmas.

Naturally most service companies have not one but several concepts of personnel. The diversity of jobs and job requirements can be very great. A very common dilemma is the difference between the situation of the customer contact personnel and the calls that are likely to be made on them and the situation and demands facing the back-office staff. Contact with customers requires great flexibility and perhaps an appetite for social interaction, and the job may bring both rewards and frustrations. An entirely different type of person, and a correspondingly different culture, may be necessary for the back-office jobs. To reflect this difference, and yet to be able to manage the interface between the two groups, is a challenge that must be met by the successful service company.

PERSONNEL IDEAS MAY NEED TO CHANGE

Personnel ideas may need to be developed or reassessed either because of change in the business needs of the company or because of changes among the personnel. The following is an example of how business needs can change:

One very large and successful European computer service company was able to grow quickly because of the enormous enthusiasm and energy of its employees—mostly young, bright and ambitious engineers who had joined the company because of the fascination which computer technology and machinery held for them. However, as the business scene changed and machine orientation became less important as a success factor than service orientation and involvement with customers' problems, the company had difficulty in developing its personnel idea. There was no self-evident source of new recruits. Besides which, the technically oriented group had become something of a *status quo* force and a hindrance to growth.

Sometimes the personnel idea can be ill-conceived from the start:

A small but exclusive chain of conference hotels systematically recruited young hostesses from the upper social strata, preferably from the aristocracy. The company gradually developed a reputation for bad service and a poor atmosphere, and this was having a definite impact on its bottom line figures. It was found that most of the conference guests tended to come from lower social strata than the hostesses, who were therefore inclined to look down on them. This set off various vicious circles.

Obviously the life needs of these young aristocrats were not being satisfied by the business of this particular hotel chain!

Airline stewardesses represent a group which has engendered many complex problems. Solutions related to certain redefinitions of the job, to new recruitment groups and to the creation of 'beautiful exits' have all been needed.

Many airline companies had problems because they were not able to improve their personnel idea with regard to their stewardesses. As the glamour attaching to the idea of being a stewardess declined, and as many stewardesses were clocking up perhaps 20 years in their jobs, the work context was unable to arouse the necessary enthusiasm and emotional energy. For many employees at least, the job failed to fit in very well with a more mature life situation. Better exit philosophies and more temporary personnel arrangements have been designed by some airlines, allowing for the fact that people's needs change as they pass into new phases in their lifecycles.

As an example, many flight attendants have transferred from in-flight service to check-in and other ground service. One benefit to the employee is regular work hours which allow a normal family life. The company benefits from this career path too; check-in personnel will now understand the situation of the flight crew, an advantage in some ticklish situations with customers. For example, certain check-in procedures which are required for in-flight safety may be irritating to passengers, who find them unjustified; former flight crew members can understand the need for these regulations and can explain them to complaining passengers.

THE PERSONNEL IDEA AS A TOOL FOR BUSINESS IMPROVEMENT

So far we have made many references to concepts such as 'human needs', 'life needs', 'solving the life problems of the employees', and so on. We have not done this from the angle of the kindly personnel manager or the Human Resource Management (HRM)-oriented organizational consultant. Nor have we been referring to a limited functional problem related to personnel management. Rather, *our perspective has been that of the general manager* responsible for the overall operation and design of a business, and we have tried to show that the personnel idea can be regarded as the tool of a hard-headed management, used to improve the results and the growth rate of the service business company.

In the service business company the personnel idea is no mere ornament; it is an integral force at the heart of the whole business. Sometimes it is the best single expression of what a service business is all about, in the sense that it is the most powerful explanation of failure or success, or the strongest weapon in fostering growth or reversing the fortunes of an ailing company.

There is no doubt that we shall see a proliferation of innovation in this area in the future. Again, this is not solely due to factors such as an increase in social awareness; rather, there is a growing understanding of the special management problems of service businesses, and particularly of the unique 'human-energy transformation function' that is so important to companies of this kind as compared with manufacturing operations. Certain new types of service company will be based mainly on innovative personnel ideas. However, an equally fascinating development can be seen in certain very traditional service businesses such as banking and insurance, which in the 1990s were facing rapid structural change and were forced to make great efforts to develop new types of services and new ways of functioning. To support these new services they will have to develop new types of service delivery systems—and in many of these the personnel idea will be a key component. For example, it is the absence of purposeful innovation in connection with the underwriters that now largely blocks the development of many insurance companies from new areas.

A new business approach will be needed, but one that includes great sensitivity to the source of human energy and to life situations as well as the creative identification of market niches for new service concepts.

THE MORAL DILEMMA

The following two comments refer to one and the same company in the cleaning business.

Ah, that's the company that exploits the difficult situation of immigrants who don't even know our language.

Without that company the unemployment and other social problems in this city would certainly have been worse. We're lucky to have a company which can give these people a change, and the possibility of an ordered existence.

The possibility of using the personnel idea as a management tool encourages managers to look for sources of human energy—and to use that energy for their business needs. Obviously the line between the immoral exploitation of people's situations and the provision of meaningful opportunities is sometimes a fine one. More work and conceptualization is needed in this area, but nevertheless it is interesting to note that in our experience there is at best a genuine exchange—a 'win-win' situation rather than a 'zero-sum' game—between the employee and the company. Within a single framework, a business need for the company and a personal need for the individual are being fulfilled, and often in the context of providing a service of true value to society.

7
Getting people to grow

Even fairly traditional types of service company are beginning to understand the meaning of the 'moment of truth'. One large bank has invented the slogan, 'The difference in money is people', and in our group we have had many opportunities for seeing the tremendous increase in investment in personnel development that leading financial services, health care, and telecommunications companies, for example, have shown over the last few years.

Since much of the quality of a service company depends on what happens at the moment of truth, several ways of assuring the required quality have evolved—apart from the one discussed in the previous chapter, which involves sending the perfectly recruited and equipped bullfighter out into the arena. The following are examples of such approaches:

- trying to remove as much of the production as possible from the moment of truth; locating more of the production in the back office, perhaps in machines,
- reducing the discretion allowed to the contact personnel; standardizing their situation and their behaviour,
- making it possible for the contact staff to use their discretion as creatively as possible; i.e. improving their ability to solve problems and to treat each situation in a customer-oriented way.

In the present chapter we shall be preoccupied mainly with the third of these approaches. For in our experience, well-managed service companies are not afraid to give their personnel freedom to handle customer situations in a flexible way. But freedom of action must be backed by competence, tools, and understanding. In addition, certain fundamentals must always be present, so that as a customer you find the same service-mindedness in company employees whether in Sweden or Singapore.

TRAINING

The importance of developing and training the people who will be supplying services is so great that many service companies organize their own schools. Hotel chains, as well as relying on well-known schools such as Cornell University, organize schools of their own. An example is the Holiday Inn University. McDonald's has its own impressive 'Hamburger University'. Disney World, Marsh & McLennan, and Cable and Wireless have their unique 'universities'. And there are many other examples.

One of the tasks of these institutions is to teach the *technical skills* needed in the particular business. In 'universities' or 'learning centres' of this kind, employees are taught such things as accounting systems in hotels, underwriting procedures for facultative reinsurance risks, or cash management techniques. Operational rules which have proved efficient in the running of a local establishment, in whatever service business it may be, are stored and transmitted to new employees.

But there is more to training than mere technicalities. It is especially important in service operations, where the moment of truth necessarily implies a great deal of uncertainty and where situations are difficult to program completely, that employees are also taught various *interactive skills.* Many airlines provide their cabin staff with training in transactional analysis, to help them to cope with difficult, demanding clients in unexpected situations. Many companies also use role-play, creativity techniques and conflict simulation as training tools. Not a few even advertise the fact that they have such training programs, trying to communicate to the customer that their service delivery system is designed to cope with almost any situation that could possibly arise.

Depending on the type of service business, the emphasis may be on either of these aspects, the technical or the interactive. McDonald's, the prototype of the 'industrialization' and standardization of services to achieve a cost-effective level of quality, is an interesting example. The contact staff at McDonald's learn to have eye contact with every customer and the training is so efficient that I have never known it to fail. You could almost certainly go to any of the thousands of McDonald's anywhere in the world and turn to any of the employees in them and you would always make eye contact.

It seems that the ideas upon which most advanced service companies are basing their internal training have a distinctly behavioural bias. In many areas it has been popular (and generally useful) to teach concrete technical skills on the one hand, and on the other, various ideas and techniques to improve self-insight and to change attitudes, especially in interpersonal relations. The popularity of transactional analysis is an example of this last. No doubt the theory was that a change in attitudes would induce a change in behaviour. Now, however, the prevailing doctrine tends to emphasize concrete behavioural skills, with a view to moulding behavioural patterns into 'role models' for different types of jobs (Rosenbaum, 1982). Our own experience suggests that long-term effectiveness is best served by a combination of 'personal growth techniques' and 'behaviour modelling' inputs, complementing each other but perhaps with the stress on one or the other depending on the particular business and personnel category involved.

For companies which understand the effectiveness, in business terms, of their employees' personal growth, training is by no means the only instrument available. Personal development issues may be discussed regularly as part of individual performance reviews (formal reviews may be made as often as four times a year in some companies). Another approach is reflected in the following observation that stems from a large international service company:

It is essential to perpetuate the enthusiasm of the employees, and we have a number of programs for that. We have one service company, for example, which allows any employee or family member of an employee to call and talk about any problem—alcohol, family, insurance, or anything that would influence the image or productivity of the company or the employee—for 24 hours a day, seven days a week, from anywhere in the world.

A third function of training is to *infuse the employees* with values, and to focus their attention on such things as being crucial to the success of the business. We shall return to this theme in our discussion of company culture in Chapter 15.

Even though there is an impressive list of 'universities' and 'learning centres' in service organizations, most of the training probably takes place on the job. Services cannot easily be demonstrated to customers; the provision of services cannot easily be taught. In both cases there is no substitute for real life experience. Mentor and master–apprentice systems, whether formalized or not, are therefore of great value in service organizations, as is emphasized in the vast body of literature on learning in organizations.

THE GOALS OF TRAINING

There is no doubt, as we have seen in our work, that well-designed training programs for 'contact personnel' can often have a profound and immediately positive effect on the performance of the whole company. And yet we often find that we have to warn clients against adopting such measures. Contact-personnel training is a superb instrument in the service organization provided it is very well designed and adapted to the unique situation and business of the company, and provided it is regarded as an integral part of a system of change rather than some kind of universal weapon. The three following comments, issuing from top executives in three very large and successful international service companies, illustrate these points:

We have found that when training tends to break down is when it is event-oriented rather then part of a larger program.

We have given this course to all of our contact personnel, and it has worked out very well. But I can tell you from experience; if this course is the *only* thing you plan to do about better service—by all means don't give it!

Courses only have value if the superiors of the participant can be brought to share the same values. When one of our international units wants training for its front-line people we say yes, we will be happy to give it, but not unless we have had sessions with the superiors and top executives also.

Various studies have shown that it is almost impossible to develop and even more to maintain a particular kind of climate and relationship between front-line personnel and customers unless the same climate and basic values prevail in the relationship between front-line personnel and their supervisors (Schneider, 1980; Dupuy, 1999). If one behavioural code and one set of values prevails inside the organization and another in external contacts with clients, then the contact personnel will find themselves in a more or less impossible 'double bind' position. The ambiguity of the situation will tend to reduce the quality of the service, as well as work motivation and client satisfaction. Climate is crucial, and climate must be pervasive.

In fact, supervisory roles are among the most difficult to fill in most service industries. Supervisors so obviously affect the behaviour of the front-line personnel, but their own situations often lack many of the excitements and rewards associated with customer contact. In addition, the role of supervisors has changed considerably in recent years. With greater decentralization, and the use of information technology to provide various kinds of information to contact personnel, the latter can now assume much of the responsibility for day-to-day operations, either individually or as a team that coordinates the work of the group.

TAILORED TRAINING PROGRAMS

In the best service companies internal training programs fulfil a precise and well-understood purpose related to the total business situation and strategy of the company. *Operational* needs at the various levels will have been analysed and programs designed to meet them. Difficult interface areas between different categories of personnel, different functional and regional departments and different organizational levels will have been studied and programs and workgroups composed to improve the relevant contacts and to create a holistic, interfunctional and interdepartmental understanding of business problems and operational pro-cedures. Programs are uncompromisingly business-oriented, aim-ing to produce better service and productivity and having job satisfaction and motivation as intermediary variables.

Training programs have to be regarded in a *strategic* as well as an operational light. A large innovative company in the insurance field, which has grown rapidly as a result of acquisitions and which has developed services that are far more advanced and complex than they were only a few years ago, has used a training program as one of the main ways of 'unfreezing' established structures, achieving inter-unit communication and a harmony of values and culture, and promoting new 'role models' adapted to the radically altered business situation. In a chapter in which we discuss image, we shall look at two further examples, one in an insurance com-pany and one in a bank, of training programs created specifically to support or even to make possible a new strategy. Such new training programs will also effectively create a new image of the company directed towards new groups of employees, thus making it easier to implement the new or modified personnel ideas necessary to a different business orientation.

Thus it is not only the operational issues that must be carefully analysed before a training program is launched. It is also necess-ary to consider factors such as the current stage of development in the industry and in the specific company, as well as the overall service management system of the company. Training programs are only one of the many tools with which management can make an impact on the organization, and the programs must be thor-oughly understood within that total context.

FOLLOW-UP AND REINFORCEMENT

Providing people with training (which perhaps has an immensely exciting impact on them) and then simply forgetting about them may result in a serious backlash. Thus, another feature of the appropriate context for a training program concerns what hap-pens to the people who have gone through it. Obviously we could say that training should continue and that the programs should be renewed, but that may not be enough.

A crucial concept is *reinforcement*. Some companies and consultants who have specialized in running training programs make a point of literally measuring at regular intervals the behavioural effect on the people who have taken the courses, in order to discover what kind of reinforcement will have to be applied: perhaps reward systems favouring the desired behaviour patterns, or regular feedback on individual performance, performance group and company performance (in terms of relevant variables such as growth, profit and service quality). Other reinforcement mechanisms may involve the training of supervisors, meetings and 'tours' by senior executives which include question-and-answer sessions, or frequent videotaped programs stressing the required values and behaviour. One large company established a pattern whereby 'dilemmas' were exposed and former course participants were asked to say what they would do. Or, after the course is over, participants might be given the chance to join interfunctional workgroups dealing with specific problems or with general issues such as, 'How can we improve the quality of our service to customer category X?' And there are many other possibilities. Many of these themes will be touched upon again in Chapter 15 where we discuss organizational culture.

JOB DESIGN AND ROLE DESIGN

In the previous chapter we saw how effective service delivery systems are characterized by a good 'fit' between the special needs and motivations of particular employee target groups and the special features of the job in question. The relationship works in both directions, and the fit may be achieved either by changing recruitment strategies or by changing the role of the job, or both.

Where motivation is lacking and people are not developing, it is always worth investigating whether jobs and roles can be redesigned to make them more interesting and enriching to the employee. To be rewarding and attractive, jobs should contain the possibility of situations in which the employee can learn; for example, interesting contact work with clients or the chance to work with knowledgeable seniors.

A related concept is that of role models. In good service companies there will almost always be a clear idea of 'the model employee' for different types of jobs, the employee who lives up to the specified criteria necessary to do a good job and therefore to achieve success. In the case of the insurance company mentioned above, it proved very difficult to achieve any understanding of the new strategy throughout the company until an easily understood 'new role model' evolved which could be communicated to people. In fact, it also had to be shown that people corresponding to the new role models did exist, or could be developed, before the strategy became credible.

CAREER DESIGN

The career problem in service organizations may not be very different in principle from the corresponding problem in other organizations, but it is usually accentuated. Service jobs are often intensive; they involve a lot of customer contact, which means that they may be very rewarding or very wearing for the employee and they are often both at the same time.

A special problem that was mentioned in the previous chapter concerns the 'beautiful exit'. Something should be done about people who find themselves in a trap as regards their own personal development. We have come across many companies in which individual people or whole categories have become almost indispensable to the operation; they are thus kept in their jobs, although their personal development would really benefit from a change. Nor would it appear desirable in the long run for the well-being of the company to be dependent on unmotivated but apparently indispensable employee groups.

The problem outlined above can be formulated as one of learning how to capitalize on the competence of seasoned staff. These individuals have learned the business and gradually acquired a thorough understanding of how the company operates. While they generally remain loyal, they know by experience that an overly 'simple' policy statement from on-high should be taken with a grain of salt. Management, particularly new management, should recognize their competence. There is no shortage of service companies where the eagerness of new management to put its own stamp on the business has led to widespread resignations of veteran employees—and also cost the company some of its customers.

The analysis of successful and unsuccessful internal recruitment policies and ensuing careers is usually a rewarding exercise, from which many conclusions can be drawn about career and role design. For example, one savings bank has bucked the trend followed by all others in its industry by seeking to recruit older staff with prior experience—'minimum age 55'.

PERSONNEL: SUMMARY

We have devoted two full chapters to the role of personnel in the service delivery system. Basically we have been thinking of employees, but as the EF Education example shows and as we shall confirm in the next chapter in discussing the role of the client, many participants who are not employees may be involved in supplying a service. The points we have made here apply to these categories as well.

The most important thing that can be said about personnel in service companies is probably that personnel policy can never be regarded as an auxiliary or merely supportive function. For top management it is a crucial strategic issue. It is hard to conceive of a successful service business manager—much less an entrepreneur or innovator—who is uninterested in personnel matters. Even minor questions related to personnel policy are usually vital to the service business, and the way personnel are treated and the location of responsibility for human resources management in the organization should reflect their importance.

8
The client as customer—the client as coproducer

CLIENT PARTICIPATION IN SERVICE OPERATIONS

In the service management system the client appears twice: as a consumer in the market segment and as part of the service delivery system. The two aspects of the relationship with the client are interconnected, since it is of course the totality that the client himself will evaluate. Part of what the client sees as the output of the service company consists of *how much* and *in what way* he has to participate in the provision of the service, and what problems and satisfactions are involved in this process.

The concept of client participation, although an old one, has perhaps been most vividly described by Toffler, who uses the telling expression 'prosumer' to designate the increasing integration between the functions of production and consumption (Toffler, 1980). Toffler sees the rise of the prosumer as part of a general trend towards a reorganization of society whereby much of the specialization of industrialized society is being swept away by 'the third wave'.

Another explanation has been suggested by Zeleny (1978), who sees increased 'self-service' as the only possible way of maintaining the performance of people-intensive services with a limited potential for productivity improvements. According to Zeleny, the price mechanism for labour does not function in Western societies according to classical economic theory; in people-intensive service sectors, costs will rise more rapidly than productivity, and the market will not be able to bear the increase;

it will therefore prefer self-service. The problem has been described from the point of view of the individual company by Lovelock and Young (1979) who advocate increased client participation as an active strategy for achieving cost effectiveness.

Given that the client is both a consumer and a producer, the management of the company–client interface becomes an extremely important and delicate task for any service organization. Interface design is a crucial variable which determines much of the strategic positioning of the company, and it has profound operational consequences. In this chapter we can only begin to indicate some of the issues involved.

We can use Figure 8.1 as a first rough illustration.

Client Company	People	Equipment
People	Conventional training	Repair and maintenance service
Equipment	Automatic bank-teller	Automatic carwash

Figure 8.1   Different types of company–client interfacing

Different types of positioning along the dimensions of people or equipment interfacing between the client and producer can be envisaged. Education services is an example where conventional training can be extended to include an 'equipment-to-people' interface. Many IT companies perform a 'people-to-equipment' education process *vis-à-vis* their clients, and there should no longer be any problem in visualizing computers interfacing with computers in an education process. The same kind of positioning exercises could be applied, for instance, to food, security and financial services. Each strategic shift in this interfacing space entails fundamental shifts in operational problems, and generally calls for a thorough redesigning of the service delivery system and even of the service management system as a whole.

The people–equipment dimension is only one of a large number of dimensions which can be used to characterize the company–client interface. The degree of freedom of choice, the degree of integration, the duration and other temporal aspects of the relationship, its spatial characteristics, who dominates the interfacing process and how—these are only a few of the more obvious examples of crucial dimensions. We shall return to some of them indirectly later in this chapter in discussing market segmentation, which is of course only another manifestation of strategic positioning.

In terms of *function* the client can participate in many different ways (Langeard *et al.,* 1981; Chase, 1978; Lovelock and Young, 1979). See Figure 8.2. One is in the *specification* of the service, as is the case in most customer-tailored services. The role of the client in the specification of the service is sometimes limited to participation in the diagnosis of the problem, or even to providing the data for a diagnosis, as in cases of health care. It is always an important operational choice for the service company to decide

Mode / Function	Physical	Intellectual	Emotional
Specification			
Production			
Quality control			
Maintenance of ethos			
Development			
Marketing			

Figure 8.2   Modes and functions of customer participation

how far the client should be allowed to participate in the specification. At McDonald's he can specify which of the items on offer he wants to eat; at Troisgros the client may go quite deeply into the specification and problem-solving.

A second function concerns pure *coproduction,* whereby the client does some of the (physical) work which could conceivably have been done by the service company. The consulting firm has to decide whether the client's staff or its own should collect the data for a product/market analysis; in self-service retailing and banking, the client substitutes for the employees in performing certain physical or intellectual acts himself.

Thirdly, the client may be involved in *quality control.* When cleaning companies substitute daytime cleaning for cleaning outside office hours it is not only because they save labour costs. When cleaning is done while the client looks on, there is an element of quality control built into the service delivery system.

The fourth function could be termed *'maintenance of ethos'.* The service company may decide to incorporate client participation and client interaction as part of the service delivery process for the simple reason that it provides benefits to its employees in terms of interesting experiences, excitement or valuation feedback. Our Troisgros example demonstrates this function.

A striking example of how the relationship between the contact person and the client may influence ethos, motivation and productivity is provided by this statement by an airline employee involved in the system of passenger check-in:

In the morning there is always the decision about who is going to be at which check-in desk. You might believe that everybody would want to go for the first-class desk, but it is exactly the opposite. The first-class passengers seem to find every reason to look down on you, to somehow increase their own status, and by noon you feel deprived of all your dignity. It is exactly the opposite when you check in the inexperienced special fare passengers, even though they are less elegantly dressed and have rucksacks and crying children. You feel they need your help and they are grateful for it and you are happy to give it—you go out of your way to help them, and you feel all the better for it.

In the chapter on service quality we shall see that designing the company–client interface in such a way that 'virtuous circles' emerge in the face-to-face interactions is of key importance in incorporating quality maintenance and quality control into the service delivery system.

The client can also participate in the *development* of the whole service system. In fact, we know from experience that in professional service organizations such as consultancy firms, advertising agencies and auditors there is very little chance of developing genuine excellence in the service system unless the company is able to work together with knowledgeable and demanding clients. The 'good client' is as essential to successful development as anything else.

Finally, the client may participate in the selling or *marketing* of the service to other clients. This can be done by word of mouth or by formal reference. Because of the special characteristics of services, a good reference of either kind from a positive client is always a particularly valuable marketing tool, both for services to individuals and for professional services to institutions.

In addition to the various functions that the client can perform in supplying the service, we can distinguish between various *modes of participation.* We have already mentioned several examples of *physical* participation, such as self-service, and of *intellectual* participation, as in the case of an advertising company. *Emotional* participation may sometimes be as important as the other modes (Eiglier and Langeard, 1975). Ramirez (1987) would say that the company has 'aesthetic' properties—in a broad sense—which mobilize the customer's emotions and involvement.

We have found that an ability to involve the client appropriately and emotionally is very often what makes the difference between success and failure. For example, in a comparative study of successful and unsuccessful housing administrators, in which success was measured particularly in terms of economic results and client satisfaction with service, the main feature that distinguished the good companies from the bad was clearly the ability of the former to get the clients (the residents) genuinely interested and active in maintaining the housing areas. In the 'successful' cases there was a general alertness-to-problems among the clients; they tried actively to cope with any minor emergencies that arose such as small repairs and signs of vandalism, whereas in the other cases the clients were comparatively passive and indifferent.

Referring to our earlier discussion of the service concept, the case of the housing administration companies is a good illustration of the composition of a service package. The successful companies managed to transfer not only service but a great deal of know-how (so that the client would know what to do when problems arose) and even more important *social organization*. This last was provided in terms of behavioural norms and cultural reinforcement of values which have proved effective. Consciously or unconsciously, these companies had developed a number of simple and concrete methods of transferring and reinforcing the culture and climate necessary to cost effectiveness and to high-quality service.

We are dealing here with a phenomenon not unlike that of the good schoolteacher, who controls his class by identifying the forces that promote the right kind of behaviour and 'learning climate' and by carefully building on these forces; the result is a self-functioning system that appears to require little effort. To put it another way: work with nature not against it.

RELIEVING LOGICS AND ENABLING LOGICS

In the first and second chapters we introduced the idea of 're-lieving' versus 'enabling' roles of provider *vis-à-vis* its customers. In essence, this means that a provider has two different ways of making business out of the fulfilment of a certain function or task.

The first is to do it for the customer. In this case the role of the customer is to order the service, perhaps including some specification work. The provider then does the work. This is what we call a 'relieving' logic (see Figure 8.3), since the provider relieves the customer of the need to do something that needs to be done and that the customer may have done for himself before.

It is of course possible that this movement of activities from the customer to the provider in a relieving relationship brings with it a change in the definition of the task, or in its cost and its quality. Typically, relieving relationships are established for activities which are outside the core activity of the customer, thus leaving the customer with the possibility to devote more of his resources to his core business. This practice is customarily termed *out-sourcing*.

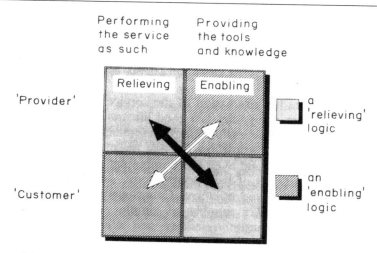

Figure 8.3   The determining logic of provider–customer service

But the service may also be provided in an 'enabling' relationship (see Figure 8.3), which means an entirely different set of roles for the customer and the provider. In this case the business of the provider is to deliver the *knowledge* and *tools* necessary for performing the task *per se,* which is now done by the customer. A management consultant who takes a problem and produces a solution is a reliever; a consultant who gives the client the analytical tools, frameworks and other skills to solve the problem and produce a solution is an enabler.

The baker is a reliever; the producer of the household breakfast roll machine is an enabler. Retirement clinics are relievers; home health care providers are enablers. And so forth.

The basic tasks of producing a service, and the possible divisions of work between provider and customer, are visually depicted in simplified form in Figure 8.4. Relieving relationships are well known from the industrial era of business. I predict that enabling relationships will become more prominent in the future, and that 'relievers' will get tougher competition from 'enablers'. From a rational, societal point of view it is clear that enabling logics are very interesting insofar as they contribute to a better overall resource utilization—and we can see that the cases we have referred to, and many other good service companies, are characterized by many elements of enabling.

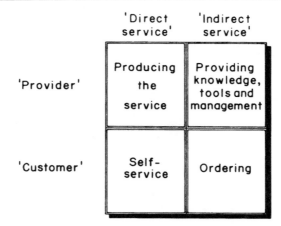

Figure 8.4   The division of work between provider and customer

But why would a company want to be an enabler, since this might mean that it loses business to the customer?

The first answer is that it might have to. Going from being a reliever to being an enabler may be a defensive act to maintain some of the business when the customer has become more able to do things.

A typical case is the explosion of securitization in the financial markets. As business companies have increased their level of competence and their information about the markets, they have tended to issue securities on their own rather than go to the bank to get loans. To keep some of their business and the customer relationships, banks have often re-defined their business, helping their customers to access the capital markets by selling them services and advice on how to do this. Similar developments have taken place in the industrial insurance markets with the rise of captive insurance schemes.

But an enabling strategy does not have to be a defensive strategy even if the client takes over some of the functions that the provider used to perform. It may very well be that an enabling offering helps to cement the customer relationship and makes the customer more successful. If the customer is more successful and grows this will usually mean broadening and lengthening the client relationship.

MAKING THE CLIENT PRODUCTIVE

How can the productivity of the client be increased, and how can he be induced to participate? The most important inducement is probably cost: he will participate if he can save on it, or if he can achieve a more favourable price/quality ratio. But, in addition, participation may be an interesting or even stimulating experience. Serving oneself in a self-service retail store has a number of effects: it involves more physical effort and takes more time, and it presumably saves some cost, but it is also a kind of learning experience. The client has an opportunity to learn about the supply of goods, prices, changes in assortment, and so on. He may be happy that less social interaction is involved. An intermediary, a filter, has disappeared between the customer and the goods.

The client can be made more effective if he is educated. An increasing number of service companies send not only their employees but also representatives of their clients to their 'universities'. Service-oriented product companies such as IBM and Xerox educate their clients so that use of the company equipment will be cost-effective. Insurance companies educate their clients in risk management.

The client may be given various kinds of tools—forms to fill in, perhaps, or checklists to influence his behaviour and facilitate his work. The physical setting may also be designed to evoke the appropriate kind of behaviour in the client, a point which will be expanded in the next chapter. Finally, designing the service delivery process so that the status and self-image of the client are enhanced could be an important inducement for him to participate usefully. The airline check-in example cited above was obviously a failure in this respect as far as the first-class passengers were concerned.

Sometimes several clients are part of the service delivery system at the same time. In a restaurant, for example, the other clients represent an important part of the total ambience, and therefore of the service experienced. This is one reason why strict control of the type of clients who are 'let into' the club and who are not—in other words market segmentation—is often called for. If the behaviour of client B is important to the service experienced by client A, then it must be possible to control both the entry and the behaviour of client B. Similarly, a service company may have an interest in keeping certain clients out altogether—or sometimes in asking them to participate less than they are willing to, so as not to interfere with the streamlined service delivery process.

In general, managing the client is not very different from managing the company's own personnel. Table 8.1 gives examples of questions which have proved useful to us in discussing the participation and productivity of clients. (Several of these questions have been discussed by Eiglier, Langeard, Lovelock and Young in articles mentioned earlier.)

Table 8.1   Examples of some questions in 'client management'

1. Can the timing of demand be influenced?

2. Does the customer have spare time while he is waiting?

3. Do clients and contact personnel meet unnecessarily face to face?

4. Are such contacts used to maximum effect?

5. Are contact personnel doing repetitive work which the customer could do himself, for example with customer-operated machines?

6. Do the clients sometimes try to 'get past' the contact personnel and do things themselves? Could that interest and knowledge be better utilized?

7. Do the customers show interest in a knowledge about the tasks of the contact personnel?

8. Is there a minority of customers which disturbs the service delivery system and its effectiveness?

9. Do the customers ask for information which is available elsewhere?

10. Can the customers do more work for each other, or use the resources of 'third parties'?

11. Can part of the service delivery process be relocated to decrease, for example, the cost of premises?

12. Can the customer be given an opportunity to choose between service levels?

CREATING CUSTOMERS

The iceberg principle

We could perhaps compare the situation of a customer buying a service to that of someone watching an iceberg. The person buying a product, such as a car or a pen, may concentrate his evaluation process on the product itself. It is there, it is tangible, and it can be tested and investigated from every angle. Although factors such as an after-sales service may be difficult to evaluate, the product is still there. And there is no need for the customer to ascertain the existence of the factory where it was made, nor to check the quality of the supervision or the type of people working there. Most of the influence and knowledge of the factory employees has been transferred into the physical product.

The customer who wants to buy a service is in a different position. The service is not yet there to be experienced—it cannot be demonstrated without being sold. The decision-making process is therefore also different. The potential client has to base his judgement on a number of incomplete clues—he can only see the tip of the iceberg, and starting from this he begins to form a mental picture of the rest of the iceberg so that he can make a decision.

From the client's point of view, therefore, the process of becoming a customer is a very active one. He is concerned with evaluating potential benefits and with reducing uncertainty and risk. The service organization must develop tools to make this process effective. The company must understand the nature of the process, and the task of the client must be influenced and facilitated. Clients seldom exist; they have to be acquired or even created. We consider Table 8.1 as a tool for use in such a process.

A service cannot be demonstrated like a car, but the service concept may be described, orally and for example in brochures. Although no substitute for the real experience, such descriptions can conjure up something of the experience itself. Another way of describing the service output is to refer to related transactions and to produce a list of records. A successful service company which can point to satisfied clients, and with a confirmed record of supplying benefits to previous clients, is in a much better position than the less successful service organizations. This is yet another mechanism whereby service organizations tend to fall into vicious circles or virtuous spirals.

The potential client will want to know what other types of client have been involved with the service organization before. He will want to ascertain that those who have appreciated the experience of being customers share his own problems and values. And he will be influenced, whether consciously or not, by the 'club' experience; both its external image and his self-image will be affected by the nature of the other customers. The image that the company projects is therefore already a tremendously important tool in the pre-selection of potential clients in facilitating the start-up of a new contact.

An important and essential difference between a customer buying a product and a customer buying a service is that the latter will seldom be content to study the service concept and its benefits alone; he will also be interested in evaluating the service delivery system. The service is intangible and difficult to evaluate, but the potential customer can discover clues by assessing the service delivery system. Equipment, premises, financial resources and, particularly, important human resources will all be closely scrutinized and subjected to tests.

The good service firm is aware of this and plays the game of the customer. In its crudest form, 'hard' features in concrete, brick and marble may be displayed in abundance to reassure the client, as a substitute for the more intangible 'soft' ingredients. This sort of display is often practised by banks and insurance companies. The client tends (sometimes quite mistakenly) to transfer these qualities to the more important soft features. In professional problem-solving services such as engineering or management consulting, the seller generally takes care to present the client with visible signs of his basic theories and his more or less complex and rigorous methodology, all in order to show that the outcome will not be the result of haphazard or subjective judgement. The medical doctor reassures his patient by his long university training and the impressive range of heavy books on his shelf.

Nonetheless, the most important clue tends to be the contact personnel with whom the potential client interacts. Their behaviour, their ambitions and skills and style will be closely watched. This process has been compared to the courtship before marriage (Wilson, 1972), but there is more to it than that. Particularly in the case of professional services (where, by definition, there is a know-how gap between the service provider and the potential client which makes evaluation of the service especially difficult for the client), two aspects of the behaviour of contact personnel are of decisive importance. One is the amount of interest and emotional empathy that is shown, the willingness to go to great lengths to serve the client. Slogans such as 'We try harder' and 'We work for you' are excellent, but only if they are genuinely put into practice.

The client who is a skilful buyer will find many chances of discovering whether such norms are really applied, or he will create situations to test them out.

The second key principle is that of 'instant mini-delivery'. The whole complex service cannot be experienced and demonstrated in its entirety, but the skilled contact person will find or create, and then take, the opportunity to demonstrate what he can do for the client. He will show that he and his company can give him value and bring him benefits. An empathic and creative diagnosis of the client's problem, a sensitive and well-chosen suggestion or proposal, or an appropriate display of other skills based on the client's situation, will create confidence in the company's capacity and problem solving ability and will promise more value to come. The principle of instant mini-delivery is one of the most difficult to learn and practise, but it is also a very effective tool in creating a customer since it simulates as closely as possible the real situation.

Further stages in creating a customer—cultivating your existing customers

By managing the 'iceberg principle' correctly the service company will open the doors to a good client relationship. However, as in marriage, the process of maintaining a relationship and making it constructive in the long term is as important as the process of initial courting; and it also takes commitment, patience and some special skills.

Time after time we have been able to demonstrate a close correlation between high client turnover and profitability problems. Surprisingly many companies fail to appreciate fully the value of a satisfied customer, and therefore get their priorities wrong. The process of applying the iceberg principle (which is needed to get new customers) may involve quite a heavy investment, and it is generally much more expensive to acquire a customer in this way than to repeat sales to existing customers. Since the process of changing supplier involves an investment on the part of the customer also, he will often be favourably inclined towards the service company; the pool of loyalty shared between himself and the company may act as a buffer for quite a long time, perhaps even inducing him to justify to himself the wisdom of remaining a client although the current provision of services no longer satisfies him. The existence of this loyalty pool (stemming from earlier good service, or from the investment made in the initial courting process, or both) explains why customer turnover and expressed dissatisfaction may not always immediately reflect a drop in the quality of the service. This is a very dangerous situation, since the service company is not receiving the right signals.

Many service organizations are uncertain as to how much effort they should devote to existing customers. But in our view the answer can generally be discovered by making quite simple economic calculations and analysing the existing customer base.

In the course of a customer relationship, substandard service, misunderstandings or other problematic situations may arise. Ideally, of course, such situations should be avoided, but when they do occur they should be well handled. In fact, they should be regarded as opportunities for strengthening and deepening the client relationship. (We have seen several examples of service business intentionally creating instances of slight client discontent, because they know how to turn the situation into an advantage!) Some well-known service organizations have developed an enormous skill in dealing with complaints which replaces a higher degree of care and excellence in the normal day-to-day provision of services. Anyone contemplating such a strategy should at least recognize that, for a variety of reasons, express complaints are a rather poor indicator of client satisfaction or dissatisfaction.

MARKET SEGMENTATION

Good service organizations have a carefully focused market segmentation built into their service management systems from the start. As we shall see later in our discussion of diversification, every move to extend or change the market segment has to be considered with the utmost care, in order not to disturb the often delicate balance and harmony of the successful service management system.

In defining market segments in service businesses, certain particular characteristics have to be kept in mind. In such businesses the interaction between producer and client is generally deeper than elsewhere, and as a 'prosumer' the client often does a great deal of the work. We have seen that the service provided may include organizing and managing the customer, which means that market segmentation must be based on the needs of the client in this respect and on his willingness to allow another organization to effect his way of functioning. The service concept may also include the transfer of skill or knowledge, which means that the customer's level of knowledge is a particularly important feature that distinguishes between market segments.

Thus, the general rule is that market segmentation should be conceived not only from the point of view of the 'needs' of the customer but also in terms of his *willingness and competence to participate* and his *participation style*, all of which are highly dependent on his level of knowledge and his way of utilizing it (Lehtinen, 1983; Langeard and Laban, 1981).

Finally, we have already indicated that part of the perceived benefit to the customers is the sense of 'belonging'. He will observe the other customers, and he will be unwilling to become a club member unless the other members somehow live up to what he expects of them. In light of this, we have found the following points highly relevant to any discussion of market segmentation in service industries.

The mixture of service, knowledge transfer and management transfer in the service package. For example, one bank may specialize in performing purely financial services for smaller companies, while another may design a package which includes a very high level of knowledge and education transfer (for example in cash management or international business) to smaller companies without specialists or without very much experience of their own. I would not take some of my foreign friends to certain French restaurants which obviously dislike serving people who do not know much about wine and are unfamiliar with *cuisine* jargon; instead I would take them to another restaurant which enjoys skilfully transmitting knowledge and helping the client to get organized at the same time as serving him with food! Some of the clients of consulting firms simply need some expertise, some good advice and perhaps a little reassurance, while others not only need but also want to have their way of working thoroughly called into question; others, again, really need someone to take over more or less the entire management of their firms.

The service level and the price/quality ratio. This is an obvious dimension. The Concorde passenger will be transported more rapidly and get a much higher level of service than the charter airline passenger, and he pays for it. The essential thing is not to get too far away from the price/quality function that customers consider reasonable. As the great French chef Paul Bocuse has said: 'There are two ways of conducting a restaurant business that I respect: McDonald's and mine.'

However, the price/quality ratio can never be taken for granted as a basis for segmentation. An innovation in the service delivery system will often shift the whole price/quality relation, so that large new market segments are opened up. We saw an example of this in the case of EF Education.

The style and image that various customers are trying to live up to. Reinforcement of self-image and self-esteem may be one of the functions fulfilled by a service organization, and this creates a natural opportunity for market segmentation. *Haute coiffure* services are an obvious example, but it is hard to find any type of service where self-image reinforcement does not provide at least part of the basis for market positioning; health services, financial services, and many others.

This dimension is seldom isolated but is implicit in the package; other segmentation dimensions are made more explicit.

This can be exemplified by the introduction in 1981 of the Scandinavian Airlines System's new 'Euro Class'. The product was specifically aimed at the 'businessman', deliberately profiling SAS as the 'businessman's airline'. Admittedly, the standard of service was noticeably raised (also *vis-à-vis* competitors) at no extra cost to full economy-fare-paying passengers. On the other hand, the possibility for the frequent business traveller to use a special fare ticket and 'crossed' tickets disappeared, unless he wanted to take the very noticeable and subjectively discriminating step of not going 'Euro Class'. This very successful new act of market segmentation was obviously based not only on rational price/quality relationships but also on the building of visible status barriers to exit and inducements to entry based on the customer's self-image.

When seeking to introduce a new high-class mobile telepone service, 'DOF', in 1998, Telia based its marketing heavily on what it assumed to be the principal personality traits of people in the target group; the typical DOF customer would be youthful, forward-looking, and individualistic.

The stage of development or lifecycle passage. What stage of development has a particular customer reached? And consequently, what particular needs and energies does he have that can be catered for, and exploited, in the joint creation of the service? As we shall see, banks and insurance companies are sensitive to the idea of developing differentiated standardized packages for clients at different stages of life. The stage of development is also a crucial variable in distinguishing between the needs of many institutional customers. To take another example from the financial service industries, we find that some service organizations are perfectly capable of helping the small entrepreneur with good ideas but no capital; but it is by no means always certain that the same companies will be good at solving the growth problems of the five-year-old successful entrepreneurial company struggling with difficult management problems and entering a new stage in its growth. In fact, the appropriate service packages for these two situations, as well as the delivery system and the whole service management system, tend to be completely different.

The participation style. What kind of participation style appeals to different customers, and how far are they prepared to go as participants? Different market segments prefer different trade-offs in terms of what the service company does and what they do themselves. For physical, economic, cultural or social reasons, they may like or dislike certain interaction patterns. Some people, for example, prefer the ease and lack of social obligation attaching to automated banking transactions, while others feel that an important quality has been lost to the interaction process if they cannot meet and talk to other people when they go to the bank.

The internal organization and decision-making structure of the customer. This segmentation dimension, obviously relevant to institutional customers but certainly not irrelevant to household services in which whole families are somehow involved in the decision-making, is a familiar one to advertising agencies, many types of consultants, IT companies, cleaning and security service organizations, to mention but a few. Does the technical or the financial director make the decisions about purchasing a certain type of service? Is the budget for this type of service flexible or fixed? Is the decision making process rapid and individual-centred or is it 'Japanese style'? What companies have high ambitions for excellence in this particular area, and how is this reflected in their decision-making structure? For example, the managing director of a highly successful advertising company specializing in industry-to-industry advertising said:

Most manufacturers of industrial goods do not understand much about advertising, and do not care much about it! We consciously try to pick only those companies where there is a seriousness, a genuine awareness that the right advertising can make a decisive difference! That is our market segment and I believe it is important to our image—both internally and externally that we do not shop around outside it.

The basic logic here is that in service industries it is very important to understand the deeper, psychosocial aspects of the market segment, since the clients are not only consumers but also producers, and since their behaviour must be controlled.

INDIVIDUALIZING SERVICES

But what possibilities are there to go even further to cater for every customer more or less individually? Obviously this depends a great deal on the nature of the service involved and on the customer structure. We have to distinguish here between individual people or household customers (mass market or consumer services) and institutional customers.

In the first category each individual account may be so small that any kind of adaptation seems impossible. The main strategy must therefore be one of focused market segmentation: to have the Concordes and the charter airlines, the Troisgros and the McDonald's, all focusing on their own particular segments. In a surprising number of consumer services this approach has rarely been followed. (Our hypothesis is that with more educated customers and more differentiated and specialized banking service systems, both the quality and the results of the banks would increase, but so far few have been willing to test this.)

And yet some systematic approaches to individualizing consumer services do exist. One step along this path is to develop a set of preconceived and standardized packages, each reflecting the total needs of one well-understood customer segment. Several insurance companies are taking this approach, basing their market segmentation on a model of the lifecycle of the individual and on the various needs of lifecycle passages. Thus, the individual customer is identified in terms of the market segment to which he belongs and is then offered a fairly well adapted but still standardized package.

Another approach is to assign customers to *individual contact people* within the service company. A few banks do this ('the personal banker'), and so do some high-status *haute coiffure* establishments. The most promising approach to 'large-scale individualization', however, could be described as 'computerized individualization'. An interesting example is the American mail-order company Fingerhut (Meyer, 1980).

This mail-order company has a computer system and a general approach different from that of other such firms. It does not send out a catalogue; the computer picks out a dozen or so sheets, each describing a particular product, for the individual customer. The sheets are selected according to the presumed needs and situation of that customer. If the client is slow about paying his bills, for example, the computer will notice this and will gradually select lower-priced items. If a customer moves to a new neighbourhood, the computer has information about the special characteristics and status attributes of that area and selects accordingly. If one of the children is going to have a birthday, the computer knows about it and will type a special letter to go with the product sheets, congratulating the child by name and getting the birthday date right, suggesting that it will be happy to send a present with the next order; and so on.

This an interesting example not only of pre-programmed assumptions but also of programmed learning. There are certain to be many such innovations in mass-market individualization in the future based on a greater understanding of differences in life-styles, life passages and desired modes of participation, as well as on refined learning programs.

Most mail-order companies have been less radical than the firm in the example above. They continue to mail out their catalogues, but add fliers with offers adapted to the personal profile of the addressee.

Obviously, both services and physical products can be highly individualized with the help of modern technology. The Dell personal computers are based on such a concept. Levi's is beginning to offer tailor-made jeans (industrially manufactured!). In pharmaceuticals people are beginning to talk about producing medicines to match the needs of individual patients.

In providing services to institutions, the size of the account often permits or even necessitates individualization. Apart from various methods of market segmentation, the system of assigning one 'account executive' to be responsible for all interaction with a particular client is quite common, for example, among advertising agencies and consulting organizations. On the whole there is probably great potential in further innovative developments here, whereby institutions interact to produce and develop services jointly and to transfer knowledge, skills and management principles and practice.

9
Technology, tools and setting

We shape our buildings, and afterwards our buildings shape us (Winston Churchill)

Although a service may be intangible and best described as an act, equipment and buildings can also play as important a role in its 'production' as they do in the manufacture of goods. Many service companies are equipment-intensive (in a survey, the source of which I have forgotten, the service industry of 'pipeline transportation' was listed as the world's most equipment-intensive industry). Transportation, computer services and medical care can all fall into this category. This does not invalidate the basic principles outlined above. In fact, the more equipment-intensive and capital-intensive the service operation, the more likely it is that its effective use of the physical resources will depend on the ability to focus and direct personnel, information and clients.

In this examination of the role of physical aids in the service delivery system we shall distinguish five factors which are invariably influenced by the physical setting and the technical tools used in service delivery, specifically:

- cost rationalization
- quality enhancement
- beneficial customer linkages
- behavioural implications
- technology adaption.

There is a tendency for these factors to blend; however, management can gain a much greater appreciation of the role of such aids and the opportunities which they may present by examining their individual effects.

While these basic factors are operative regardless of the technology, there is one caveat: one must always be alert to technologies which, although not traditionally a part of the competitive sphere, might have a transforming effect on one's business. This phenomenon is particularly evident in manufacturing: the vacuum tube technology was displaced in a matter of a few years by transistors, and in a shorter period integrated chips replaced discrete transistors. The ubiquitous silicon wafer is found in cars, televisions, computers, kitchen appliances, door locks, power tools, and 'smart' credit cards. Many manufacturers are no longer in the business they were in a decade ago; some are not in business at all. They are victims of their own lack of vigilance for such transforming technology and/or their inability to make the dramatic adjustments required.

Services have felt the indirect effect of the technology dislocation experienced by their customers, and they are increasingly encountering direct effects. Information technology has altered the landscape in services radically over a relatively short period.

THE POWER OF INFORMATION TECHNOLOGY

Information technology affects every part of the service delivery equation, from concept and strategy to quality, cost, production and delivery. As evident in the McKesson case presented in Chapter 3, information technology can restructure and redefine a whole industry, thoroughly changing the roles of suppliers, intermediaries, customers, and customers' customers. Today the entire financial services sector is being redefined.

As shown in the bar chart in Figure 9.1, the cost structure of service industries is changing. In simple terms, service business used to be people sitting in buildings, and using some transportation equipment. The major long-term changes in the cost structure are related to the growing importance of investments in information technology. It is easy to underestimate this trend based solely on the cost structure, since it has to be taken into account that the information technology that can be bought for

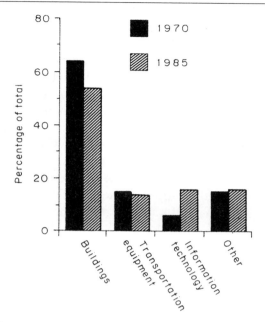

Figure 9.1 Comparative capital investment distribution by asset type in service industries, 1970/85. Source of data: ESIF

one cost unit today bears no resemblance to what could be bought for the same amount of money 10 years ago in terms of its information handling capacity and inherent productivity.

If we position this change in the matrix of the first chapter we can discern two major functions of information technology in the service sector. First, this technology fulfils the same role as it did in the industrial economy; that is, it enhances the task productivity of individual service workers and contributes to economies of scale by standardizing and mass-production techniques. In this sense we can talk about the 'industrialization' of services. This type of impact may significantly alter the service concept and the implementation strategy. In most instances, however, the degree of change falls short of a transformative impact.

Secondly, as the example of McKesson shows, information technology serves to reinforce the inherent logic of the service economy: to customize, to integrate with the user process of the customer, to adapt to the increasingly complex coproductive relationship. In this area in particular, information technology has potentially transformative impact. The potential for pursuing both of these trends should be great.

Thirdly, customers are now less dependent on their suppliers. New actors are entering the market, bringing about 'disinter-mediation'. Customers can seek information or act on their own. They can link up to each other and form new value-creating networks.

Higher technology intensity in service provision does not invalidate any of the basic principles outlined earlier in this book related to personality intensity. We are not dealing with an either/ or, but with a both/and relationship here. As we have stressed, the full potential of one type of knowledge resource in a company can be realized only if it is appropriately leveraged by other resources. Businesses increasingly take on a systemic character.

In this examination of the role of physical aids in the service delivery system we shall distinguish five functions, which are often intermingled. This framework aids in understanding and capitalizing on physical effects and technical tools.

COST RATIONALIZATION

Just as in the agricultural and manufacturing sectors, technology and physical equipment can be used in the service industries as a substitute for manpower with a view to reducing costs or increasing efficiency. This substitution may be introduced into the interaction with the customer, as in the case of the automatic car wash or the automatic cash-dispenser; or it may be used for office tasks as in computer simulation. It may also be possible to redesign the service delivery process so that parts of it can be automated and done behind the scenes (where it can often be more easily controlled) rather than in interaction with the client.

One industry in which technology is profoundly changing the whole service delivery process is security. The development of electronic sensor systems, information transmission systems and electronic central alarm stations has not only shifted the former emphasis on selling patrol-hours to selling security systems, but it has also totally changed the demands on the guards and the roles involved in supplying a security service.

In Oulu, Finland, the use of new communications and information technology in the health care sector has led to some very interesting results. For example, it was possible to achieve substantial savings in transportation costs by using a 'telemedical' method of transmitting X-ray images.

MORE EFFECTIVE QUALITY CONTROL

The introduction of a machine as a substitute for people may make it easier to control and standardize the quality of a service. Dealing with an automatic cash-dispenser may not be as satisfying as dealing with a really pleasant cashier, but at least you know what you are getting. One of the 'secrets' of the McDonald's hamburger restaurants is the way the physical tools and the layout have been planned with a view to ensuring complete consistency in the behaviour of the staff. There is usually only one way to do things, depending on the design of the physical equipment: the right way. On the other hand, technology can put a ceiling on the level of quality that can be attained: at the turn of the millennium McDonald's is finding it necessary to change their technology simply to make it possible to improve the taste of their food.

MAKING HIGHER QUALITY POSSIBLE

The automatic cash-dispenser, the automated 24-hour branch office or—to take the next step—the Internet bank, which is always open, are examples of technology that permits a higher level of service (in this case round-the-clock operation) which would be impractical or too expensive if people were doing the same jobs. Computer information systems permit banks and insurance companies to supply their customers with more data, as well as data that are more rapidly available.

Similarly, with advances in technology it has become possible to make new types of service available to the client which would otherwise have been impossible or too expensive. Examples of this are legion, ranging from Concorde and the new technology in the rapidly growing information industry to machines for process-ing enormous quantities of medical laboratory material at a frac-tion of the previous cost.

CLOSER LINK-UP WITH THE CUSTOMER

Financial service companies can link their information systems to those of their clients, thus integrating the client more closely into the service system. The same applies to other areas, for instance security services.

Companies operating in the goods distribution or wholesale fields may install order terminals, inventory-control terminals or other equipment at their customers' premises, thus providing the client with better service while also achieving a more closely integrated client relationship which would be rather difficult to dissolve. With the new 'supply-chain management' technologies, it is not easy to see the boundary between supplier and customer.

A related strategy is to design new peripheral services which are equipment-based and which link the service company and the client more closely to one another without apparently affecting the core service. A large wholesaler, for example, has designed a computerized system for local-market analysis and local-market strategy design for its own retail customers. There is no doubt that this genuinely helps the customers, but it also gives the wholesaler a very broad database, and this knowledge puts him in a strong position *vis-à-vis* his clients.

TECHNOLOGY AND DESIGN AS A FACTOR AFFECTING BEHAVIOUR

Finally—and this function is usually given less attention than it deserves—technology and physical aids can fulfil a key function creating the desired human behaviour. When the quality of a service is highly dependent on a specific type of action or interac-tion, certain physical tools can be used to promote the right kind of interaction or social behaviour.

A company which has clearly understood this mechanism is Club Méditerranée. The company is aware that its service involves the creation of special sets of social relationships amongst its clients and between the clients and the company's *gentils organisateurs*. Its attitude to any kind of status relationships (or rather the way it plays down such relationships) makes it possible to create new social linkages without threatening or overwhelming the client. The policy of Club Méditerranée is to design and control the physical setting in which its service is supplied down to the smallest detail. The design of the dining-room tables is an example of this. By tradition, all the tables are made for eight people, because it has been found that smaller tables do not promote new social contacts, while at larger tables closed subgroups will form. At tables for exactly eight people, the desired interaction pattern emerges!

Disney World has spent a lot of effort trying to determine how to organize queuing systems so as to create a less negative—and preferably positive—experience for the visitor.

As well as increasing productivity and efficiency, technology and physical tools may be used to enhance the status and motivation of employees to enrich their jobs. Word-processing machines do away with the tedious elements of secretarial work, and security guards are transformed into electronic-equipment operators. A good example of this mechanism at work is illustrated by an experience I had at Helsinki airport:

I had to wait a few minutes in the departure lounge, and I found myself idly watching a member of a large cleaning company polishing the fabulously elegant parquet floor. He was sitting on a small tractor-like machine. I then noticed how he started to work on a particularly complicated part of the floor, manoeuvring his machine between handrails and into small corners with great skill. The machine turned round in practically no space at all. Suddenly I noticed that I was not the only person watching; a small crowd of waiting passengers had stopped wandering around and gathered to watch the cleaning act. It occurred to me suddenly that the man on the machine had ceased to be a mere cleaner, and he knew it. He was an artist performing to an audience and getting its full attention. The machine had helped him to transcend his previous role and he was enjoying the situation to the full.

The physical tools employed for creating the desired type of social behaviour can sometimes be extremely simple. By going round with pieces of chocolate or a menu as soon as the passengers have boarded a plane, the cabin attendants have an opportunity for personal contact with every passenger from the outset. The design of the menu in a restaurant can greatly affect the interactions between waiters and guests, as well as among the guests themselves (if a dish is described as 'Delice Aga Khan' it will certainly generate much more interaction than if it is described as 'Poached sole with a champagne sauce on a bed of sliced onion lightly sautéed with honey'). The interaction patterns, and consequently the service experienced, will be quite different.

In general, equipment and physical tools and premises can all be employed to facilitate and create any of the different types of client participation discussed in the previous chapter, and we have found that concrete ideas usually result from a systematic survey of the various possible functions and modes of participation. At a strategic level, physical aids can certainly contribute to the strategic positioning of the company (design of buildings, equipment used, etc. all add something to the image of the company). Bank branch offices can be designed so as to facilitate subsegmentation of the market; customers with different needs (especially as regards knowledge transfer) will be automatically channelled into the appropriate service delivery system without any costly 'sorting mechanism' and without disturbing the smooth running of other service delivery processes which they do not happen to need just then.

Designers of home pages generally expend a lot of energy on trying to understand how different customers look for information and on making that search easier. An illustrative home page may be a rather accurate reflection of the company itself and thus an effective display window.

Clearly, the equipment used by a service company also serves to position it in the human-resource market. It can serve a status-enhancing role, as was the case in the Helsinki example above or in personally assigned vehicles used by employees of J-C Decaux. It can standardize production and quality and at the same time allow for employees with lesser skills than those otherwise required by a similar service based on a different personnel idea. In other cases equipment and technology activate whole new role sets, linkages and opportunities for utilizing human energy.

IKEA's stores are designed like blazed learning trails for their customers and are thus pedagogical enablers. For many electronic products, however, the opposite holds true. My new car has a thick and comprehensive instruction manual. But the manual for the car's hi-fi system and radio is even thicker. There is no end to what can be done with the many buttons; there are countless sequences and functions. But the effect on me, the customer, is essentially to make me feel stupid. Not only that, but to manipulate all the controls and see what adjustments are necessary, I have to take my eyes off the road. In this way, industrial design, rather than being an enabler, can be an obstacle.

Design and aesthetics influence not only the physical and social behaviour, but intellectual and emotional behaviour (what we think and feel) as well. The art of directing a performance, pedagogy, stage design, and rhetoric are examples of competencies which—in combination with physical design—have an impact on the effectiveness and quality of service delivery.

The conscious use of physical setting and technical tools is admittedly common among successful service companies. And yet we have found little discussion or conceptualization of technical systems and physical tools as critical components in the concept, strategy, product offering, or delivery system of services.

THE INTERNET AND THE FUTURE

At the turn of the millennium, writing about the Internet and what it will mean to the services of the future, and, in a broader sense, for the business of the future is to set yourself up for failure! Developments are proceeding so rapidly. The second edition of this book was published less than 10 years after the first; much of what had been further developed related specifically to the importance of new information technology for the creation of services. Now—again less than 10 years later—the new examples and scenarios of the second edition are almost entirely obsolete.

The pace of development will probably accelerate further in the next 10 years. Even the most radical examples in the present edition will probably be outdated in a few months. What then can be said about something which hardly anyone today has the imagination or knowledge to predict, and when all we really know is that the resulting changes in the lives of virtually every human being will be far-reaching? My approach will be to limit the number of examples and to discuss the major trends more generally.

The Internet revolution and, in a broader sense, the digital revolution, basically means that one of mankind's oldest dreams is coming true: the separation of information from physical objects. Nicolas Negroponte has expressed the idea of this disengagement in an excellent way: we can dissociate 'bits' from 'atoms', information from the mass to which it has previously been bound.

The result was in many respects a detachment of the virtual world from the physical world, something that people have been trying to achieve for a long time. The Roman Empire was based to no small degree on an effective system of transportation (roads throughout Europe—'All roads lead to Rome.') Gutenberg's art of printing, a product of the Renaissance, was revolutionary; the new medium of the printed word made it possible to disseminate knowledge much more widely than before. It is well known how the Rothschild family established and consolidated its position of power by virtue of a superior system of communication by carrier pigeon—it came in very handy after the Battle of Waterloo.

And now we have the Internet, virtual reality, the possibility of communicating in real, global time, global markets for just about everything.

Internetrevolutioner (Internet Revolutions) is a book in which two of my colleagues, Lennart Nordfors and Bert Levin (1999), described different scenarios for the new world of the future. These scenarios are: 'The electronic communities', 'The Wild West', 'The power of the portals', and 'Politics takes command'. The scenarios are based in turn on hypothetical assumptions about how two critical issues will be resolved in the future: whether power will be concentrated or dispersed, and whether the development of the Internet will lead to a society of isolation or one of community (see Figure 9.2).

The purpose of this book is not to describe the societies of the future, but to discuss the premises for service production and value creation today and in the future. What is certain is that the new information technology, and the Internet in particular, will provide a radically new *platform* for new businesses, new services, and new forms of value creation.

The Internet does not—and I weigh my words carefully, hoping that I will not later be considered a mental dinosaur—imply any

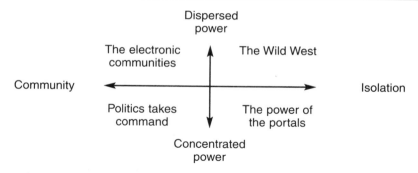

Figure 9.2 A diagram taken from Nordfors and Levin (1999)

contradiction to what has been the theme of *Service Management*. On the contrary, information technology underlies and reinforces many trends and business logics treated in this book.

The new technology has three features which are relevant to our subject:

1. It is a *real-time economy* in which different activities and the activities of different actors can be compressed in time.
2. It is leading to increased *interactivity*, so that more activities can take place simultaneously and in parallel rather than sequentially.
3. It is weightless and—once the infrastructure is in place— extremely cost-effective, so that it is becoming *global*.

These features have many consequences. One is that the boundary between customer and supplier is tending to dissolve. Another is that it is becoming increasingly possible to individualize offerings to customers by mobilizing resources globally for each individual case. This individualization may be achieved either by companies which can skilfully combine Internet technology with advanced database technology, or by customers themselves.

Thirdly, the new technology reinforces a trend already mentioned several times in this book: the growing impossibility of drawing the line between manufacturing and services. The following are two examples:

General Electric's aircraft engines can now be serviced through a global system in which the engines generate data on their own condition and use, and on the basis of these data, optimal servicing is automatically provided. It is thus possible to optimize flying times, fuel consumption, and use of assets.

Xerox attracted a lot of attention in its transition from analogue to the digital economy. The first step was to let different machines 'talk' to each other, thus moving from copying to document-handling in a broad sense. Another tendency is that machines are becoming much more 'intelligent' and are being linked in real-time to service centres, which monitor the use of the machines and can continuously assess servicing needs and adjust performance. In parallel with this technological development, a growing proportion of machine parts are being designed so that customers themselves can service the machines and replace defective units, a task which previously required company personnel to visit the customer. And further developments of this kind can surely be expected.

In structure, these examples are representative of the IT- and Internet-based businesses of the future. On the other hand, many of the companies which are so highly valued by the stock market today, whether or not they are making much money, are doomed to fold or be bought up unless they can redefine themselves. Presently, at the turn of the millennium, the world of business is going through a period of adjustment, and to some extent one of euphoria, which will not last.

Why? Very many traditional companies, whether they sell financial services, automobiles or furniture, have been based on non-transparency in pricing, bundling of 'atoms' and 'bits', and overpricing of 'commodities'. When transparency in prices of standardized products becomes almost total by virtue of the Internet, the effect will be twofold. First, many new companies will be attracted into existing markets and offer various products and services at what will seem to be astoundingly low prices; these markets will be ones which ecomomists would term 'imperfect'— in other words, protected by a monopoly position or a lack of perfect information. Secondly, many large, established companies will be affected by this invasion of their previously protected territory.

But the trend has already turned; today the question is no longer which companies will be involved in 'e-business' and which ones will continue to do business in more traditional fashion.

Above all, for some time the new e-business invaders will fulfil the function of correcting previous market imperfections. Many established companies will learn from the experience and will radically redesign their business. New, invading companies which initially based their operations simply on exploiting market imperfections will run into trouble unless they rethink their businesses and develop genuine new competencies. (During this process many established companies will surely lose a lot of ground, to say the least.)

The Internet revolution in business will thus bring a relatively limited period of prosperity to companies capable of concentrating on the virtual world of 'bits' as long as established firms remain largely in the world of 'atoms' and physical processes. But this stage, during which the two worlds disengage, is a transitional one. The future will belong to those who can reintegrate the virtual world and the physical world. For the true value of 'bits'—or information—is that they can be used to control processes in the physical world. The dissociation of the two worlds will be a distinctive feature of a transitional phase which may last five, seven or 10 years. Skill at reintegrating them to create genuine new value for customers will determine in the long run which companies will be successful.

INTRODUCING NEW TECHNOLOGY

Automation and new technology—in particular information technology—have great potential for making many services more cost-effective and for increasing their quality. Nevertheless, frequent examples have shown that the introduction of new technology into an established service management system is a very delicate process. Since services involve social actions, and are perhaps embedded in social and cultural patterns on both the employees' and the customers' side, new technology must be accompanied by other changes in the total service management system.

Social interaction patterns, such as that between bank clerk and customer, may disappear, possibly with unexpected consequences; some of the vital but intangible rewards that the contact personnel get from their direct interaction with customers may vanish.

There is thus a danger in leaving less scope for the 'tacit know-ledge' in a social interaction.

The status of whole professional groups may be threatened or even swept away altogether. (It was difficult enough for the people responsible for pricing in insurance companies when they were replaced by computers; no doubt doctors and lawyers will resist even more violently as many of their tasks and activities are demystified and computerized in years to come.) These are some of the pitfalls.

When new technology is being introduced into a service man-agement system, many, if not all, of the other components in the system will generally be affected. But if a holistic view is adopted, and if the new technology is skilfully employed to enhance and promote rather than to disturb the kind of social process that typifies effective service organizations, then the potential will be very great.

10
Image

IMAGE AS A MANAGEMENT TOOL

We can now turn to the fourth component of the service management system—its image. Image is a much used and much abused concept, so let us start by investigating its meaning. Kenneth Boulding used the concept of image as a mental representation of reality sustained by an individual or a group. In other words, the image is a *model,* signifying our beliefs and our understanding of a phenomenon or situation.

This mental model upheld by a specific person or a specific group may be a good or bad representation of reality, but whatever it may be it is always significant because it guides behaviour. True or false, useful or not useful, clear or hazy—we act (or choose not to act) according to our own perception of reality. If the image is not an exact equivalent of reality, it is at least a 'social reality'. Since our actions subsequently affect and even create 'reality', the boundary between image and reality is diffuse (cf. Berger and Luckman, 1967; Maturana and Varela, 1987).

It is therefore appropriate at this point to discuss what the concept of reality actually stands for. Is there any objective reality outside of us, or is it all a product of the human mind? The latter alternative is a starting point for Berger and Luckman's (1967) thesis that we are always dealing with social constructs. Many of these are so taken for granted that they have become 'objective'. What we generally term reality should then preferably be referred to as the prevailing views of reality. Another important consequence, provided we accept Berger and Luckman's point of departure, is that what people once conceived can be reconceived as something else.

This is why image can be a powerful weapon with which to exert influence. More specifically, it is an instrument of communication. 'Management' is the art of making things happen by way of combined and coordinated human action; obviously, then, influencing people's images—the way they perceive reality—is a management tool with great potential (Kets de Vries, 1980).

Another interesting property of the image and 'social reality', which should be mentioned here since it is relied on heavily by managers (and for that matter by politicians and propagandists in general), is its tendency to reinforce itself and, once it has become established, to become self-fulfilling as well. 'Image' generates purposeful behaviour which, if successful, tends to justify and therefore to reinforce the image. Moreover this behaviour is visible to others and will thus also influence *their* perception of reality. Images which generate firm, visible and successful action not only contain an element of the 'self-fulfilling prophecy', they also exert a considerable snowball effect.

In the light of all this it is easy to see why 'image management' is so important in service organizations. Services are obviously less well defined than physical products, and rather more difficult to try out. To induce the appropriate action in a client and to arouse the (from the company's point of view) desirable preferences in him, it is necessary to communicate with him and to influence his perception of reality in more sophisticated ways than merely showing him a product.

Moreover, because of the vital importance of human motivations and actions in service operations (what we have dubbed their 'personality intensity'), management's ability to steer its own staff's perception of reality so as to create the self-fulfilling snowball effect is absolutely crucial.

WHAT MAKES THE IMAGE?

There is no doubt that the most important factor determining the image or social reality is the currently prevailing conception of reality. To the extent that their cognitive and other mental processes function with reasonable accuracy, people will try to form useful mental models of 'reality'; models which generate action which in turn is reinforced by positive feedback. Inaccurate models will naturally generate less successful action and will probably be discarded or modified.

But of course there will always be inaccuracies; and in any case every phenomenon or situation can be described in an almost infinite number of ways, all perhaps equally accurate but leading to different kinds of action. This constitutes the very foundation of politics and all types of persuasion.

The image that the service company creates in the minds of its own staff and its environment will be largely determined by the nature of its service, its organization, its culture and its members, and by its market segment (the users of its services). This is illustrated in Figure 10.1. In the long term these will be almost the sole determinants. By taking specific action to communicate and direct various aspects of the company image, management can strengthen and clarify the image and thus affect people's behaviour.

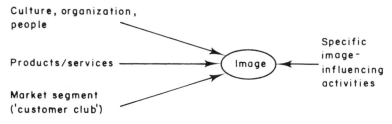

Figure 10.1 Determinants of image

However, in certain circumstances management may choose to create a deliberate mismatch between the prevailing conception of reality and the image, in the hope that a strongly projected image *will actually create behaviour of such a kind that the prevailing conception of reality is in fact questioned and reshaped.* This is a dangerous strategy which is often used in the wrong way; but we have also seen it being used creatively by skilful and innovative managers. The success of the strategy will depend entirely upon whether the image can actually make reality change and quickly enough to maintain management's credibility.

The borderline between good management and what could almost be described as downright fraud is sometimes a very fine one. If the projected image is not supported by the generally accepted view of reality, there must be a watertight plan to make the new image self-fulfilling. Many service organizations launch campaigns to convince clients of the exceptional excellence of their staff or their 'caring' attitude to clients when in fact they are no better than other organizations in these respects and have done nothing to ensure that they will ever be so. False images of this kind tend to bring their own backlash among the staff and the customers.

In discussing management in later chapters we will again note that skilful managers are able to exploit the complex dialectic relationship between reality and image to advantage. The accepted view of reality creates images, but images can also be used to create a view of reality.

FUNCTIONS AND TARGET GROUPS

Figure 10.2 shows the target groups at which 'image management' can be aimed. As we shall see, there are several different purposes for which the image can be used in relation to each target group. Briefly, however, the main uses of the image are:

- strategic positioning;
- more effective market penetration;
- facilitating access to various resources, and/or lowering the cost of access; and
- focusing behaviour to increase motivation and productivity.

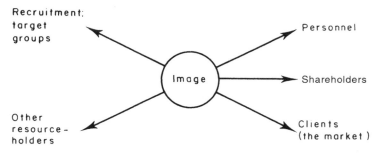

Figure 10.2 Groups at which the image can be aimed

For all these purposes, and in relation to all the target groups, the methods are basically the same: reinforcing virtuous circles, and exploiting the snowball and the self-fulfilling prophecy effects that readily attach to images.

The predominant group at which the image is aimed is probably still the market; i.e. present and future customers, although personnel and shareholders are rapidly becoming important targets too. The president of a large and well-known American service company told me: 'We do run a lot of ads and in fact they are aimed more at our own people than at the customers.'

If the image of the company is so clear that it can activate the customer and help him to *see himself* as a member of the 'club' connected with this particular service company, then a great deal has been gained and less effort will be needed in other aspects of selling.

As well as creating an image in the minds of its own personnel, the company can create a profile on the recruitment market. In discussing the personnel idea above, we saw that an appropriate positioning on the market for potential employees can have a double effect; employees are more positively focused ('this is the club I want to join because it fits my aims and life situation'), and recruitment is easier and possibly less expensive.

Publicity campaigns demonstrating the typical 'good' employee are very common in service and information organizations. Individual employees may be presented in advertisements, with information about their backgrounds, their hobbies and their perceptions of the job. If well designed, such campaigns can make an impact on all the target groups we have been discussing: they demonstrate the company's interest in its employees and provide role models for other employees; they provide a model against which potential employees can measure themselves; and they display essential aspects of the service delivery system and the company culture to present and future customers, reducing some of their uncertainty with regard to the service organizations. They attract investors.

In our experience, such campaigns are successful only if they genuinely reflect the company's profile. A few years ago a large American service conglomerate announced that they were starting a campaign of this sort, and that they would be presenting some of their outstanding and excellent employees, who would reveal their personal views. A series of advertisements followed, filled with dull pictures and incredibly boring and ridiculous statements from senior executives. The campaign conveyed no message except that the company felt a need to advertise, and was proof in itself that the company was in difficulties. We can compare this with an advertising campaign launched by Atlas Copco (a production company which is intentionally becoming more service and problem-solving oriented and therefore, in our terms, more personality-intensive), which presented employees from different parts of the world, describing their personalities and their hobbies in some detail and pointing out any particularly outstanding solutions or creative achievements they had been responsible for. A very definite message emerged from this campaign.

In the Atlas Copco case the image emerges of a company which is more creative than its competitors, that is committed to problem-solving, and whose structure and resources suggest that the customer is likely to acquire something special or even unique in his dealings with it. The Avis 'We try harder' message has another content; here there is less emphasis on originality or uniqueness but all the more on the energy that will be at the customer's disposal—often an effective and useful message in service industries. The customer is assured that in the uncertain situation of buying a service somebody will be fighting for his interests. An industrial risk insurance company with which we once worked owed much of its success to the fact that it was able to convey the idea, which it could also support in practice, that 'this company does not start arguing among the wreckage'.

Another way of reducing the uncertainty of the client is simply to demonstrate resources and concrete achievements (these last should logically be proof of the existence of adequate resources). Banks and transportation companies display their networks; or a bank illustrates a great dam project which it has financed or otherwise supported. Airlines display route maps; and so on.

In the art of image creation, one of the smartest gambits is making your competitors work for you! In its simplest form this strategy can also be illustrated by the Avis slogan, 'We try harder', which was of course as much a statement about the main competitors as about Avis itself. Another more advanced form of the same image-creating strategy is provided by the Swedish financial service company, Independent, where the image was reflected in the name of the company. When Independent was first established, its Swedish competitors were all subsidiaries of the big banks, burdened with many of the policies and much of the inertia of the parent organizations. The whole point of Independent was to be different from the banks, to be more aggressive and creative, to be sales-minded, to help customers and to really solve their problems, to allow their employees a degree of discretion in decision-making which would be unthinkable in a bank. The whole image was beautifully envisaged, starting with the company's name. In this case, the energy and expectations raised in the clients and (potential) staff were skilfully and extremely successfully exploited to turn the image into a self-fulfilling prophecy.

But there are even more subtle ways of making the competition work for you. If a service company tries to redefine an industry by introducing a radically different service concept and/or service delivery system, then the reactions of competitors may be extremely strong. This very fact can be exploited to advantage.

The Swedish company IKEA, designers and distributors of home furniture, is a case in point. By establishing a completely new and different distribution outlet, and by designing a full new range of furniture that combined contemporary Scandinavian design with simplicity, self-service and a range of production contracts with furniture manufacturers, the company enjoyed a resounding success. The conservative establishment in the industry did everything to stop IKEA. Attempts were made to block supplies from the manufacturers and to rush through new quality regulations. IKEA reacted to this by extending its production-contract strategy to other countries in order to achieve even lower production costs and by becoming a pioneer of furniture quality norms itself. But perhaps the most important benefit that IKEA acquired from its rivals was the boost to its own coherent company ethos, which formed in opposition to the 'enemies', and the enormous publicity in the mass media. This story has been more or less repeated each time IKEA has established itself in a new country.

Another typical illustration is provided by the Scandinavian Airlines System (SAS), which in 1981 introduced its new 'Euro Class' concept (then a distinctly improved level of service for passengers paying the full fare). The reaction of some competitors was violent and conservative; it was claimed that the new service concept infringed the IATA rules, and serious threats were issued by various other airlines and (on their behalf) even by governments. At least one competitor embarked on a price war, advertising heavily in Scandinavia. The front-page coverage in the newspapers in Scandinavia and in other European countries could not fail to make every potential customer aware that one airline was fighting for the right to give its customers more service without raising the price. Mass media reports on emergency meetings between governments were not harmful; rather, they reinforced the image which SAS had been trying to create.

As an instrument the image is not directed only at customers and (potential) employees. An appropriate image will also help in negotiating for access to resources in general and in bargaining for low-cost resources. It is hard to conceive how John DeLorean, a maverick in the US automobile industry, would have been able to raise capital and other support from so many sources for his car-manufacturing venture without his skilful image-building. In General Motors he had already proved his ability to play the game of the establishment in the car industry, and when he set out to play against the establishment he seemed a good bet to many optimistic and adventurous resource-holders. With his image he was able to exploit innumerable dreams! But the end of the story proves again that if the general view of reality cannot be brought quickly enough into reasonable accord with the image there will be a harsh backlash. The idea was attractive but the product banal.

The image of a company/businessman may thus be misleading to outsiders. We would very much like to believe in someone who dares to break with established notions. This someone seems to incarnate what we ourselves would want but have never had the courage to try. In the Bible, David defeated Goliath. But that image alone will not create a new IKEA; for that, there must be a well-functioning whole. The image is important, but still only one of several parts of such a whole.

INTERNAL MARKETING

In discussing the target groups for image-building we have stressed the idea of using the company image to influence employees. This is a suitable context to extend our argument to the wider concept of 'internal marketing', which is becoming very fashionable in service companies and other personality intensive businesses (Grönroos, 1982).

It is a common saying among farsighted business leaders in the service sector that 'what you can't sell to your own staff you can't sell to the customers either'. This is not only relevant in connection with products or services; it also applies to 'selling' the company's essential idea to its members. Let us illustrate the complex mechanisms at work here in a slightly edited example from a company with which we have worked.

Suppose that a customer enters a restaurant and orders a dish from the menu. Let us also suppose that he is neither very knowledgeable nor very discriminating about food, and that he is a one-time visitor who is just passing through the town.

Suppose that just today the restaurant happens not to possess the perfect faultless ingredients needed for this particular dish—it is a bit of a gamble whether it will be up to standard or not. The chef hesitates but decides to serve the dish. He may have done a fine job; the normal standard may have been exceptionally high; or the customer's lack of knowledge and low standards have come into play; but, whatever the reason, our customer walks away happy and satisfied. So is everything all right?

No, because something extremely significant has happened: a new norm has been established in the company, stating in effect that 'It's all right to cheat the customer a little, especially if he doesn't seem to notice'. The customer may not notice, but there is no way of hiding what goes on from the employees. Such an incident (probably quite rightly) will be seen not as a single occurrence but as a symptom of prevailing professional and ethical norms in the organization, and this will have a profound effect upon the way employees perceive the organization and on the kind of reputation it will eventually have among potential recruitment groups. Employees with high professional and ethical standards will not see this company as a place in which they could be happy and, in the long run, develop. The grapevine will spread the news to the professional community.

It is easy to see how in the slightly longer run our little incident will influence the personnel structure and professionalism of the restaurant and, consequently, *its genuine ability to provide excellence*. In the end, the service itself will be affected—and finally the customers will notice. Sloppy internal marketing will affect the external market position.

Mechanisms of this kind are continuously at work in all organizations that depend on the motivation, the productivity, the professionalism and the ethics of its employees for the maintenance of the given quality standard in its service. Internal and external marketing are intimately linked.

The purpose of internal marketing can thus be summarized as follows:

1. It maintains the standard of quality in the provision of the service.
2. It achieves cost efficiency by way of higher productivity.
3. Motivated and professional staff represent an important part of the image *vis-à-vis* the customer. This promotes selling and reselling, which in turn usually has a significant impact on commercial success.
4. Recruitment thus becomes easier.

When is internal marketing appropriate? Obviously it should take place continuously; it should be part of everyday life in a service organization. But as is the case with external marketing, there are occasions when special campaigns are called for.

One such occasion arises when a company needs pulling up out of what has perhaps been a generally lethargic state. Ailing service companies can sometimes be rescued without any dramatic changes in strategy or market positioning. A general tightening up of quality standards and behaviour patterns, leading to higher motivation and productivity, may be quite enough and may be achieved by well-designed internal marketing campaigns.

When strategic repositioning and/or the launching of new types of services or redefined service concepts are called for, special internal marketing campaigns also become necessary.

In the commercial section of a large insurance company a new and advanced service concept, which included radically new ways of interacting with customers, was developed to cope with a dramatically harsher competitive climate. The most difficult thing about the new concept, however, was finding the means of actually supplying it. Established behaviour patterns and roles in the company and in the industry in general were totally inadequate. A varied 'internal campaign' was launched, including a series of seminars and conferences in which the demands of the new situation and the necessity for the changes were made clear to the personnel. A new 'role model'—a new type of contact person with special qualifications and tasks—was introduced and gradually legitimized, and the employees who were intended to behave according to the model (some of them new and some who had already been working in the organization in other jobs) were put into a specially designed 'internal university'. The organization structure was modified. A new external advertising strategy also aimed at explaining and reinforcing the change to the employees. Internal news media were involved.

In a bank traditionally geared to retail business, we helped to develop a new, offensive strategy aimed at the commercial market. Many obstacles had to be overcome, quite apart from developing new resources, identifying market segments and elaborating the appropriate service packages. The bank's branch network was suddenly going to have to handle two businesses instead of one. Status relationships were challenged. The fear of dealing with new types of customer had to be overcome. Again, a whole range of activities was co-ordinated in a massive campaign aimed particularly at the personnel. The president himself was heavily involved. A special internal newspaper was created, elaborating the whole strategic situation of the bank, the logic of the new strategy and the coming change process. Almost half the latest annual report was devoted to the new business and to the interaction between the new and the old.

A multiplicity of means thus exists for internal marketing. Among the most usual are internal schools and 'universities', special advertisements, internal publications, massive programs involving major conferences at which top managers appear either in person or on video or both, and the manifest day-to-day priorities of senior managers. The role of the customer, new internal role models, new dimensions of quality and new quality standards all appear on the internal discussion agenda. 'Little red books' with management philosophies or personal statements from the chief executive are other common tools.

As we have already suggested, external media can also be harnessed to the internal marketing.

When Jan CarIzon became the new chief executive of the ailing Scandinavian Airlines System (SAS), the fame of the company and various novel ideas about management which he immediately expressed made him a popular target for journalists. The innumerable articles about him in the mass media seem to have been studied more thoroughly by his staff than equivalent articles in internal publications would ever have been. Moreover, they drew SAS employees into discussing the company and the new interesting management ideas with people outside SAS. In many cases this has obviously served as a source of reinforcement, whereby employees have crystallized and internalized the ideas more strongly after having a chance to defend them against the world outside.

As in our earlier restaurant example, we have here an illustration of the close interdependence of internal and external marketing. The clever company can achieve both at one blow.

11

The art and science of pricing

The relationships between producer and client in service and knowledge oriented businesses are unusually complex, and as a result pricing tends to assume several important functions apart from simply putting a price tag on the service. The increasingly competitive service environment demands that service providers examine the strategic role of pricing. It is no coincidence that the chapter on pricing follows the one on image.

The price of a service is a strong element of the service product offering which interacts in multiple, complex ways with all parts of the service management system: the guiding principles, the service concept, the market segment, the image and the service delivery system. In the most successful service businesses pricing is used as an active and purposeful management tool both strategically and operationally. Why, then, do we see so many instances of service offerings which appear to be merely tagged with a price?

WHY IS PRICING DIFFICULT?

Several factors render the pricing of services more complicated than the pricing of products. With products there is generally a clearer relationship between the cost of production and the price. The intangible character of the service itself makes it difficult to understand what the package actually consists of, and consequently what we are putting a price tag on. The provision of a McDonald's hamburger is a fairly precise and understandable event with clearly identifiable cost components; but the pricing of that hamburger reflects McDonald's strategic decisions regarding target markets, business concept, market penetration, volume sales and image omnipresence, all of which have strategic pricing implications. They have strategically conceded the high-price low-volume 'gourmet' hamburger market to competitors even though that market has expanded significantly as a spin-off from the high profile they have generated for the hamburger. Other companies had tried variations of this strategy but none with the success of McDonald's, which resulted in large measure from their highly successful reproduction formula.

If we turn to health care or banking or consulting services, we may find that both the client and the supplier are at something of a loss if we ask for a detailed specification of the content of the service and of exactly how its provision is achieved and its cost accounted for. Generally, the higher the intangible component in the service offering, the more loosely coupled the relationship between costs and prices.

Pricing in service businesses is less influenced by cost than it is by the customer's perception of 'value' or 'worth'. In order to optimize service pricing, the service provider may use his cost generators as a price bottom; however, the actual pricing is better determined by matching the customer's perception of 'value'. It is possible to develop a sense of the customer's 'value' determinants, although the tools for doing so, and the results, are not nearly so precise as is cost accounting for a manufacturing concern. The service concept, the product offering, the target market all shape that 'value'-creation, 'value'-definition process. The basic pricing strategy will mark the producer's position in the competitive field; if the producer deviates from that strategy, he will have to differentiate his product offering. The customer will ask himself: what reason can there be for this high price? Or: can I count on the low-price supplier.

Few service transactions are identical; standardization of services is harder to achieve than standardization of products. Customers who ask for more may get more, and at the same price. For this reason some customers may very well be subsidizing others, without any differentiation in the pricing. This can provide openings for competitors with alternative market segments and other pricing strategies.

Pricing is always uncertain or even arbitrary when the cost of production is different from the value to the customer—something which is not uncommon in service industries. The cost of selling risk management services rather than pure insurance may be much lower to the insurance company or the broker, while its value to the client may be considerably higher. As more service concepts are coming to contain a greater element of knowledge and management (rather than simply the transfer of manpower), costing and pricing are becoming increasingly complicated. Furthermore, as research and development in the service industries are also on the increase, the marginal cost of producing a service has less direct connection with the average total cost. Owing to the relative ease of entry into many service industries (because it is, comparatively easy to acquire enough know-how at least for small-scale operations), it is difficult to price services which have been developed at the cost of considerable front-end investment.

If they are finding it difficult to sell their capacity, many producers are tempted to use part of this capacity at marginal cost. In such situations the service company is in a poor bargaining position, unless it has succeeded in making its primary services unique and their value to the client exceptionally high. As many airlines have introduced a complex array of discount fares in order to fill their aircraft, they have encountered more than a little objection from their full-fare-paying customers who perceived they were paying a substantially higher price for substantially the same service. Airlines were violating their customers' perceptions of 'value' and integrity. They responded by enriching the product offering to the main client base, the business traveller. We saw the introduction of frequent flyer bonus programs, advance seat allocation, and differentiated in-flight service (wider seats, different coloured head cushions, menu choice, complimentary alcoholic beverages). Interestingly, telephone companies have been able to adopt similar approaches to utilizing their capacity with little negative impact and almost no enhancement of the basic service.

And just to make the art of pricing even more complicated, the cost structure of the service company is difficult to assess. What is the real cost to the consulting firm of allocating a star consultant to one assignment rather than another? How can part of the total costs of a bank which is really a 'systems business' be attributed to one particular service or customer segment?

The competitive pressures are tending to create differentiated, more specialized market segments. As service firms un-bundle their product offerings in order to respond differently to the different markets, both the pricing decisions and the allocation of overhead and development costs become more complex.

THE PHILOSOPHY BEHIND PRICING AS A MANAGEMENT TOOL

The following points must be considered in every pricing strategy:

1. First, the strategy must build on a profound understanding of *how the profitability of the company is created.* There are two aspects to this. What is the cost structure like, and how do costs arise? And how does the customer's willingness to pay manifest itself, and how can it be influenced?
2. Secondly, pricing strategy is *an instrument for influencing behaviour.* Pricing must be employed in such a way that the service company uses its key resources to the maximum, and pricing strategy must be employed on the market to make the desired client behave in the desired manner.

An analysis of the cost structure has to be made in order to answer the question; 'How can the service company make money?' The analysis will reveal areas sensitive to intervention and help the company to understand how the utilization of key resources should be directed. As a part of this process the service provider has to be highly conscious of the much shorter lifecycles of both the equipment and technology he uses and of service offerings themselves.

If a business is characterized by high fixed costs (perhaps very high equipment costs) and big variations in demand, pricing can be used to direct demand towards certain times, certain areas and certain services. This tactic, as we referred to earlier, is used by airlines and telephone companies, which try to change customer habits or attract the non-business or non-affluent potential customer by special price arrangements at times when their equipment would otherwise be idle.

Banks nowadays offer alternative distribution systems for their services. For instance, you can take out money by going to the local branch or by using an automatic dispenser. Since the latter is generally a great deal less costly for the bank, suitable pricing could be used to steer the behaviour of the customer to the advantage of the bank's economic equation. In fact it would generally be both realistic and profitable to reward every customer who used the automatic dispenser for routine transactions rather than the branch office concerned.

If a service company normally has high costs for its sales to new customers but relatively low costs for repeat sales to existing customers, then the pricing strategy should be adapted to reflect the situation; i.e. rewarding the development of existing customers. Strangely enough, this is contrary to the internal reward systems of most service companies today.

Pricing should reflect and promote service differences connected with *market segmentation.* It is logical that costs are different for services rendered to different market segments. But such effects alone do not always account for many price differences, particularly where there seems to be a considerable 'snob' or status component. Sometimes, however, what could be perceived as a snob effect is really something different; perhaps, for example, one market segment is willing to make a trade-off between price and participation in the service transaction.

Pricing must reflect the decision-making system and the decision-making process of the client. On specific markets there are often fairly well-established rules with regard to pricing and tendering. In such cases the service company, at least at a certain stage in the development of the client relationship, will have to adapt to the expectations of the client and follow the established rules. If a client is used to regarding his purchase decision as a choice between prompting service companies, then there may be no alternative but to join in the process of bidding. But more often the service offering has to be adapted to the freedom of action of the person or unit in charge of purchasing the service.

Sometimes pricing strategy can be used as an active means of influencing the decision-making system of the client. The following are a couple of examples:

By deliberately failing to follow the rules of the game (for example in a tendering process), or by starting on purpose at a higher price level than the client's negotiator has the right to decide about, the service company may be able to lift the decision-making process on to a higher level in the client organization. This, in turn, can pave the way for new types of communication with the client.

It is often possible to arrange the different components of the total price in such a way as to reflect more precisely the decision-making system of the particular client.

In the case of institutional services, it might be possible to discuss how much of the price should be regarded as an investment and how much should be ascribed to the operational budget. Adjustment to the customer's decision-making structure can be made by discussing the alternatives of leasing or selling equipment. An insurance company can let a customer choose between higher insurance premiums (charged to the operational budget) or a combination of lower premiums and a higher investment in loss-prevention equipment.

TYPICAL ELEMENTS IN PRICING STRATEGIES

There is no single or simple solution to the dilemmas and problems discussed above. The following are some of the elements of pricing strategy that can be used in various combinations.

More precise specification of the service concept. To ensure that prices are really reflecting the value to the client, it may be necessary to specify more precisely what the service package consists of, and to make sure that the customer understands the value the service company is giving him. He should then be less inclined to concentrate on the marginal cost of production in the service company. However, this can seldom be achieved without some form of concrete development of the service package as such.

Un-bundling. Banks, insurance companies and securities companies, for instance, always used automatically to include a number of peripheral services in their service packages without specifically charging for them. However, there has been a gradual

trend towards a more precise specification of the various components of the service package. Each one is priced separately and
the client is asked to take his pick. In this way he also decides his
own price. The 'bundle' of services is untied and sold bit by bit. It
is thus possible to adapt price and value more realistically to suit
the needs of each customer. This is, of course, also a way of
segmenting the market.

New price carriers. Many service packages are designed in such a
way that a particular component formally bears the whole cost. In
the security and guard business, for example, the guard or the
guard-hour has been the typical price carrier. To open the way for
negotiations with the client about value and price it may be
necessary to introduce new components into the service package,
each of which can have its own price tag.

Examples could be technology and training. 'Value adders',
which visibly solve important problems for the client, may be
included in the package. A distribution company may introduce a
computer system and then lease or distribute terminals to its clients to increase the efficiency of the ordering routines. In some
cases it may be possible to identify areas in which the client has
problems where it would be possible for him to make money and
then to develop the service packages to help him in just that area.
This kind of component in the service package may be priced
separately or may make it possible to renegotiate the price of the
total service.

Success-fee pricing. Reducing the uncertainty of the client is a
crucial part in the sale of many services. A pricing system which
allows the client more control, or which reduces his uncertainty
in some other way, is therefore often an effective sales weapon.
Various kinds of success-fee pricing, linking the price to what is
actually achieved, may help to reduce some of the client's uncertainty about the relation between the price of the service and its
value. It would be quite feasible for a security company, for
example, to link part of its price (according to some agreed
formula) to statistically demonstrated reductions in pilferage
and crime in the client's organization; a consulting company
could link part or all of its price to the increase in its client's
profitability.

Incentive pricing. In this case the uncertainty is reduced by linking the price to the activity of the client. There may be a bonus attaching to an increase in the client's participation in the service operation, or some kind of profit sharing if the client's participation improves the results. Such pricing formulas are clearly relevant in insurance as well as in health-care services. Pricing strategies of this kind are very well suited to services in which the involvement of the client really affects results.

PRICING STRATEGY AND PRICING TACTICS

The service industries abound in pricing, payment and bidding formulas in all conceivable combinations. In many services, factors such as the date when the client is actually billed, the designation of the services for which he is charged, whether he is billed at intervals or in a lump sum, can all be of the utmost importance. Such things not only affect taxes and cash flows (some service industries are particularly attractive to enter because fees are paid before the service is performed, which makes the business a great cash-flow generator) but also have a psychological impact.

The reader interested in pricing tactics with diverse ethical or moral implications will find an interesting exposé in Wilson (1972). Among tactics of this kind which are by no means uncommon are 'loss leaders' (deliberately launching a new relationship at a low price in order to get established, with the intention of raising the price later), 'offset pricing' (low price for the basic product but high prices for the peripheral products which are added later) and 'price lining' (keeping the price constant but deliberately varying the quality and thus the cost of the service according to what the client is found to accept). If a company adopts such tactics, however, there is a risk that the customer will see what is happening and take advantage of it in the short run; of course, the business relationship will never last beyond the first losing transaction. Competitors may enter the market in peripheral products while avoiding the basic product line. Thus, ethically dubious practices may also prove to be of dubious long-term value from a business standpoint.

12
Creating, reproducing and refining business ideas

The entire book is an examination of the processes of creating, reproducing and refining business. Chapter 2, 'The new economic equation', provides an initial insight into innovation and its key driving forces, and the process of creating a product offering. In this chapter the focus is on the business lifecycle, the reproduction formula and incremental development of the product offering.

THE BUSINESS LIFECYCLE

In most cases it can be fruitful to envisage the individual business company as passing through a series of evolutionary stages, from the invention or birth of a new business idea, to maturity, redefinition or death. Growth-stage models of this kind are not so exact that they can be used for simple predictions; in fact many variations and sequences are possible. But they can help us to understand the nature of growth problems, and thus to recognize that management problems do vary according to a certain logic.

There are at least two important reservations that should be made in applying the classical S-shaped growth-cycle model to service businesses. The first is that a service business is often an intermediary business. It fulfils a broker function, linking different groups to each other to permit them to interact; or it fulfils a transfer function, mediating flows—of information, money, know-how or human resources—from one context to another.

What happens in these 'institutionally complex' contexts, which may be quite turbulent, is so important to the mediator that the mediator's own S-shaped curve may have almost no significance at all. However, the S curves of the business for which the intermediary functions are being performed are critical. It is likely that the mediator can better understand the sensitivity of his service to such turbulence by examining the S-curve phenomenon of his customers and their competitors.

With regard to customer relationships, the S-curve reflects the time required for a customer to enter into a new relationship, and also the inertia that retards the break-up of a long-standing relationship.

Secondly, when discussing the growth cycles of manufacturing firms, innovation and continuous growth are usually associated mainly with the product itself. Growth cycles connected with technologies and production processes have also been conceptualized and in times of rapid change may be more instructive. Richard Foster (1986) has exposed these many dimensions of technological innovation in some depth.

The service provider may, by monitoring the technologies and production process used directly in the service offering, identify future product offerings and future competitors. By monitoring these factors inherent in the operation of those for whom he is performing a mediating role, he will surely increase his anticipatory powers. This type of analysis is specific to each situation, and although it is not always a particularly useful predictive tool, it can be very helpful in identifying points of vulnerability in the system. When the increased productivity benefits from the costs of tweaking a technology or a production process becomes marginal, you can be assured that someone, somewhere, is working on the new product, service, technology or production process which will displace the existing one.

In essence, the service provider has to develop new measurement systems that help him make his strategic decisions. Accounting, with its historical information base, often gives us the wrong information—too little information—too late. In service businesses, innovation tends to be associated at least as much with the way the service is produced; i.e. with the process or the service delivery system. From the client's point of view there is no clear distinction between several of the elements of the service management system (e.g. the service concept, the service delivery system). Ordinary school education, Berlitz courses, Linguaphone courses or EF Education all seem both close to one another and yet fundamentally different. The goal of teaching the client a new language may be the same; but the process whereby it is done, the service delivery system, the way the client participates in the process and, consequently, his whole experience—all these are completely different. The innovation and growth problems of service organizations may have more to do with service delivery systems than with 'products'.

Bearing these reservations in mind, we can nevertheless use the S-shaped growth curve of Figure 12.1 as a framework for identifying a number of typical growth problems. In the case of the individual business, the curve may assume quite a different shape and the various problems encountered may appear at stages other than those we have indicated.

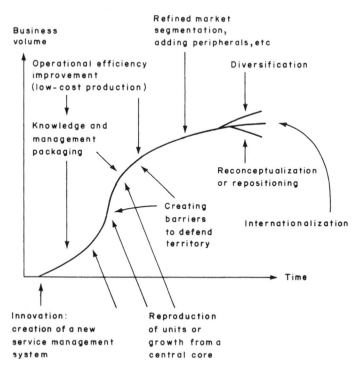

Figure 12.1 Typical problems encountered during the lifecycle of a service business

REPRODUCTION

Once the service management system has been established, the service company may have its most difficult and challenging task ahead: growing.

The nature of the problem at this stage is very different from the one that faces a product business manager. Growth in manufacturing can be achieved by adding sales outlets and increasing the size of the factory; exports can be achieved by packing the products in boxes and shipping them across borders. But in a service company, growing is something else again. The service is produced as a set of social actions made possible by people—employees and clients—who not only have to be motivated to participate but also have to be supplied with the right behaviour programming. The social innovations and the ethos intrinsic to the efficient functioning of a service management system may be possible to reproduce in one place and for a certain length of time; to reproduce them in new places, keeping quality consistent over time, is something altogether different.

We perceive the service business system in terms of the service management system consisting of a service concept, a service delivery system, a clear-cut market segment, an image and an appropriate culture and management system. But in order to grow, these and other elements generally have to be multiplied by way of a *reproduction formula.*

It should be noted that there are ways whereby a service company can grow other than by reproducing the same service management system. It may be possible to grow by adding more services rather than by expanding territorially. It may be possible to expand activities and client interaction by travelling more or extending other communication techniques. (See Carman and Langeard, 1981.)

Sometimes the service management system may be so delicate or so exclusive as to be virtually irreproducible (or the service company may have chosen to project such an image, perhaps in order to maintain a very exclusive market segment which would regard reproduction with suspicion). This is mainly true of service ideas involving such a high degree of problem-solving as to border on the area of artistic endeavour. A research-oriented consulting organization such as Arthur D. Little or our old acquaintance

Troisgros are good examples of this. If such companies are successful, their reputations may become even higher, and the temptation to grow will increase. Gucci lost its exclusiveness by trying to overexploit its image, but has subsequently attempted a comeback. When Bernard Loiseau, the three-star chef, went public with his company in 1998 in order to exploit his image, some of his regular guests stopped coming to his establishment.

Some of the traps attaching to such strategies will be analysed in Chapter 13, 'Diversification and internationalization'. Nevertheless, it is possible to grow while maintaining a single centre, although growth will never be as rapid and uncomplicated as it is when a really innovative reproduction formula is applied.

So what is the nature of reproduction, of recreating a service management system on a local basis and with a continued guarantee of performance and quality?

Obviously it has something to do with the nature of the service management system as such. I have indicated that service systems which include a very high degree of professional problem-solving or an element of artistry may be particularly difficult to reproduce. Since the original formula often depends heavily on the ability to create certain social interaction patterns, it may also be highly dependent on local culture or a local institutional structure. Health maintenance organizations (HMOs) were created in California but have not so far succeeded in breaking into Sweden. Cultural patterns and institutional restrictions have acted as effective barriers.

On the other hand, what could be more American than McDonald's hamburgers? But in this case there is no institutional complexity, in the sense that other organizations have to be linked or adapted to the system (except in the marketplace), and the idea is therefore easier to recreate. It is difficult to conceive a more successful exercise in reproduction than of McDonald's hamburger restaurants. The way in which the process started can be regarded as a turning point in the history of service business management; the principles were not perhaps revolutionary, but the way they were conceptualized and systematically applied was probably unique.

The story is usually connected with the name of Ray Croc, and rightfully so, but it should be remembered that one sample of the service management system as such had already been created by the McDonald brothers. Ray Croc, at the time aged around 50, was selling milkshake machines to fast-food restaurants. He had been thinking about a change and had been looking out for 'The Big Deal'. He had also been speculating about different ways of achieving it.

One day he came to the McDonald brothers' restaurant to deliver one of his machines. The big 'M' consisting of two golden arcs immediately caught his eye, and when he went in he was struck by some of the things he saw. Instead of just delivering his machine and going on his way, he stayed in the restaurant for two days, observing, taking notes, thinking. At the end of those two days he asked the McDonald brothers whether they wanted to become partners with him.

In the history of service management this may well have been the moment of transition from the level of the single service management system to the reproduction formula, when the technology for large-scale operations in services was born.

The first step in reproduction is to analyse the service management system down to its bare bones, finding 'the single logic', the few key characteristics that are necessary for it to function. Of course this may lead to a simplification of the system. (At the present stage of knowledge many formulas are naturally conceived with the idea of reproducibility in mind from the beginning.)

The second step is to conceptualize ways in which this logic, the key success factors, can be adequately formulated and controlled. The third step is to acquire the concrete instruments—management systems, support systems—which will make reproduction feasible.

The second and third steps can also be regarded as a process of 'packaging' the service management system, including the knowledge and skill needed to manage it, so that it can be readily unpacked and used. Because of the very varying nature of different service management systems, there is no single way of packaging or creating a reproduction formula, but we can list a number of items that seem particularly important:

1. A description of the service, and the service levels and quality standards that are to be achieved. The description must be very clear, with a view to efficient internal communication.
2. Maintaining central control of certain components which are absolutely essential and for which local discretion is not

necessary. One example is the purchasing of meat for McDonald's hamburgers; another is the personal selection by the founder of the Retravailler company of all the educators working in this French organization for the education of women intending to go back to work. (This second example shows that there may be some limits to reproduction formulas, since the founder does not have unlimited capacity.)

3. Creating and communicating central policies or success formulas, perhaps in the form of instructions or by maintaining control in key areas such as recruitment procedures and the personnel idea, image, physical layout, etc. Standardized technology and physical layout can be used to check unnecessary discretion (which may only lead to confusion and unwanted variety) in the local units.

   We can take two examples to show that this sort of control mechanism can assume a variety of forms. McDonald's (or for that matter many restaurant chains and catering organizations) employ a very precise technology in their kitchens, which steers people's movements exactly so that they have to do things in one way—the right way. EF Education provides a very different example of the same basic logic. In the middle of the company's very successful international growth process, its president and founder said: 'I personally, and increasingly one or two other key people around me, think I have a very clear understanding of what makes EF Education's sales office so successful. It definitely has to do with leadership and social climate. Perhaps my main role at this moment is to guarantee these things in the new offices that we open up. As an example, I personally recruited practically all the new office leaders during our first few years of international growth. And I believe a lot in things such as how the physical layout can influence our climate and internal image; it may sound strange, but I have personally been involved in the decoration and choice of colours and furniture in all our offices!'

4. Developing information systems and reporting systems which focus on those ingredients of the service management system which represent 'the simple logic', or the key success factors, in order to direct everyone's attention continuously towards these issues. In almost all very successful multi-unit service organizations, top management will have identified a few clearly defined

qualities which they expect to find in a unit that is functioning well. These will be used as a vehicle for formulating demands, as a means of achieving high efficiency, and as a criterion for the evaluation of individual units—so called bench-marking.

5. Creating centrally located expertise in areas where knowledge lends itself to advantages of scale. In the case of a consulting firm this could mean world-wide industry specialists; in the case of a restaurant chain it could mean a hygiene control system; or in security services it could be a question of risk analysis specialists.

6. Creating infrastructure systems to take advantage of network effects where relevant; for example, a world-wide reservation system for a hotel operator or an airline.

7. Developing instruments and institutions aimed at promoting key knowledge of the business and in particular the special ethos and social climate which is necessary for success. The 'university' type of institution mentioned earlier is one example; other methods may require top management to spend a good deal of time travelling and communicating with personnel at the local units.

8. Formal contracts and constitutions, such as franchising agreements, which are designed as behaviour-controlling instruments and based on the understanding of the 'simple logic' leading to success.

9. Developing and communicating 'role models' and typical, desirable career patterns, as well as creating career opportunities between local units.

The efforts to achieve reproducibility may themselves disclose unnecessary complications in the formula. But during the process of reproduction or at some stage in it the service management system may be redefined or changed. Local conditions or strategic positioning in the face of competition may make such moves necessary.

The Holiday Inn hotel chain chose to position itself towards the top end of the market when it entered Europe. When the Swedish furniture distributor IKEA went abroad, it had to decide whether or not to adapt its very Swedish concept. Since the company realized that it did not have the resources (or, perhaps, the ambition) to achieve as high a market share in other countries as it enjoyed in Sweden, it decided to be totally uncompromising and to reproduce its original Swedish concept with one exception only; it emphasized its image as being different and Swedish, e.g. advertising itself in Germany as *das unmögliche Möbelhaus aus Schweden* (the impossible furniture house from Sweden), thus making its position absolutely crystal clear and uncompromising.

However, there is always a dilemma in deciding how far such changes should go, especially in view of the great effort that may have been made to permeate the whole organization with one, streamlined formula. There is also the question of how far the system should be adapted to local conditions. During a stage of rapid growth in relatively unsaturated markets, it may be possible for the leaders to go on reproducing their idea for quite a long time with little or no modification, as companies like Benetton and McDonald's have shown. When a more mature and therefore more competitive stage sets in, however, it may become appropriate to exploit the benefits of a more distinct market segmentation and differentiation between competitors, of closer interaction with clients, or even a fairly substantial repositioning of the service system. But there will always be drawbacks. Steps of this kind can lead to a costly complication in the service system and to internal confusion as the balance is disturbed in a closely knit social system that was originally built up around a unique formula.

Sometimes the core service may be very difficult to reproduce, while some peripheral service might prove easier. For example, a consulting firm with an advanced and complex method for strategic and organizational development (which was also closely linked to the local culture of the country of origin) found out that its core service was virtually impossible to reproduce. Getting it over to potential foreign customers or employees was, at best, a long process. At the same time an important peripheral service was connected with fairly straightforward industry studies and concrete information collection. Once the company had realized that it would have to discard any idea of reproducing the core service and turned instead to creating a satellite system of offices specializing in the much simpler but complementary peripheral service, it was able to build up a viable international structure.

Experiences of this kind, and the example of the American Health Maintenance Organizations described above, show that service management systems which are highly dependent on a particular culture and which at the same time have to be linked into complex institutional networks are very difficult to reproduce.

The examples of EF Education and McDonald's illustrate another important point. Some kind of differentiation in management structure almost always has to be introduced when a company sets out on a reproduction scheme. Some distinction is necessary between the 'old' operative management of the original unit and a management structure catering for the reproduction process with all its crucial needs and characteristics. This fresh structure must operate as a new 'mother' which can give birth to new units.

REDEFINITION AND CONTINUOUS DEVELOPMENT

The lifecycle of a service business may be prolonged by judicious redefinition of the service management system. The service concept itself may be developed, with careful changes in the package including the introduction or adjustment of peripheral services. It may be possible to define the market segment more clearly and to make adjustments in it, for example by going into borderline subsegments. Recruitment procedures, career systems, reward systems, mechanisms for promoting culture and other management tools having an impact on the service delivery system can be streamlined. The use of technology and physical aids, with a view to redefinition in any of the five areas mentioned in Chapter 9, should also be kept under constant review. The image can be changed to strengthen the strategic position, or simply to call attention to it without disturbing the system.

Work on all these fronts is the essence of day-to-day research and development in a service organization. Obviously, social technology is a key factor in this process.

Many of the schemata introduced in this book can be used as rules of thumb for redefining and improving a service management system. For example, the schema outlining different types of company–client interfaces in Chapter 8 (Figure 8.1) can be useful as a rough basis for the company–client interaction: can interaction be moved from one context to another, and what consequences—positive and negative—will there be? Likewise, the schema connected with Table 2.1 in Chapter 2, showing the driving forces for innovation, can be used as a checklist in a search process for sources of further innovation.

To bring the number of 'search matrices' up to three, let us add the 'cost control dilemma' as depicted in Figure 12.2. This refers to the management of human energy and excess capacities, which is a key success factor in many flourishing service businesses.

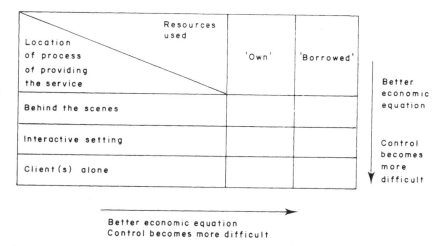

Figure 12.2   The cost-control dilemma, or a schema for discovering potential innovations in service management systems

The 'production' of a service can take place behind the scenes, or in an interactive setting, or in the client on his own. There is usually a combination of these three possibilities.

The physical tools (including locations) and the people involved may belong to the service company, or to the client, or to some third party. According to the principles of 'human energy management' and 'utilization of excess capacities', one might be tempted to try to shift as much as possible of the actual provision of the service down towards the lower right-hand corner: the client doing most of the work himself, using the tools provided by himself or by others. Clearly, from a cost point of view this would be the optimal solution. The role of the service company would then consist of transferring knowledge and organization to the client so that he could get things done, and then sending in the bills.

The dilemma is that the closer we get to the lower right-hand corner, the more difficult it is to control what happens.

Depending on the service concept and its complexity, and on what the market is willing to pay, the service company has a choice. Club Méditerranée, for example, decided to use mainly an interactive setting and the company's own resources, i.e. the holiday village (although the other clients are a crucial part of the service from the point of view of any one client). It was then deemed necessary to keep full control over the process of supplying the service and thus over the physical surroundings, the on-site payment system, etc. to ensure that the company could really provide the service it had promised.

Banks used to operate mainly in the 'own/interactive' box, with customers coming into the branch office and talking to the employees. A present trend in banking is to move much of the process out of this box, so that more takes place behind the scenes, while clients interact to a greater extent with machines which may be reached by the Internet from almost anywhere.

The problem in many public service systems is that too much of the job of supplying the service has been moved into an interactive setting where the system's 'own' resources are used, which neglects the potential energy of clients and their families and the available physical facilities such as people's homes. 'Overcontrol' has been achieved at tremendous cost in areas such as health care, childcare, care of the old, labour market agencies, and so on.

A company such as Weight Watchers has designed its system so that most of what goes on takes place in the lower right-hand corner. A purely interactive system (refrigerator guards?) in specialized locations would be hopelessly expensive. Instead, the company has to rely on back-office work for its systems development, on social control, and on the transfer of 'self-management norms' to its clients. Social innovation and the skilful management of human energy and available capacities have made it possible to realize this business idea.

By juggling with the design of its service concept, new approaches to control and innovations in 'human capacity management' in the design of its service delivery system, a company may be able to reposition itself in the matrix and discover new ways of improving its business ideas.

13

Diversification and internationalization

THE DELICATE BALANCE OF THE SERVICE MANAGEMENT SYSTEM

We have now dealt with most of the components of the service management system and with its reproduction and refinement. Some topics relating to culture and leadership are addressed in Chapters 15 and 16. The effective service management system is characterized by harmony and by the good fit between its components. All these components enhance each other; and they must all promote the fundamental ideas which constitute the basic logic and success factors in any business. Up to now we have not touched upon the problems that can arise when two or more service businesses (service management systems) coexist within a single company.

Service companies can grow by fairly drastically changing their service systems as a result of strategic repositioning or a reconceptualization process, or by diversifying. Strategic repositioning is an inherently difficult process in service companies, in which a uniquely focused culture tends to be a pervasive feature, so that a difficult process of 'unlearning' or even a 'cultural revolution' may be necessary. Adding to the service operations of a company also entails changing the service management system with the risk of a consequent imbalance. We can now investigate in more detail what this means and what risks are involved.

The mixing of service management systems is a hazardous process. This does not mean that it cannot sometimes be done; but when it is done—and we shall be looking at some successful examples—the utmost care and sensitivity are needed to avoid disharmony or any disturbance in the functioning of the success formula.

Such disturbances can result from changes much less dramatic than diversification. For example, when new technological components are being introduced into service delivery systems in the security industry, very delicate changes and adaptations have to be made. The efficiency of the guards has traditionally been highly dependent on the ability of the company to select and motivate its personnel, to provide status and a feeling of importance. For some role occupants in security companies the introduction of high technology has meant an increase in status and in the respect commanded by their jobs, but for others the effect has been the opposite. The patrolling guard, whose role has been reduced to adjusting switches and who is no longer viewed with as much respect by the client, has often lost part of his motivation. The profession has become less attractive in many ways, with the result that personnel costs have tended to go up (higher personnel turnover, for example) and service quality to go down. Thus the introduction of even one new component into the service delivery system has necessitated fundamental changes in the whole system. Similar processes can be seen in banking and insurance, where large categories of personnel have been affected by new technology.

We have already seen how a modest diversification by the introduction of new peripheral services into the operations of a bank can have profound effects which only gradually become apparent. Let us now look at some more typical examples of diversification

A large conglomerate, well known for its tough (some would say almost terrorizing) management style and its strict financial control, acquired a number of companies in the cleaning business. It had noted that this was a growing area with a high return on investment and interesting cash-flow possibilities. Not many weeks had passed before all new companies had embarked on vicious downward spirals and were showing economic losses. It soon became clear that the culture and management instruments applied by the conglomerate to its new members were completely inappropriate. The effective functioning of a cleaning company requires a management style that is highly sensitive to the needs of people at all levels in the organization, and there was no way of achieving a good fit between the success formulas of these companies and that of their new parent.

The large Danish service company, International Service System (ISS), which has traditionally provided two basic services—cleaning and security—tried to achieve greater operational synergy by integrating the two businesses more closely. However, this caused more confusion than profit, and it was found that there were after all big differences between the services. The company returned to a management system which, operationally, kept the two sides of the business more clearly apart.

A striking example of a failure to diversify into what seemed at least superficially to be a closely related area is provided by the French Borel company.

Jacques Borel was the pioneer of building efficient self-service restaurants and low price motels in France. (It was said that he was inspired by a visit to Pompeii, when it suddenly struck him what an efficient catering system the canteen for the slaves had been!) The Jacques Borel establishments were very successful in France, and a period of rapid international growth also followed, all due to their general efficiency and low cost. Services of a reasonable quality were being made available to a cost-sensitive market segment. On the other hand, Jacques Borel became something of a symbol of everything that was threatening what many people regarded as the fundamental values and quality of the French lifestyle. A popular film highlighted the situation by confronting the values and style promoted by the *Guide Michelin* with those represented by Jacques Borel.

Things started to go wrong for Jacques Borel when he decided to diversify into the hotel business, and bought up the Sofitel hotel chain. This modern, well-known and highly-regarded hotel chain operated at the top end of the market and its hotels were generally in the four-star bracket. After the take-over, the Sofitel name was changed to 'Sofitel Jacques Borel. The problem was that the Sofitel hotels appealed precisely to the market segment which saw Jacques Borel as an enemy of their lifestyle, and they did not want anything to do with him. Many guests arriving at the Sofitel Jacques Borel hotels literally turned away at the door, and visitor ratings fell catastrophically. It did not take long before the whole Borel group was ruined, and was acquired by a bank.

Several years later the Sofitel hotels, now under their old name, were acquired by the successful Novotel chain (now in the Accor group). This company had also had considerable experience of the art of mixing service management systems. They had started out with a clear concept of mid-market hotels for the travelling businessman on the outskirts of towns, and had then, for example, launched some tourist hotels in holiday resorts. Again it was found that the whole idea was utterly confusing both to the market and to the company's own staff, who no longer knew what the Novotel concept really stood for, and success came only when this second type of hotel was kept more clearly apart operationally and was given its own name and image.

The difficulties facing the professional service firm that tries to mix different service management systems are well known. When it launched a major headhunting business alongside its traditional management consultancy operations, the firm of Booz Allen and Hamilton found itself in conflict with many of its own customers as well as becoming involved in internal value conflict. The solution in this case was to get out of the headhunting business. Another example is that of the well-known friction between Arthur Andersen's traditional auditing activities and the consultancy business of Andersen Consulting.

And history is full of advertising agencies like Saatchi & Saatchi, accountancy firms and others which have tried to extend their services to work for their clients in other more general areas such as organization or strategic planning. In Sweden, Indevo and SIAR-Bossard similarly sought to become 'full-service houses'. Although this might seem to be a logical step from the market point of view (and there is often a market pull reinforcing the temptation to go ahead), such attempts generally fail. The reason is that the service delivery systems, and the prevailing culture which embraces skills, people and values, tend to become confused between the various businesses. In the end, the companies are providing poor consultancy services while also lowering the quality of their own original business.

The moral of these and many other examples is clear: it is difficult to mix service management systems, which represent delicate formulas for poised success, without destroying or disturbing something valuable in the process. If diversification is to be devised, it must be done with the utmost sensitivity, so as to maintain the integrity of the existing service management systems. Even mixing images can lead to great confusion on the external market and among the present or potential employees of a company. In service businesses, where the service on offer may be abstract and intangible, clean and concrete images are vital to success.

SOME DIVERSIFICATION STRATEGIES

Diversification became a popular mode in the 1960s, and there was a time when large corporations seemed to lose their self-respect unless they could call themselves 'conglomerate'. The casualties of the diversification and conglomerate wave have been many. There is no doubt that diversification was often a kind of pastime or even an escape strategy for top managers who were not able or prepared to take the necessary time to investigate the development possibilities often essential to, the strategic repositioning of their original businesses. Diversification into areas which the managements did not really understand led to problems not only in the new areas but often also in the established core business, which suffered a severe dilution of crucial management capacity. These are general observations; in the previous section we looked at some specific explanations of failure in service companies. But a number of service companies have succeeded, and we can now identify some of the viable strategies that we have come across in the course of our work.

Basic to the whole concept of diversification is the idea of synergy; i.e. of somehow using or exploiting various elements in the business as it already exists. In our terms this means exploiting the existing service management system or some element or elements in it. This will be possible if care has been taken to defend (or even enrich) the existing system.

We will not examine the idea of *financial synergy* in any great detail here, although in fact it sometimes provides a very important reason for diversification in service businesses. One idea is to mix businesses which exhibit different but complementary cash-flow patterns. For example, this could be one of the reasons for a financial company in the credit card business to acquire a life insurance company. Because of the type of agreement it has with its clients, the first company may have to tie up large financial resources to cover the time lag between cash-out and cash-in. The insurance company, on the other hand, is characterized by its notably positive cash flow; premiums are generally paid in long before anything is paid out. In many other services, too, it is possible to make interesting payments arrangements whereby the services are paid for before the company is faced with their cost; this generates liquid resources which it is tempting to use for other purposes.

Perhaps the most common kind of diversification in service companies is *client-based diversification.* The main rationale here is that an established client relationship is one of the most valuable assets any service company can have. A cleaning company dealing with industrial customers will often offer various auxiliary or complementary services in addition to its basic cleaning operations; maintenance of grounds and lawns, provision of flowers and plants, curtains, and so on. In financial service businesses there is a marked trend towards supplying the individual client with a broader range of financial services, once he has become a member of the clientele.

Companies like American Express and Merrill Lynch are successfully providing their customers with additional services, so as to offer them an integrated financial–service package. Sears & Roebuck sought to use its intimate knowledge of its customers and its established customer contact, obtained via its catalogues and millions of company credit card holders, to become a diversified financial services company. But in so doing, it may have overlooked the potential for improvement in its principal business area of retail trade.

Another approach to diversification, also based on the customer, stems from the idea of *main and auxiliary* services (which is related, but not necessarily identical, to the concept of core and peripheral services). An airline company certainly regards passenger (and cargo) transportation as its main service idea, but peripherals have included lodging and food (both inside and outside the aircraft). New businesses such as hotel chains and airline catering have therefore been developed, originally to support the main business but later becoming important individual businesses with their own core and peripheral services. In our terms, they have developed their own service management systems more or less independent of the main business.

But here, too, there is a danger that development of supporting businesses will divert attention from the original core business and claim management and financial resources that might have been needed there. For example, SAS sold its catering operation and took on a new partner (Radisson) in its hotel business. Neither the catering nor the hotel business was in any kind of crisis at the time. Still, in light of their development needs and market potential, SAS was probably not the most suitable owner for either of them, considering the massive financing requirements of SAS' core business of air transportation.

The other side of the coin is that auxiliary businesses of this kind may find it difficult to escape the often rather dominating culture of the original business. The conglomerate and the cleaning companies were cases in point. This is a classic problem. As in all diversification, there is a dilemma; should the distinction between the main and the auxiliary business remain; should the distinctive culture of the main business continue to pervade the whole organization, or should the auxiliary businesses be allowed to grow on their own terms? If they are not allowed to do so, then they may sooner or later fall into the 'appendix syndrome trap', i.e. they may never reach a real breakthrough in their own development, remaining essentially subordinate to the main business (Normann, 1977).

Yet another type of diversification involves using the same type of *basic knowledge* to cater for different market segments. In the case of Jacques Borel, there was nothing fundamentally wrong about acquiring the Sofitel chain. As a few other hotel companies and later developments in the Novotel chain and its owner, Accor, have shown, it is quite possible to run simultaneously hotels aimed at different market segments, but only on certain conditions: there must be no ambiguity in the *image* presented to the public or to the employees; also, internally, there must be as little mixing of operations as possible. The Swedish retail group NK-Ahlens (now renamed and under new management) could have used some of its back-office facilities jointly and advantageously for stores in its two chains. The stores could even have been in the same neighbourhood but aiming at different market segments. In this particular case things went wrong, however, because the difference between two success formulas, including the images to be presented to the public, was insufficiently understood. Moreover, too much weight was given to what was wrongly regarded as potential operational synergy.

We have already seen that the first step towards reproduction is to identify and clarify the 'simple logic' or key success factors of the service management system. This sort of understanding is equally indispensable to diversification. Some service management systems share important elements in their basic success formulas, and a company which recognizes these common aspects, and the perhaps small but certainly important differences. may have found a basis for differentiation. Let us look at some types of 'simple logic' to be found in individual service management systems which we have seen servicing advantageously as the basis—the crucial synergy—for diversification.

- The addition of large-scale or quality-raising effects to hitherto local or 'handicraft' types of business. This is a service idea which has so far remained largely unexploited in many service areas. Car service garages, speciality stores and local hotels are examples of local establishments in which the need and the opportunity for achieving large-scale effects in quality-raising systems (such as personnel policy, education, standard setting, marketing and image creation) have been identified. Service organizations and multiservice companies have therefore turned their attention to business of this kind.
- A related service idea is to link unconnected local establishments providing substantially the same service in certain ways which could benefit from operations on a larger scale. Transportation (including taxi companies), real estate offices or hotels are possible examples.
- Yet another related example is to link unconnected local establishments offering different types of services together based on one common element—having the same target markets. This affinity linking is created by conceptualizing a common value-adding mechanism, such as a discount card which allows card holders to make purchases at participating business establishments, or gain access to special benefits. Such service ideas are offered to expectant mothers, college students, airline 'frequent flyers', etc.
- Some 'service-idea families' are founded on a special insight into lifestyles or popular images. The most obvious examples

occur in the entertainment industry. where a 'theme film' or a sports team may generate a particular style of music, dress or toys, or a multitude of other items. However, it is fairly unusual to see the same company operating all the service systems arising from such opportunities. Royalties and trademarks are generally sold to specialized companies.

- Advanced and *versatile technology* could also be a fruitful basis for diversification in services, as demonstrated by McKesson. However, in McKesson we should not exaggerate the role of the computers and the information processing technology. The company's success in breaking into new service areas also stems from its culture and personnel policy; without these, any attempts at developing new technology-based services would probably have ended in failure.
- A growing number of multibusiness service companies build on the concept of *service management.* An interesting example is the large American service company ARA, which operates and manages a wide range of services including restaurants, municipal transport maintenance, nursing homes, catering for a great variety of institutions, and so on. One restriction which ARA appears to have imposed on itself is not to market services to individual households. Instead, it administers services where there is a captive market or where the marketing is mainly taken care of by the client organization. A few other companies seem to have grasped the basic logic of several such services. In this sense we could call them genuine 'service management' companies.

Frequently used as a base for diversification are the *customer relationship* and the *identification of complementary needs* of the customer. An illustration is found in financial services, where the concept of the 'financial department store' emerged in the 1980s. At that time, more and more people were discovering that the products offered by various types of financial institutions—savings accounts, investments (stocks, bonds, and mutual funds), and life insurance—were competing for the same money. Moreover, customer needs in this sphere were complementary. In the Nordic countries, these trends led to banks' aquiring insurance companies, and vice-versa. At the outset, many mistakes were made. For instance, when nation-wide insurance companies like Trygg-Hansa or Topsikring (subsequently known as Topdanmark) bought up local banks, the synergy benefits failed to materialize, leaving only the problems of the acquired banks to deal with. Gradually it became evident that nation-wide banks, with their superior distribution systems, had much to gain by acquiring even a small life-insurance company. By contrast, the insurance companies were not using their own distribution systems to sell banking services to any significant extent. Also, it soon became apparent that while banking services and life insurance logically belonged to the same 'family', property and liability insurance was the odd bird in the nest.

The list of 'service family' businesses which are different but still somehow related could be extended further. It is natural for banks to provide several services, because the 'systems' character of their business necessitates several types of transactions with the raw material, money. Intermediary organizations (for example consultancy firms) which have created linkages, perhaps between a number of knowledge users (e.g. industry), may then use these for other purposes as well. But the rule is clear: diversification should be based on a genuine and profound understanding of the existing service management system, and it should build on the formula rather than destroy or disturb it. And it is not possible to compensate for a fundamental weakness in the basic business by diversifying into others.

INTERNATIONALIZATION OF SERVICES IN A MACRO PERSPECTIVE

There is probably enormous unrealized potential in the export of services. The following is a statement from *Business Week* (1980): at a time when people were beginning to realize the possibilities in this area:

. . . the fastest-growing element in the US trade account is the export of services. Last year export of services—insurance, engineering, communications systems, movies, banking, and accounting—racked up about $36 billion for US corporations. This year service exports are expected to hit about $45 billion and will be a major factor in generating a $2 billion surplus in the US current account, the first since 1976.

We have continued to see growth in the international trade of services as the industrial economy assumed a global orientation throughout the 1980s. The growth, and particularly the potential. have precipitated some rather dramatic restructuring in some services. We have seen major advertising agencies intent on establishing a pre-eminent position internationally acquiring agencies based in other countries; in the accountancy, financial and investment services, consulting and law we see similar acquisitions or new strategic alliances amongst firms seeking to respond to the service needs of their clients or new dynamics of the marketplace. The trend is clear and the stakes are high!

But in international trade, services clearly account for a much lower proportion of the total than their usual share of the gross national product—in spite of the significant growth of the 1980s. There are a number of reasons for this imbalance, and it is outside the scope of this book to analyse them in detail. However, a couple of factors deserve special mention.

One is that, paradoxically, success in the area of services is probably reflected most visably in the export of goods! This can occur in various ways. For instance, successful R & D efforts of companies and independent organizations, and in the academic world, lead often to the development of more advanced, competitive products which therefore have great export potential. All statistics show that the 'knowledge content' of products is growing; for this reason, we can rightly say that today's advanced products consist essentially of 'services in solid form'.

But these mechanisms may also be considered in other ways. The American diplomat Richard Holbrooke is said to have declared that the competitive strength of the United States is based primarily on the country's universities rather than its economic might. A very large proportion of university students from different countries who study abroad go to the United States. The various ties that they establish there, and the knowledge that they acquire, can later have an impact on international trade. For example, physicians who have studied medicine in the United States have also become accustomed not only to American practices, but also to American products and equipment: it has been shown that on returning to their home countries, these doctors encourage the import of those same items.

While this book is primarily about the individual company rather than the economy as a whole, another issue regarding the export of services should be raised here. For it is obvious that the opportunities for exports of services, and for international trade involving integrated 'clusters' of services and products, are heavily influenced by the way in which society and business enterprises are organized and run.

For example, where business by tradition often 'outsources' needed services, specialized service companies will tend to spring up. And such companies naturally tend to internationalize. This rarely or never happens when the service is performed by an internal support unit of a manufacturing company. Sweden and the United States have a rather clear and widely adopted philosophy of outsourcing, whereas in Germany, for example, the outsourcing-based service sector by tradition is relatively underdeveloped. An illustrative case is that of ABB Service; here service functions were transferred to a special unit of a manufacturing corporation and then offered on the open market—one with high potential for internationalization.

The same mechanism also applies to society as a whole. One of the largest areas of the modern economy, and one of the fastest-growing ones for the past few decades, is 'welfare services', which include health and medical care, education, and pension systems, as well as other sectors. A number of European countries, perhaps Sweden most of all, have clung firmly to their traditional philosophy that government, or the public sector, not only is solely responsible for such services but even has a monopoly on their production. This policy has a number of implications. One is that development does not occur primarily in response to competition and market demand, but is governed by regulations and controls. Furthermore—and relevant to the internationalization of services—no specialized service companies with the potential and ambition to internationalize will spring up. With Swedish companies like these absent on international markets, a force which could have promoted the export of related Swedish products will also be lacking.

Because of this restriction on the manner of organizing and producing social services, welfare services, and services to local governments and communities in Sweden, there are almost no Swedish companies on the immense and fast-growing international markets for welfare services; the few that are present play only minor roles. Large, successful international exporters of 'services to cities and local governments', such as J-C Decaux, Lyonnaise des Eaux, Vivendi, and Anglian Water, could hardly have come into existence in Sweden. Swedish companies are only marginally present as international competitors in the health-care sector—a natural consequence of how Sweden has chosen to organize itself. There are a few exceptions, to be sure. For instance, EF Education and Mercuri sell educational and training services internationally, and Skandia through AFS has created a highly innovative international business in the savings market. But these cases have arisen in spite of the way Swedish society has been organized, rather than because of it.

As is evident from this discussion, there are two major prerequisites for the development of a strong and internationally successful service sector. First, there must be a fundamental understanding of how the economy works; secondly, these mechanisms must be reflected in the way in which society and businesses are organized. That having been said, we shall now turn to issues concerning the internationalization of the individual company.

INTERNATIONALIZATION ISSUES AT THE INDIVIDUAL COMPANY

Few services can be exported without also exporting the service delivery system. The general rule that we have discussed in connection with service company growth, namely that multiplication is needed not only of the 'product' but also of almost the whole service management system, applies to internationalization as well. This makes the task more difficult to handle for the manager of a service company.

In services, as in other businesses, there are many reasons for going international. Internationalization may be an ego trip or a personal challenge to key people; it may even be necessary to keep up their energy. Or growth in the home market may be blocked for some reason. Or customers may internationalize, so that the service company follows suit in order to give its clients comprehensive service. This is often the case for banks, insurance companies and consultancy organizations. Or internationalization may often start more or less by accident. A request may be made, or a letter arrives from somewhere, or a local entrepreneur wants to buy a licence. Or sometimes internationalization comes as the logical result of a superior success formula on the home market which has obvious international potential.

Almost any initial driving force such as one of the above can result in successful internationalization if well handled. But I must emphasize that I have never seen a successful attempt to internationalize which has been based on the idea of 'exporting away the problems at home', or in which the main driving force has been a surplus supply of cash.

In the process of internationalization it is particularly important to distinguish between two stages: the initial feelers and the actual 'business breakthrough'. Almost any opportunity may be used for learning and testing out whether there is any possibility or potential for genuine internationalization. However, there will never be any real business breakthrough unless three conditions are fulfilled:

1. The company has some kind of superiority, manifesting itself in a service management system which has proved successful in the home market; it is necessary to build on this formula, but it is also necessary to be sensitive to the need for changing it and adapting it to local conditions.
2. There are strong personal ambitions to internationalize among powerful key people in top management. Without such support successful internationalization can never take place (unless possibly as an extremely lucky accident).
3. There is willingness to set aside the resources and the considerable time necessary to achieve a breakthrough.

In the breakthrough stage of internationalization, focus and priorities are all-important. Many corporations with interesting success formulas in the home market which have roused great interest abroad can still come to a standstill because they have been unable to focus their efforts or to put in the resources necessary to achieve a true breakthrough in any single new market. A common trap is what might be called 'the enchantment of the first stage'. Requests are made and little projects tend to pop up all over the place, as management realizes the potential of its home-market success formula and knowledge. But neither interest, nor even projects, make a business.

A major problem in internationalization, once the primary conditions outlined here have been met, is to adapt the service management system to new conditions. All the special features of services—their intangibility and the consequent difficulty in demonstrating them, the element of social action perhaps based on a particular culture and particular human energies in staff and clients—all these are often highlighted during an internationalization process. The personnel idea and the 'client participation idea' may have to be thoroughly re-examined; and there is very little chance of this happening in any real sense without the participation of key resources in the parent company and, as is often the case, of some deeply committed local entrepreneur or a strong and ambitious local partner.

On the other hand, the benefits to the service company of internationalization can be very great (Figure 13.1). The company may be able to serve its clients better (in the end internationalization often becomes a condition for keeping important and progressive clients). Efforts to reproduce the success formula abroad

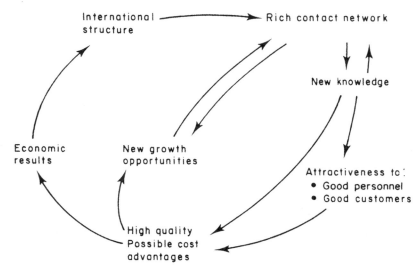

Figure 13.1 A typical 'virtuous circle' resulting from successful internationalization

can sometimes help to streamline the service management system even more in the home market. Tackling new markets may raise general quality levels, including the quality of the people in the company. The image may be enhanced, not only in the eyes of the customers but also in the eyes of the staff and, even more noticeably, on the markets for potential recruits. Some personnel ideas may even be impossible without internationalization. An international structure with a richer contact network also opens up opportunities for attracting new types of resources and customers and for the further development of knowledge and ideas. Once over the threshold, there is a strong 'virtuous circle' working for the international service company. But the threshold may be remarkably high.

14
Quality

TWO BASIC PHILOSOPHIES

Quality is a topic of burning interest in the world of management today. The cost of low or inconsistent quality and the value of high and consistent quality are both being reassessed. It is the concept of quality that has finally helped Japanese management philosophy to make an impact on the management thinking of Western societies (Ouchi, 1981). It is interesting in this context to remember that the Japanese learnt their basic ideas about quality control from a couple of farsighted Americans who discovered after the Second World War that the Japanese were more eager to listen than the Americans.

But what is meant by quality and quality control? While the importance of quality is recognized everywhere, the concept seems to refer to several different areas:

1. the quality of the *product* (the output);
2. the quality of the *process*;
3. the quality of the *production* or *delivery system*; and
4. quality as a *general philosophy* pervading a whole organization.

The Western company in its stereotyped version focuses on the first of these, while the Japanese company as ideally conceived leans towards the fourth. But good service companies tend to be very 'Japanese'. The wave of 'business process re-engineering' (BPR), has evened out these differences.

The difference in basic philosophies between the two stereotypes is considerable. Insistence on control of the product or outcome implies that low quality and defects may occur (which, in turn, means that they are in a sense accepted and legitimized). An important consequence of such a philosophy is that control easily becomes a specialized function, differentiated technically and socially from the rest of the organization. At the other extreme, quality is a general philosophy and mode of thinking built into the whole organization. It becomes a way of life, having a pervasive impact on everybody and on all everyday activities. Quality and excellence apply not only to the product but also to price, security, planning strategy, management, human relations and the whole system of production or delivery.

The above distinctions serve to pinpoint two basic views of quality which we may term the *mechanistic philosophy* and the *philosophy of service systems based on social innovation*. The first focuses on the measurement of outcome, on quality control as a specialized function, and on technical quality specifications and measurements. The second is a mode of being, an existential philosophy.

The reader will have guessed that my own inclination is towards the second, holistic philosophy. This is correct, but it is important to note that I speak of an 'inclination' only. Part of the 'mechanistic' or 'technical' type of philosophy can and should be used in service companies, for the simple reason that it is well founded and can serve to communicate certain aspects of the service which are of crucial and unequivocal importance to the client and which can be easily specified. The following are some simple examples:

- the number of minutes before a McDonald's hamburger is thrown away if it is still unsold;
- the 'block off time' statistics of an airline;
- how many days it takes to replace a lost American Express card.

These are examples of 'hard', unequivocal measures which have a direct impact on the customer and a clear symbolic impact to employees. However, the service package is usually a complex and multifaceted affair, generally including various very 'soft' and even implicit intangibles. For example, whilst almost everyone would agree that the general friendliness and helpfulness of contact persons is important to the overall quality of many services, how can such properties be specified, measured and controlled? There has been no lack of attempts: several organizations specify the minimum number of times that their contact staff should smile at, and have eye contact with, a customer during a transaction; and at least one major airline has specified the number of passengers to whom the cabin attendants should have spoken before and after takeoff.

While such measures and rules can doubtless help to focus people's attention on the importance of skilful social interaction, some serious questions must also be raised. Are they compatible with more general (and perhaps in the long run more functional) goals of human dignity? Could such measures serve to divert attention from more genuine attitudes of care and helpfulness? Do they lead to a type of behaviour which some customers find repellent? Do they contribute to an internal climate of trust or of control, and which climate is relevant in specific situations? In what cultures could such measures work, and where would they not work?

There is also the question of consistency between the conduct of face-to-face contacts and behaviour in the rest of the service system.

In one large well-known hotel, the customer checking in receives a smile plus the comment 'It's a nice room, Sir!' so consistently that it is obviously a question of routine. Apparently the customer is supposed to feel good about this information. However, the regular customer soon discovers that the smile and the comment constitute a ritual applied independently of the quality of the room, and unfortunately the quality of cleaning and room maintenance has lately deteriorated. . . .

A SYSTEMS VIEW

A comprehensive and balanced approach to quality might include all the aspects of Figure 14.1. We can thus distinguish 'soft' and 'hard' features of the service package, interaction and the service delivery process, and the whole service management system. Hard and soft aspects of quality influence one another, and naturally the properties of the whole system will influence the service delivery process, and thus the service package as perceived by the client. Quality can be viewed in relative terms—relative to expectations, to the competition, and so on—or in absolute terms. Whether the absolute or relative approach is the most appropriate will depend on the situation.

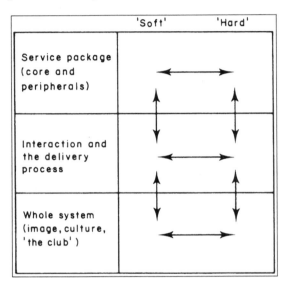

Figure 14.1   Soft and hard measures of quality can apply to different aspects of the service and the company

In the early stages of developing a superior and innovative service business idea, absolute standards of quality are often paramount. Companies such as McDonald's or EF Education originally developed new concepts and set new standards of quality, and their challenge was to live up to their own high standards rather than those of their (more or less non-existent) competitors. At a more mature stage, local and competitor oriented adaptations may be necessary. For example, an airline will have to keep a close eye on the competition and on customer satisfaction (the two are of course closely related) separately on all its routes, adapting its service package and its quality standards to maintain the relative position that it has set itself.

We have already discussed the importance of maintaining quality in relation to expectations in the chapter on the service concept. Let us remember what was said there: that performing below standard in one respect and therefore 'getting one minus' will need '12 pluses' to compensate.

STARTING FROM THE MOMENT OF TRUTH

The quality experienced by the customer is created at the moment of truth, when the service provider and the client meet in a face-to-face interaction. The most perfectly designed and engineered service delivery system will fail unless things work out then. Thus, any enquiry into quality must start from the microsituation of client interaction, the moment of truth. The important question is: what mechanisms lead to and reinforce the client's experience of quality and good value in that microsituation? There is a well-known dynamic in interpersonal interactions whereby positive action creates positive reactions, which in turn leads to mutually positive feelings which in turn leads to mutually positive interaction. Or the reverse can apply. A positive attitude and efficient action on the part of the service supplier will encourage the client to participate more, and more effectively, which in turn encourages the service supplier, and so on. A 'virtuous circle' has started.

Several steps to influence quality can be taken specifically in connection with the company–client interaction situation. The following are some examples.

Creating empathy with clients

One of the best and most important features of the idealized model of Japanese management philosophy is that the employee learns to regard the client, and not the company, as the one who pays his salary. Consequently problems are regarded not only in terms of how they affect the company and the employees, but also and particularly in terms of how they affect the client. Part of the idea behind the famous 'quality circles' is to get the employee to empathize with the client's needs and to find ways to adapt accordingly.

Using tools to create and enhance interaction and motivation in the microsituation

An airline hostess distributing newspapers to the passengers at the beginning of the flight has an automatic pretext for 'interacting' and chatting with the clients. The menu in a restaurant can be designed in such a way as to promote interesting and challenging discussion. In the Troisgros restaurant described earlier, the physical design of the premises has been used to create an unexpected type of interaction between the kitchen personnel and the guests, enriching the experience on both sides. The president of a large cleaning company once told us:

The cars, with our colours and logo, running around in the streets are very important to us. When our employees meet their friends in their leisure time and one of the cars passes by in the street, he or she will point at it and say: 'Look, there's one of our cars!'

Thus, systems and tools which reinforce the position of the service provider, creating and enriching the interaction with the client, can enhance both the motivation of the contact person and the satisfaction of the client. Such measures are therefore an important part of quality management.

Feedback linkages

Feedback is necessary to those who can influence quality. Simply by creating opportunities for interaction, the possibility of positive feedback to the employee is increased. But some of the feedback mechanisms of the creative service organizations can also be quite sophisticated. There are top managers who systematically use the press or well-known personalities from outside to talk about their company; this provides employees with feedback from authoritative external sources. One result can be that families also become involved in raising the motivation and loyalty of the employees.

Such feedback methods can complement the more obvious ones, such as reports on quality measures and customer satisfaction polls for the appropriate people involved in the provision of the service.

Managing the client

The moment of truth represents a social event, whose dynamics and outcome are determined to a great extent by the skill, the mood and the expectations of the contact personnel and the client. One element in quality management therefore consists of shaping the expectations of the client and preparing him to enter the interaction in such a way as to contribute as much as possible to the social dynamic that engenders his own quality experience. If passengers are in a good mood when they enter an aeroplane, this will have an immediate impact on the cabin crew and on the level of service the passengers will receive during the flight.

Choosing measures on the basis of your customer's process, not your own production process

All too often the language, including measures of quality, used by service companies clearly reveals that their frame of reference is production-oriented, not customer-oriented. Here are some examples:

The store managers of the Danish Co-operative chain stores are traditionally called *uddeler*, or person charged with 'handing out'. The users of such language are still mentally living in a society where there was a shortage of goods and customers obediently stood and waited for the *uddeler* to 'hand out' their rations.

French service companies, from Air France to my own local taxi co-operative, try to induce customers to join their 'programmes de fidélisation', which are programs designed to ensure customer loyalty. The name chosen for these programs expresses the value of the 'product' in *the company's* terms, not *the customer's*. For the company it is obviously of significant value that I am a loyal customer; for me that has no intrinsic value whatever. Although such 'programmes de fidélisation' naturally provide rewards for loyal customers, the fact is that the language used by the company clearly emphasizes what is valuable in terms of the company's production process, not what is valuable to me as a customer. Actually, the concept of 'customer loyalty program', used in this way, expresses a fundamental arrogance. While fortunately this attitude may be unwitting rather than deliberate, the use of such language is of no help to a service company in refocusing its thinking.

Another example of how criteria of quality can reflect production-oriented thinking and a by-gone era can be found in the world of air transport. Airline schedules always show departure and arrival times for the flight itself but tell you nothing about when you have to be at the airport before departure or how soon after arrival you may expect to leave the airport (not to mention when you should leave your office or home, and when you will arrive at your final destination . . .). On an airline with which I often fly, the chief steward proudly announces to passengers that the flight has landed at the Paris airport right on time. What he does not tell them is that the plane may have to taxi for another eight or twelve minutes before coming to a full stop, and that a bus will then take them to the arrival gate. Throughout, the language used by the airline indicates that mentally its employees are still living in a world in which being up in the air was a unique experience, whereas today's passengers are naturally concerned with how long altogether they will have to remain seated on board the aircraft and how much more of their time, in addition to the flight, will be taken up by airport procedures.

Climate displayed outwardly and climate prevailing internally

It has been shown that the quality experienced by the client increases if a positive, open and service-minded climate pervades the service organization and *is displayed to the client* (Schneider, 1980). On the other hand, it is exceedingly difficult for a contact person to express an attitude towards the customer that does not match the climate actually prevailing in the company. Thus, unless the kind of social logic conducive to high service quality and efficiency in the client interaction genuinely pervades the whole company, the contact personnel may find themselves in a very ambiguous or even 'schizophrenic' situation.

I once interviewed the manager of a local unit belonging to a large service company, and he spoke of the progress they had achieved in employee attitudes to clients. I knew, however, that there were definite flaws in the service quality provided. One clue to this appeared quite clearly during our conversation. Three times during the hour that I was with him there came a knock at the door and three different employees wanted to talk to him. And, although the picture he was painting to me spoke of an excellent climate, characterized by helpfulness and dedication to the client and cooperation among personnel, each time one of his subordinates came into the room his whole posture and tone of voice changed; he became curt and bureaucratic, essentially (it seemed to me) telling them to buzz off as quickly as possible.

A service organization can hardly expect its employees to show an attitude towards clients different from the one which management and supervisors show to the contact personnel. In the long run, 'double signals' to the contact personnel cannot avoid creating a measure of role ambiguity which cannot be hidden from the client, and which will eventually reveal itself in deteriorating employee satisfaction and in lower quality as perceived by the client.

The importance of the contact personnel to service quality and to the efficiency of service organizations is becoming increasingly widely recognized. The mechanisms we have been discussing here show just how important it is to consider and to influence other personnel categories as well, particularly supervisors and middle management. Programs of improvement aimed solely at the contact personnel can only too often lead to a serious backlash.

DESIGNING QUALITY INTO THE SERVICE MANAGEMENT SYSTEM

Quality in the components

We have indicated how feedback mechanisms can be built into the service system and how production and climate can be made visible in such a way as to promote mutual support and reinforcement between client and employee at the moment of truth, which in turn improves the satisfaction of all the parties involved. Obviously, then, in the long run the mechanisms that influence the personnel and client structure are crucial to quality. The *service concept* as such and the appropriate *market segmentation* are therefore really the first factors to consider in any discussion of quality.

Recruitment and *personnel development* are also particularly pertinent. Motivation and climate are generally founded on respect for human dignity and on allowing for personal development and opportunities for self-fulfilment in the design of every job. Because the strain and tension of service jobs tends to be high and unique, it is very important to ensure that the right people are in the right jobs from the start.

Quality on-stage and backstage

A common problem in service organizations arises from the difference between the requirements of client-interaction roles and back-office roles. The client–interaction role often requires a rather special type of personality, probably someone who accepts a very uneven workload and irregular working hours, who gets satisfaction out of interpersonal relationships and who can take abuse without breaking down. Back-office jobs may call for something very different. They generally lack the thrill that attaches to the moment of truth, with its immediate feedback and the pressure to adapt rapidly to new circumstances. For managing quality 'on-stage' the aim is usually to identify and reinforce mechanisms that lead to virtuous circles at the moment of truth; for backstage jobs alternative strategies are called for. Japanese-type 'quality circles' are examples of instruments that can be used. In addition, it is usually necessary to design recruitment systems and personal-development and career programs geared specifically to on-stage or backstage.

Quality from the top and from the bottom

There are many reasons why a quality-improvement program in a service organization should be started and supported from the top. Certain clear-cut quality dimensions can be selected and communicated rapidly to all parts of the company. And without simple, concrete and visible demonstrations of desirable behaviour from the top, ideas about quality are unlikely to have any lasting effect on the staff. Unless quality improvement is firmly entrenched at the top, ambiguity and near-schizophrenia are almost inevitable.

On the other hand, the idea of a quality-improvement program starting from the bottom is certainly a valid one. Experience shows that once certain simple quality dimensions have been 'unbundled' from the service package, it becomes increasingly difficult to say exactly what is meant by good service and how it is to be achieved in the individual instance. And in any case, every moment of truth is slightly different from every other. The idea of 'quality circles', for instance, is thus particularly appropriate. It involves regular meetings among the relevant line staff to discuss performance and the service delivery process in general. In our experience successful quality programs in service organizations must work both ways: from the top down and from the bottom up.

QUALITY, COST AND PROFITABILITY

There is a common and, on the whole, largely justified idea that better quality costs more. Naturally, then, in deciding about quality levels costs must be taken into account. This is reflected in the organization of many service companies.

One large transportation company, which is well known for its consistently good service, has a service quality department largely manned by engineers. Whenever quality measurements reveal a problem somewhere, or when the subject of a change in quality norms comes up in some other way, this department calculates the operational consequences and puts a 'price tag' on them. For example, cutting the average response time for telephone bookings from X to Y seconds would probably require more telephone lines and more staff; the department can make the necessary calculations and the line people have to decide whether the higher quality is worth the cost.

This general price-tag-for-quality philosophy is often justified, but we have also seen it lead into a trap. Over-reliance on such an approach carries the risk that one of the most crucial points in the understanding of effective service management systems may be missed. An example can illustrate this point:

For several years an airline had been having serious problems with punctuality. Numerous investigations had been made and the accepted diagnosis was that flight schedules around the most important hub of the airline (its major home airport) were too tight. The alternatives were either to make them less tight or to employ more personnel and add more aircraft capacity. Both alternatives would be very costly. After a change in the top management of the company, the established diagnosis was no longer accepted. In effect, the new management decided that the cost of inadequate quality was no longer acceptable. The actual causes of the delay in a large number of concrete cases were investigated and a set of rules for handling difficult situations was drawn up. New punctuality standards were set and an intensive internal campaign was undertaken. The result was a dramatic increase in quality (punctuality) in very little time and at practically no cost at all. The main difference was that everybody now concentrated on punctuality and became aware of its importance.

Productivity and service quality in service organizations is supremely dependent on motivation and morale. As we have seen, efficient service systems are generally based on some kind of social innovation—creative ways of linking people and equipment together and creative ways of emancipating and focusing human energy. The uncritical acceptance of a given cost/quality curve may be a great mistake, because if action is taken that changes behavioural patterns and affects the whole company culture, then the entire curve itself may shift considerably. A review of the service delivery system and perhaps the creation of new types of roles may lead to new levels of quality at the same or lower cost. In the above example, for instance, a new gate-manager role was created with responsibility for punctuality at takeoff—a responsibility which had previously been divided among many people and which therefore did not really exist at all. A structural change of this kind in the service delivery system may lead to a new cost/ quality curve altogether.

Quality is not an end in itself—it is, and should clearly be seen to be, closely linked with efficiency and profitability. Figure 14.2 illustrates this relationship. Quality contributes to profitability by

Quality in order to:	Examples of effects/purposes
Define *strategic* position	Market segmentation The service concept made more precise Pricing strategy Image/feeling of belonging to a club
Increase contribution *to* and *from* personnel	Focused recruitment Instrument for increased motivation Lower personnel turnover
Increase the precision of the service delivery process (the moment of truth)	Satisfied and loyal clients Lower client turnover (facilitated 'repeat selling')

Figure 14.2 The linkage between quality and profitability

positioning a company strategically, thus defining its service concept and the associated market segment while simultaneously helping to define a suitable price strategy. Aspects of quality are therefore also a salient part of the image of the organization.

Secondly, in service companies quality has an important impact on the staff. Consistency and precision in the quality of the service can be used as a tool for raising the morale and therefore the productivity of the personnel. A product that is well adapted to the market segment, quality that is consistent and tools suited to handling clients—all these help to give employees a feeling of mastery over their situation. This in turn promotes 'virtuous circles' in the microsituation, thus improving the climate and the productivity of the organization—which is one reason why costs sometimes go down as quality goes up, especially in the case of professional services. To the extent that this helps to better the position of the company in the market for recruits, and perhaps to reduce personnel turnover, profitability will significantly improve.

Thirdly, an appropriate and consistent level of quality will make for a satisfactory and effective service delivery, and thus for satisfied customers. This should help to reduce client turnover and to improve the opportunities for repeat selling—one of the most effective ways for almost any service industry to increase its profitability.

It is important to remember that quality in a service business has long-term implications. It is difficult to build up a durable reputation for quality without long, systematic effort. And this hard-won quality image can be easily and quickly destroyed. It is an indispensable part of good quality management to form a precise and explicit idea of the relationships between the quality and profitability, in order to understand the cost and the leverage effects of quality changes.

COMMON REASONS FOR FAILURE IN QUALITY MANAGEMENT

There can, of course, be a multitude of reasons for deficient quality. After all, every rule we have proposed can be broken. At a strategic level, one of the most common failures to maintain quality stems from mixing service management systems; that is, trying to service different market segments with the same service delivery system. In the case of quality-improvement and quality-maintenance programs, however, the following appear to be the most common reasons for failure:

- *Lack of interest on the part of top management.* Without personal example and positive reinforcement of ideas from top management, quality standards are unlikely in the long run to be accepted and maintained.
- *Making quality a specialist staff problem.* It is typical of the Japanese quality-oriented management model that staffs are thin and the line is strong—a philosophy which tends to fit service organizations well. By assigning the care of quality control and quality maintenance to specialized units, a fundamentally mechanistic model has been established which destroys much of the social energy that is so essential to the functioning of service systems. The few aspects of quality that can be 'unbundled' and easily specified may have to be measured and processed and communicated by a special staff unit, but the main responsibility for quality and quality control should certainly belong to the operative units.
- *Role ambiguity,* resulting from a failure to promote between management and contact personnel the sort of social logic that is necessary to good quality in relations with the customer.

- *Lack of interest at higher levels in 'local' quality-enhancement processes.* For example, 'quality circles' will not survive unless there is some apparatus for receiving and processing and eventually acting upon the ideas and proposals which they generate. Everybody wants to see results and to know that somebody listens and is prepared to act when appropriate.
- *Failure to sustain a long-term effort.* Splendid programs may be launched for raising quality levels in record time. They may well be based on a combination of sound ideas, a charismatic leader and some effective communication tools. But there is always a risk that 'the enchantment of the first stage' will be short-lived. Unless systematic efforts are made to achieve lasting quality-enhancement and maintenance mechanisms, a backlash is only too likely.
- *Losing sight of the connection between quality, service and social innovation* and substituting a technical list of things to do instead.

SOME POINTS TO CONSIDER IN SETTING UP A QUALITY PROGRAM

Certain initial steps are important in setting up a quality program. One is to relate the concept of quality to the business as a whole—to understand clearly the impact that quality has, and could have, on the profitability of the company, according to the mechanisms mentioned above. Quality is, and should be used as, a weapon in strategy positioning.

A second step is to analyse and understand the concrete reasons why there are quality problems in the company—if there are any, and there usually are! Any quality-improvement or quality-maintenance program should include the following questions:

1. Are the quality problems caused by a lack of knowledge?
2. Are they a result of lack of motivation?
3. Are they caused by a lack of performance and quality standards?
4. Are they caused by lack of proper facilities and tools?

5. Are they caused by ambiguity between the internal culture and the demands of the client situation?

This list could easily be extended. It is perhaps interesting to note in this context that I have often been approached by service companies claiming to be uncertain whether they have any quality problems and, if so, what they are. This should not be any great problem. By far the best source for an answer is the customer, and it is seldom necessary to make an extensive customer survey. In fact many companies which devote considerable resources to such surveys seem to know the least about their customers and about their own quality problems. One very large international service company started one of the most extensive and comprehensive quality-management procedures I have ever seen by simply scrutinizing 150 letters containing customer complaints. It seems to me that going out to talk to 10 customers in the right frame of mind would usually be much more effective than sending out a questionnaire to 10 000.

A third point is more concerned with a mental framework, with an understanding that the causes and remedies for quality problems can be found at any level and in any component in the service management system. The best remedy may not always be to set up a new quality standard; instead it may be necessary to change recruitment policy, to redesign an education program or to find some way of shifting priorities or promoting new values. A change in the service management system, and in particular the possibility of social innovation, may be the most effective answer.

Any good quality-management program should be characterized by a simultaneous 'top down' and 'bottom up' approach: quality standards and quality-oriented behaviour begin with the chief executive officer, and he should be the first target for the program. Otherwise, however, programs must be designed in light of the particular problem and the culture of the individual company. Some companies in some cultures have been successful with what we have called a 'mechanistic' approach, based mainly on concrete and detailed service levels and a comprehensive system of measurements. The approach of another equally successful company with different traditions and a different culture is illustrated by the following quotation. The company had been asked how it measured service performance:

We certainly devote much effort to discussion, all through the organization, about what constitutes good quality and how you achieve it. But no, we do not measure! As soon as you bring out your rules and start to measure you change the whole culture of the organization: we believe that such an approach would give us lower quality.

I have a great deal of sympathy for this type of approach, where the emphasis is on a true understanding of what is good value in the client's terms and on activating the employees and taking steps to build quality delivery standards and capacities into the service delivery system. The danger of the more mechanistic approach, with its detailed specification of service levels, is that it bears the seed of bureaucracy. It may lead us into the famous 'vicious circle of bureaucracy', according to which precise task descriptions and minimum performance standards soon become definitive standards which breed complacency and destroy some of the dynamic force of the organization (March and Simon, 1958). By the same token, I have found that many companies that have put great effort into complying with various ISO-9000 norms have painted themselves into a corner of 'upper-level mediocrity'.

15
Culture and dominating ideas as management tools

THE ORIGINS AND FUNCTIONS OF CULTURE

All organizations, and by definition all social systems, possess a culture. Culture is the set of beliefs, norms and values which forms the basis of collaborative human behaviour and makes human actions to some extent predictable and directed towards the achievement or maintenance of some commonly accepted state. The pervasiveness and uniformity of culture may vary, but it is always there whether we want it or not.

Culture is generally fairly stable. Beliefs and values do change over time, but cultural revolutions in larger social systems are fairly rare. Culture is embedded in language, institutions, habit, social relations. Changing a culture requires a formidable effort, far beyond what is needed for relabelling certain phenomena or issuing official 'credos' (Crozier, 1964; Deal and Kennedy, 1982; Kets de Vries, 1980).

And yet, culture can be changed in business organizations, and quite effectively so, under the right circumstances.

To simplify, we can say that culture arises from two sources. The predominant source is the general environment in which an organization functions—society at large, the traditions of a particular industry, the influence of a particular technology, the set of values and beliefs associated with a specific professional group that is important to the company. Viewed in this light, culture is largely a passive product of history and context. Every industry, and every company, has something special which is unique and which can be explained by the particular circumstances under which it was conceived and developed. Most airlines have an interesting combination of military establishment and pioneering enthusiast spirit; brokers tend to have a transaction-oriented culture; and most computer service companies are struggling hard to reinterpret and even to cast off their original hardware and technology-oriented culture.

But there is no doubt that management—or in this context 'leadership' is a more appropriate term—can also be a source of culture. Given that management has effective, fresh and valid values and beliefs which are both beneficial to the business and inherently understandable to the members of the organization, and given that it possesses skill in communication and the institutionalization of such ideas, then culture can be influenced by an *act of will*.

We shall designate such conscious values, norms and beliefs stemming *from within* a company, as the company's *dominating ideas*—the guiding principles, the philosophy. A company's dominating ideas, then, are a part of culture, as well as a tool for influencing the general culture of an organization in competition with other influences. These dominating ideas enter into the 'battle of ideas' (Normann, 1977) in the company. Since it is an act of will, a tool for influencing behaviour (for the role of culture is always to influence behaviour), a company's philosophy has a normative character.

The reader will see many parallels between this definition of the concept of culture and some of the ideas attaching to the role of 'image' in the service organization as described in Chapter 10. The connection is clear: image is a communication tool, and one of the key functions of this tool may be (and usually is) to communicate culture and appropriate dominating ideas throughout the organization and often to its environment as well.

Culture and dominating ideas are always important management tools, but especially so in service organizations, for the reasons outlined in Chapter 10. The nature of the service transaction as a social process, the very dispersed character of many service organizations, the high 'personality intensity', and the intangibility of the service itself—all these reinforce the great need for rules and norms effectively internalized in individuals, for guiding day-to-day operational behaviour. Only in this way can precise, consistent and cost-effective everyday behaviour and provision of services be secured.

Culture and dominating ideas not only guide daily operational behaviour; they also structure long-term business strategy development. Recruitment and human-resource development, as well as basic guidelines for business development, are usually among the most important features of any culture. It should be clear by now that culture and dominating ideas are very practical matters, even though they may be elusive and difficult to analyse. They manifest themselves in the language used (and therefore in the thinking), in what is highly valued (and therefore in rewards, in the choice of heroes and in what is considered good or bad), and in many other practical everyday matters which have a profound and immediate effect on where people's energy is directed and how efficiently it is being used.

To make the service management system more complete, we can therefore incorporate into it the idea of guiding principles or 'normative philosophy' as depicted in Figure 15.1.

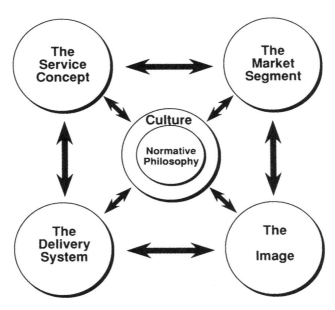

Figure 15.1   Philosophy as part of the service management system

'NEW CULTURE' COMPANIES

From personal experience and the study of successful organizations, I have identified a pattern of what seems to me to characterize the culture and management philosophies of successful service-oriented businesses. Observation of companies in many types of business, servicing a variety of customers, representing diverse service concepts and possessing different delivery systems and organizational structures has revealed *a common pattern of culture and dominating ideas*. Specifics may differ, but at a reasonable level of generalization these companies share some fundamental principles.

Starting from these observations, which admittedly have not been tested with scientific rigour, I hazard a tentative proposition: not only are the culture and normative guiding principles generally speaking a crucial success factor and a distinguishing feature of any service organization or knowledge-intensive business; there are also several specific and necessary ingredients in the culture of all such companies. Business organizations which share and effectively promote these values can appropriately be termed 'new culture' companies.

The essential elements in the philosophy of such new culture companies are the following:

1. *Orientation towards quality and excellence.* They have a strong orientation towards results and demand precision and consistency in service transactions with clients and in all aspects of the internal functioning of the company—these are both prerequisites and logical consequences of a genuine client orientation. New culture companies are not soft. They are skilled at getting the best out of people, and they do not accept mediocrity. I have often seen top managers intervene directly and visibly, paying no attention to hierarchy or formal lines of command, if they have noticed sloppiness or seen any kind of behaviour that conflicts with the philosophy of the company.

2. *Client orientation.* These companies have understood that services are not sold once and for all; rather, every aspect of the interaction with a client is part of a long-term marketing process, and repeat selling is the least expensive way of acquiring good business. They have realized that customers do not exist a priori;

rather, they are 'made' in the course of a conscious, often lengthy and laborious process, so that the client relationship represents a very considerable investment (and therefore an asset). There is no substitute for a satisfied customer.

This way of viewing the client relationship as one of the company's most vital assets is also inherent in other ingredients in the success of service organizations: for example, market segmentation, which implies a profound understanding of the precise needs and behaviour patterns of various types of customers and a genuine concern for the quality of the service transaction. With the aid of new technology, the precision can be still further refined—then each customer may be treated virtually as a 'segment in itself', a marketing approach known as quasi-individualization.

3. *Investment in people and emphasis on high social technology.* When an air-freight corporation advertises that 'People, not planes, deliver', or a bank that 'The difference in money is people', they are expressing a profound insight. Given the personality intensity of service business, there is now a strong inclination to regard people—along with the customers—as the firm's most valuable asset. Knowledge about how to handle this asset is rapidly spreading.

In this book the idea of 'social innovation' has been a recurring theme. The key to success in service businesses is always connected with the ability to identify, to mobilize and to focus human energy, for example by creating new roles or new linkages, by bringing out the energy and productivity potential of the client, by inventive recruitment, by effective communication, and by creative 'packaging' for the reproduction of knowledge and service systems. It is a distinguishing feature of new culture companies that they are skilled in this area.

In cases when really successful companies have been able to employ high social technology, we are sure to find a deep-rooted and genuine *faith in the power of human beings to develop and produce.* This becomes one of the virtuous circles we referred to in Chapter 4.

In contrast, I have seen cases in which superficially advanced human resource management techniques are apparently being applied, but where this basic trust in people is missing; sometimes there even seems to have been a fundamental hostility. The culture in such companies seems only too likely to slip gradually into a manipulative habit which can easily lead to vicious circles. I have also seen many public sector organizations where much lip-service is paid to this kind of trust but where it obviously does not exist and no demands are made on people—there is no real belief that the people might live up to the demands.

In any discussion of social technology the theme of communication must be mentioned. New culture companies are skilled in communication. I have mentioned the virtues of visible management, and it seems that this kind of management works best at communicating the dominating ideas when it is composed of two somewhat paradoxical elements. One of these could be termed *'management by simplicity'*, and is characterized by extremely clear and simple signals about the few key norms and standards that bring success. The other, for lack of a better term, I will call *'management by magic'*. This stands for the ability somehow to penetrate people's emotions and to create a social reality in the company that is beyond the rational and the ordinary—a social reality that *resonates.* At its best, it helps to focus the attention and engage the emotions so that people recognize what they are doing as an exciting part of their lifestyle. As Ramirez (1987) would put it, leadership gives an organization its 'aesthetic' dimensions.

Naturally it is not only *social* technology that is important. 'Hard' technology is a crucial basis for the development of service industries. And in fact 'hard' and 'social' technologies are very closely linked. For example, as information technology moves ahead, the challenges and the need for even more advanced 'social technology' cannot but grow. Thus the 'high-tech/hi-touch' proposition which Naisbitt introduced in his book *Megatrends* (1982) is both well founded and well expressed.

4. *'Small is beautiful on a large scale'.* Another consequence of this constellation—excellence orientation, client orientation and faith in human beings—in combination with high social technology is that control systems in new culture organizations tend to be extremely rigorous with regard to factors vital to success in the client relationship, while perhaps remaining informal and relatively 'soft' in other respects. This correlates with our earlier observation that good service companies seem to be both strongly decentralized and

centralized *at the same time,* and that in this way it is possible to arrive at a situation in which 'small is beautiful on a large scale'.

5. *Strong focus but broad perspectives.* A company that concentrates on giving the client value for money, and on tailoring its services to a particular category of clients, will automatically focus on and identify with its market segments. It chooses its market, thereby forswearing certain opportunities; it intentionally opts to unfocus from other client categories and business areas, mobilizing all its resources and energy to achieve maximum excellence in its chosen field or fields. However, this does not mean that the company is unaware of what is happening in society at large, or in alternative business areas. Focus is the result of active choice, not myopia. Constant monitoring and prospecting activities are undertaken to understand important trends and possibilities in society, but there is no ambiguity, no dilution of effort into areas which cannot be handled with excellence.

Naturally it is not enough simply to have a good set of guiding principles—dominating ideas. Skill is also needed to implement it—skill in creating a coherent and effective service management system. Not only must the dominating ideas be unique to the specific company, but also they must embrace these new culture elements and fit together in a congruent way.

These themes have been around for a number of years and clearly empirical observation confirms their validity. They seem, however, to defy the application of formulas. Peters and Waterman's book, *In Search of Excellence* (1993), translated many of these themes into normative rules. We have observed many companies which have attempted to implement such rules to little positive effect; obviously it takes more than making such themes explicit. The inertia of an existing culture is high. The personnel, the structure, the norms, the rewards and the heroes mirror the culture. The introduction of new rules very often triggers an organizational 'immune response'. If these 'new culture elements' are to be effectively integrated into the operative culture of an organization, then they must be accompanied by an internal change strategy which moves internal norms and practices unequivocally into alignment with the new rules. The importance of change strategies and leadership is addressed in Chapter 16.

16
Change and leadership

DIAGNOSIS AND OVERALL INTERVENTION STRATEGY

The service management system in itself represents a powerful diagnostic scheme for analysing the problems of service and knowledge-oriented organizations. For another angle, the three levels of virtuous or vicious circles described in Chapter 4 complement this scheme, depicting the dynamics of the way the system functions.

Employing these schemes, it can be useful to establish at an early stage whether the problems of a particular service organization stem mainly from the *operations* system or whether they are also of a *strategic* nature. It is not always easy to distinguish between these two sources, partly because the most important ingredient in the strategy of a service organization is not uncommonly an innovative formula for implementation in operations. Quite often, however, the basic strategy of a service organization—consisting of its basic market segmentation, its basic service concepts and so on—is reasonably good, while definite problems can be distinguished in operations management and in the design of the service delivery systems.

No two interventions or change processes are ever the same. In the following pages I shall briefly describe at an analytical level some typical change and growth strategies which, given the right circumstances, can be successful. We can then return to discussion of the actual *process of change*.

BOOSTING EFFICIENCY AND THE QUALITY OF OPERATIONS (THE 'INDUSTRIAL MODEL')

Traditional industrial productivity thinking is certainly not dead—on the contrary; and it can often be applied with great advantage to service organizations. A couple of well-publicized examples are the two large financial service institutions Citibank (now Citigroup) and American Express. Here, as well as in many other companies, big increases in productivity and service quality, and in the end even far-reaching developments in service concepts, have resulted from asking questions such as: What do customers complain about? What are the various activities involved in supplying this service or that one? What steps in our process could we co-ordinate, improve, eliminate?

An apparently traditional approach of this kind is useful when a company's overall strategy is sound, but the Citibank experience among others demonstrates clearly that starting such a process can have considerable repercussions on the whole company. In the Citibank case new types of market segmentation, a new organizational structure, new supporting technology and new kinds of roles were among the most prominent results, and the whole process took several years.

CULTURE SHOCK AND 'LIFT'

This intervention strategy is again best suited to companies with ailing operations but sound strategies. To take a well-known example, the reversal of trends at United Airlines as a result of 'visible management' (Carlson, 1975) is a case in point. An active mobilization of human resources on the part of a new management and a general tightening-up in the company gave the necessary boost to efficiency.

Lately, however, there have been a few cases of shock treatment strategies and 'cultural revolutions' in service organizations which have been misunderstood. For example, many managers were led to believe that a key factor in the great upturn of the Scandinavian Airlines System in the early 1980s was the much-publicized 'service course' attended by about 12 000 contact personnel within a very short time. This interpretation of events is mistaken not only because the course—an excellent one of its kind—was merely one of over 100 concrete and interrelated measures; it is also a thoroughly dangerous strategy to apply if the *real* problem in a company is not confined to the operations but has also penetrated the strategic level. If, for example, the market segmentation or the service concepts or the basic design of the service delivery systems need to be revised, then a program that concentrates on giving the staff a 'lift' by providing a 'service course for contact personnel' and similar arrangements may simply serve as a dangerous tranquillizer for top management, while the fundamental problems continue in all their disruptive force.

DEVELOPMENT OF THE SERVICE MANAGEMENT SYSTEM: A STRUCTURAL APPROACH

If the strategy of a company is ailing, then what is needed is a combination of the 'shock' or 'lift' treatment and a structural approach. *Service concepts* and *organization* and *delivery systems* need to be reviewed in the context of innovative *market segmentation.*

The above-mentioned case of the Scandinavian Airlines—now a well known and much-quoted example which later was more or less copied by British Airways—in fact comes closer to this situation than to the previous one. It would be an exaggeration to say that the strategy of SAS was subjected to a revolutionary change, but there was a very strong refocusing on a neglected market segment (the businessman) which also implied a conscious decision to reduce the focus on other market segments. The aim was to design a sharply defined service concept and a corresponding service delivery system for the businessman, with a crystal-clear image to complete the picture. The shock treatment, based on high social technology and the extremely effective communication of a new philosophy, was applied within this overall context of strategic change; one part of the change strategy would not have worked without the other.

STRATEGIC GROWTH

Fortunately, intervention is not always geared to dealing with problems; sometimes it is also a question of working on growth and
seizing business opportunities. But growth in a service organization
often implies some powerful intervention, which may well threaten
the equilibrium of a well-functioning streamlined service management system. We have already discussed some of the basic
conditions for successful *reproduction, diversification* and *internationalization.* Another common growth strategy is *customer-
oriented systems development;* i.e. adding peripheral services and
perhaps even new core services to the service on offer to a client or
a category of clients. All these strategies have to be applied with
very great sensitivity, so that they accord with the existing culture
of the organization (if it is a good one), and with an awareness of
the possible danger to an established service management system.

LEADERS AND LEADERSHIP STYLES

Two types of successful leader can be seen in service companies;
those who have grown up with, or even themselves developed, the
business, and those who have a special ability to arouse energy
and enthusiasm in other people. And best of all is a combination
of the two.

This corresponds closely with the idea of 'two-front selling'
which we have touched upon several times. To be successful the
service company must market itself to its clients and to its personnel, and good leadership in a service company calls for an ability
to understand the viewpoint of both 'markets'. Not a few successful service business leaders are greatly influenced in their perception of the business by trying to assume the role of consumer
themselves: buying one's own company's services incognito is not
an altogether uncommon custom.

But perhaps the most striking quality of service business
leaders in general is an ability to motivate their personnel and to
act as change agents in their own organizations. The following list
includes some of the action patterns that I have observed among
such leaders *(also compare* Johnsen, 1983).

Setting standards. A matter of crucial importance in any service company is to set standards of quality and to see that they are strictly followed. Standards usually apply not only to performance as such but also to behaviour and style. The idea that 'working in this company is a lifestyle' is quite a common one among the employees of service companies.

Evaluating people. Successful service business leaders tend to be skilful at judging what people are motivated to do, how much energy they are willing to put in, what their long-term ambitions are, and their capabilities. Many leaders, realizing how much the success of their company depends on the performance of individual people, are fully aware of this situation and have developed their own methods of evaluating. For example, when we asked how he evaluated people, one service business leader replied:

Well, I employ them and then I give them much too much to do, and then I see how they handle this impossible situation, and particularly how they set their priorities.

Promoting role models. Setting standards and working out methods of evaluation is important; communicating these standards and the desired behaviour effectively to other people is just as vital. Many leaders find that the best way of communicating the desired standards and behaviour is to choose good examples, or role models, and then to display them to all those concerned. This is what happens all the time in a great many service organizations, for instance in a hotel which chooses 'the employee of the month'. An exercise of this sort serves the dual function of displaying desirable behaviour, and thus setting standards, and of being part of the reward system.

Displaying role models is especially necessary when a change in strategy and therefore in behaviour is under way. In an insurance company where traditional specialization according to functions and products was being replaced by 'the iron law of client orientation', a new type of role had to be created. Consequently, an intensive campaign of internal promotion, external recruitment and education was launched in order to discover as soon as possible a few people who would be able to act according to the new strategy. Analysing and displaying the behaviour of these people internally was a crucial way of getting employees throughout the organization to understand the real essence of the new strategy and thus feel genuinely committed to it. In a large housing management company with many local units and very uneven standards of behaviour, one of the key instruments of change was identifying and displaying employees who were genuinely successful.

Setting a code of conduct by way of personal behaviour. The code of conduct established by the leader himself, both in detail and in broad lines, will serve as an essential role model. Good service leaders are extremely conscious of their own behaviour and priorities and of how these are perceived by the employees. One rarely sees a successful company whose leader openly demonstrates his lack of interest in the details of the business, or who lets it be seen that he is more interested in long-term diversification, for example, than in the quality of the service his company provides.

Defining the barricades. In a successful service company, the service management system is characterized by a few key factors which must function properly and which must be rigorously maintained. The successful leader loses no opportunity for communicating these factors to the whole company, and so in a sense he is constantly defining the position of the barricades. Nobody should be in doubt about what leads to success. In the same way, the leader can define and re-emphasize the company's special role in society, reminding his audience of those who are hostile to the goals and values which the company represents.

The actual style of communication may vary from one leader to another. Some keep a low profile, while others like to be very noticeable and sometimes even theatrically so. But some kind of 'visible management' which indicates where the company's battlefields are to be found is vital. Thus, successful leadership styles often involve the top manager in the heavy task of communicating directly with almost all employees, even in large companies. He or she may do it at institutionalized local meetings, in internal company magazines, by way of video films, or in various other ways. Many means of communication are available, and there are many different 'stages' on which to perform. Some very effective leaders actually choose to communicate with their own personnel by frequent appearances in magazine and newspaper interviews, for example, simply because they know this is to be a very efficient way of reaching them (although we have seen leaders involved in flashy publicity campaigns to less functional advantage).

When a new leader arrives in an ailing company, his or her strategy and new style often involve the identification of some feature or features of the service management system which are not working properly, followed by the vigorous promotion of knowledge and value associated with just those areas. For example, the new managing director of an insurance company which had been losing vital ground identified the company's poor and uneven client relationships and its dwindling reputation as being the key problems; his first move was thus to reorganize and centralize all handling of claims. Although to start with this was a bureaucratic and costly move, it was exceedingly effective in communicating standards and promoting new types of behaviour, and it was much easier subsequently for the new leader to launch a constructive program of improvement on other fronts—mostly in connection with the handling of client relationships.

TRANSFORMING THE VICIOUS CIRCLE INTO A VIRTUOUS ONE: THE ROLE OF MANAGEMENT

The conception of the service company as a set of interrelated dynamic processes which tend to take the form of virtuous or vicious circles provides a key to understanding the role of management in a change process. The areas of intervention are defined by the diagnosis of the problems according to the service management system model; but a good analysis and well thought out ideas about what needs to be changed will not automatically produce the social dynamic needed to distinguish the vicious circle from the virtuous one.

To bring about effective change, the leader—and management in general—must quickly establish their *credibility* in the organization. Charisma and a touch of magic may be helpful but are not enough. A good way to establish the credibility of a management and of a change strategy is to aim at some form of *early, visible success,* albeit on a limited scale. For example, when an airline rose from a position far down on the list to become the most punctual airline in Europe in only a few months, the staff realized that at least something had been achieved, and it subsequently became much easier to defend a new strategy and philosophy that differed radically from the established ones. Change strategies at Citigroup and American Express are similarly nurtured and reinforced by limited early successes in meeting more stringent quality standards, which among other things attracted new customers.

One of the most difficult things for management to bring about is the 'middle circle', the internal service circle. It seems that to begin with change processes in service organizations tend to assume an hourglass structure. It is possible for a strong management with good and viable ideas to convince a leading group at the top that change and a new philosophy are needed. And although efforts will be needed, it can also be surprisingly easy to convince the contact personnel to act in new ways, especially if they can be given new tools which will evoke virtuous feedback from customers and open the way to a 'virtuous circle'. It is often much more difficult to create the same involvement in the middle echelons of the organization, however, and thus a good deal of ambiguity and inconsistent behaviour often characterizes the service organization during a period of major change.

There is no short-cut to creating the virtuous internal service circle. All the tools we have discussed must be applied with energy and combined with effective communication to promote consistent behaviour throughout all levels of the organization. Meanwhile, management must exploit and reinforce everything positive that arises from the relationship between contact personnel and customers while also assuming a posture of extreme sensitivity. Management listens for signals anywhere in the organization, and acts on them as required.

References

Andersson, Å. and Strömquist, U., 1988, *K-samhällets framtid*, Stockholm: Prisma.

Berger, P.L. and Luckman, T., 1967, *The Social Construction of Reality*, Anchoridge: Doubleday.

Business Week, 1980, The US lead in service exports is under siege, 15 September.

Business Week, 1987, 5 October, p.52.

Carlson, E.E., 1975, Visible management at United Airlines, *Harvard Business Review*, July–August.

Carman, J. and Langeard, E., 1981, Growth strategies for service firms, *Strategic Management Journal*, No. 1.

Chase, R.B., 1978, Where does the customer fit in a service operation?, *Harvard Business Review*, November–December.

Crozier, M., 1964, *The Bureaucratic Phenomenon*, Chicago: University of Chicago Press.

Crozier, M., 1982, *On ne Change pas la Société par Decret*, Paris: Grasset.

Davis, S.M., 1987, *Future Perfect*, New York: Addison-Wesley.

Deal, T.E. and Kennedy, A.A., 1982, *Corporate Cultures*, Reading, Mass.: Addison-Wesley.

de Geer, H. *et al.*, 1985, *I framtidens kölvatten (In the Wake of the Future)*, Stockholm: Liber

Duggan, B.G., 1988, *Inside Guide*, Winter, Canadian International Airlines.

Dupuy, F., 1999, *Le client et le bureaucrate*, Paris: Dunod

Eiglier, P. and Langeard, E., 1975, Une approache nouvelle du marketing des services, *Revue Française de Gestion*, November.

Eiglier, P. and Langeard, E., 1977, Le marketing des entreprises de service, *Revue Française de Gestion*, March–April.

Foster, R.N., 1986, *Innovation: The Attacker's Advantage*, New York: Summit Books.

Grönroos, C., 1982, *Strategic Management and Marketing in the Service Sector*, Helsinki: Svenska Handelshögskolan.

Johnsen, E., 1983, En teori om ledelse av serviceföretag, in *Danmark som Services-amfund*, Copenhagen: Tidens förlag.

Kets de Vries, F.R., 1980, *Organizational Paradoxes*, London: Tavistock.

Langeard, E., 1981a, Dienstleistungs marketing, Munich, *Marketing, Zeitschrift für Forschung und Praxis*, November.

Langeard, E, 1981b, La stratégie marketing des services aux entreprises, in *L'action Marketing des Entreprises Industrielles,* Collection ADETEM Marketing Demain.

Langeard, E., Bateson, J.E.G., Lovelock, C. and Eiglier, P., 1981, *Service Marketing: New Insights from Consumers and Managers,* Boston, Mass: Marketing Science Institute.

Langeard, E. and Laban, J., 1981, *Service Novateurs et Comportement du Consommateur,* 3ème Séminaire Comportement du Consommateur et Distribution des Biens et Services, Rennes: Université de Rennes.

Lehtinen, J.R., 1983, *Asiakasohjautuva Palveluyritys,* Tapiola: Welin and Göös.

Levinson, D., 1978, *The Seasons of a Man's Life,* New York: Ballantine.

Levitt, T., 1972, Production-line approach to service, *Harvard Business Review,* September–October.

Lovelock, C.H. and Young, R.F., 1979, Look to consumers to increase productivity, *Harvard Business Review,* May–June.

March, J.G. and Simon, H.A., 1958, *Organizations,* New York: Wiley.

Maturana, H.R. and Varela, F.J., 1987, *The Tree of Knowledge,* Boston and London: Shambhala (Revised edition 1998).

Meyer, H.E., 1980, How Fingerhut beat the recession, *Fortune,* 17 November.

Naisbitt, J., 1982, *Megatrends,* New York: Warner.

Nordfors, L. and Levin, B., 1999, *Internetrevolutioner (Internet Revolutions),* Ekerlids Förlag.

Normann, R., 1977, *Management for Growth,* Chichester: Wiley.

Normann, R., 1980, *Förbättrad Samhällsservice,* Stockholm: SAF.

Normann, R., 1982, Kritiska faktorer vid ledning av serviceföretag, in J. Arndt and A. Friman, *Ledning, Produktion & Marknadsföring av Tjänster,* Stockholm: Liber (taken from 'Utvecklingsstrategier för Svenskt Service Kunnande', SIAR, 1978).

Normann, R. and Ramirez, R., 1994, *Designing Interactive Strategy,* (Revised edition 1998), Chichester: Wiley

Normann, R., Cederwall, L., Edgren, L. and Holst, A., 1989, *The Dance of the Invaders (Invadörernas Dans),* Malmö, Sweden: Liber.

Ouchi, W.G., 1981, *Theory Z—how American business can meet the Japanese challenge,* Reading, Mass: Addison-Wesley.

Peters, T.J. and Waterman, R.H., Jr, 1983, *In Search of Excellence,* New York: Harper & Row.

Ramirez, R., 1987, *Towards an Aesthetic Theory of Social Organization,* Ph.D. dissertation, University of Pennsylvannia.

Rosenbaum, B.L., 1982, *How to Motivate Today's Worker,* New York: McGraw-Hill.

Sasser, E.W., Olsen, P.R. and Wyckoff, D.D., 1978, *Management of Service Operations,* Boston, Mass.: Alleyn & Bacon.

Schneider, B., 1980, *The Service Organization: Climate is Crucial,* New York: AMACON.

Sheehy, G., 1974, *Passages,* New York: Knopf.

The Economist, 1999, 18 September, p.29.

Toffler, A., 1980, *The Third Wave,* New York: Collins.

Wilson, A., 1972, *The Marketing of Professional Services,* London: McGraw-Hill.

Zeleny, M., 1978, *Towards Self-Service Society,* New York: Columbia University Press.

Index

Accor 183, 187
affinity linking 188
airlines 26, 41, 42, 53, 59, 63–5, 68, 94,
    102, 118, 130, 163, 186, 202, 203,
    208
American Express 186, 198, 222, 228
Apple 3
ARA 189
Atlas Copco 154
Avis 154

balance of trade 16
banking 12, 27, 34, 40, 41, 79, 83, 98,
    104, 129, 133, 154–5, 163, 180, 182
Benetton 177
Berger, P.E. 149
Berlitz 171
BMW 15
Bocuse, Paul 130
Boeing 25
Booz Allen and Hamilton 184
Borel, Jacques 183–4, 187
Boulding, K. 149
broker function 169
business life cycle 89, 169–70, 164
Business Week 36, 190

Cable & Wireless 107
Carlson, E.E. 222
Carlzon, J. 159
Carman, J. 172
Chase, R.B. 117
circles
    internal service 70–71, 228
    interrelationships 71–72
    macrocircles 68, 69–70

microcircles 68–9
vicious circles 61, 62, 125, 182, 213,
    227–8
virtuous circles 62, 64, 118, 125, 153,
    195, 196, 201, 209, 227–8
Citigroup 221, 228
client, and productivity
    as critical assets 24, 186, 218
    creation 124–8
    integration 140, 201
    management 54–5, 124, 164, 201
    orientation 150, 217–18
    participation 28, 35–6, 54–5,
        115–120, 129, 131, 195
        functions of
            co-production 48, 51, 68, 118
            'maintenance of ethos' 118
            quality control 118, 130,
                199–201
            specification of the service
                117–18, 120, 166, 191
        modes of
            emotional 117, 119
            intellectual 117, 119
            physical 117, 119
Club Méditerranée 12, 26, 29, 95, 141,
    180
Coco-Cola Corporation 36
Compaq 3
computer industry 102
Cornell University 107
cost, and quality 207–10
    efficiency 208
    rationalization 138
cost-control dilemma 179, 207
Croc, Ray 173–4

Crozier, M. 52, 214
culture 182, 187, 199
    and a service company 55–7, 60, 108
    origins and functions of 214–16

Davis, Stanley M. 7
Deal, T.E. 214
Decaux, Jean-Claude 26, 28–30, 46, 51,
    56, 83, 142
DeLorean, John 156
Denmark 93
diagnosis 207–8, 221
    evaluating people 225
    growth problems 172
    virtuous circles and vicious circles
        61–74
    technology monitoring 170
Dior, Christian 20
Disney World 107, 141
diversification
    and internationalization 173, 181–3
    types of
        client-based 185–6
        knowledge-based 187–8
        main and auxiliary services 186
        synergy 185
dominating, ideas 59, 215
Duggan, B.G. 42
Dupoy, F. 110

economy
    agricultural 1–2, 4, 5–6
    formal 2, 5, 13, 89
    industrial 1–2, 4, 7, 10, 43
    informal 2, 5, 8, 89
    sectoral matrix 4
    service 2, 4, 43
EF Education 26, 30–2, 34, 46, 52–3, 54,
    70, 94, 114, 130, 171, 175, 178, 200
Eiglier, P. 18, 60, 119, 124
ESIF 3, 137

F International 32
FA-Rådet 3
Federal Express 26, 34
Fingerhut 133
Foster, R.N. 170
Future Perfect 7

General Motors 20, 156
gentils organisateurs 29, 95, 141
Grönroos, C. 157

Hard Rock Café 26
Harvard Business School 18
health care 2, 15, 26, 41, 43, 53, 57, 173
Holiday Inn 107, 176
hospitality industry 12, 32–3, 96–7, 102,
    173–4
human resource development 89–105,
    106–14
    career development 29, 94
    complements to basic careers 96–8
    exits 99, 113–14
    focused personnel ideas 100–01
    job design 112–13
    life stage transition 92–3, 94–5, 98–9
    people who have 'fallen between two
        stools' 95–6
    recruitment 72, 206, 216
    reinforcement 111–12, 153
    service universities 107, 123
    social mobility 93–4
    temporary personnel ideas 98–9
    training 107–111
    unrewarding environments 98

IBM 2, 9, 20, 123
iceberg principle 124–7
IKEA 34, 142, 155, 176–7
image 60, 111, 130, 149–60, 172–3, 185,
    187, 188–9, 196, 209, 215
    determinants 15, 150–2
    functions and target groups 152–6
    management 149–50
immune response 220
In Search of Excellence 220
Independent 154–5
information technology 3, 20, 27, 32, 40,
    53, 59, 110, 133–4, 136–8, 189
    effects of 137–8
    functions of 137
'instant mini-delivery' 127
insurance industry 12, 25, 28, 34, 35, 40,
    41, 83, 84, 85–6, 91, 104, 111, 154,
    158–9, 163, 182
internal marketing 153, 156–60
International Service System (ISS) 93,
    183
internationalization of services 16–17,
    181–96
    breakthrough, conditions of 194–5
Internet 26, 143–4, 147
    bank 139, 180

Johnsen, E. 224

Kennedy, A.A. 214
Kets de Vries, F.R. 150, 214
know-how 44, 86, 126
    transfer of 25, 27, 83–4
knowledge 7–8, 36–9, 84, 90, 129, 187
    transfer of 27, 43, 179

Laban, J. 129
Langeard, E. 18, 60, 117, 119, 124, 129,
    172
leadership 221–8
    styles 224–7
Lehtinen, J.R. 129
Levin, B. 144
Levinson, D. 94
Levitt, T. 20
Linguaphone 171
Lion King, The 12–13
Little, Arthur D. 172
Loiseau, Bernard 13, 173
Lovelock, C.H. 116, 117, 124
Luckman, T. 149

maintenance industry 12, 96, 100–01,
    118, 142, 182, 200
management, and a service and a
        company
    'management by magic' 219
    management by simplicity' 219
    Japanese approach 132, 206
    versus manufacturing management
        8–11, 19
manufacturing industry vs service
        industry 7–8
    value adding logic 9
March 213
marketing orientation 9
Marsh & McLennan 107
McDonald's 12, 15, 22, 26, 32, 33, 57, 77,
    107, 118, 130, 133, 139, 161–2,
    173–5, 177, 178, 198, 200
McKesson 26, 46–9, 53, 54, 56, 136, 137,
    189
McKinsey & Co. 12, 15, 99
Maturana, H.R. 149
Megatrends 219
Merrill Lynch 186
Meyer, H.E. 133
moment of truth 20–1, 68–9, 90, 106,
    201, 205
moral dilemma 104–5

Naisbitt, J. 8, 219

network effects 12, 26, 33, 79, 81, 176
new values, new problems and new
        lifestyles 33
NK-Ahlens 187
Nordfors, L. 144
Normann, R. 11, 17, 20, 42, 60, 187, 215

Olsen, P.R. 18, 79
Ouchi, W.G. 197

personality intensity 21–3, 59, 61, 218
personnel
    economic equation 24
    motivation 91
    personnel idea 91–3, 95–105, 153, 195
Peters, T.J. 220
Porter, M. 39
Praktikertjanst 56
pricing 88, 130, 161–8, 198
profitability and quality 208–9
public sector 17
public service systems, problem of 180

Ramirez. R. 11, 119
RCA Corporation 2
reproduction of services 27, 57, 58, 188
Retravailler 175
role ambiguity 205, 210
role design 35–6, 112
role models 225–6
Rosenbaum, B.L. 108

S-shaped growth curve 169–71
Sasser, E.N. 18, 79
scale effects 11–12, 32–3, 56–7, 81, 176,
    188
Scandinavian Airlines System (SAS)
    130, 155, 159–60, 187, 222–3
Scandinavian countries 17
Schneider, B. 70, 110, 204
Sears & Roebuck 186
sectoral matrix 4
security industry 22, 36, 84, 166, 182
segmentation, market 25, 37, 58, 88, 130,
    162, 165, 172, 177, 206, 223
self-service 8, 25, 28, 115, 119, 123, 183
service delivery, individualizing
    132–3
service delivery system
    functions of 138–43
    and service concept 86–8, 170–1,
        198–9

subcomponents of 59, 91–2
service economy, logics of 13, 46
   broadening 40–1, 46–9
   enabling-relieving 42–3, 47, 48,
       120–2
   relationing 40
   service loading 39
   un-bundling 41–2, 47, 86, 164, 166–7,
       207
service-idea families' 188–9
service industry vs manufacturing
       industry 19
service innovation
   driving forces 8, 26
       external 26, 27, 33–4
       internal 28–33
service management systems 46–60,
       84–5, 172, 223
   components of 149
   disturbance in functioning 181
   driving forces 26–34
   key success determinants 18, 24–6,
       58, 179
   'the single logic' 174
service package
   and customer expectations 76–8, 165
   code of conduct 226
   composition 18–20, 55–7, 79–82,
       129–30
   core services 58, 75–9, 120, 224
   design of 65
   peripheral services 75–9, 86, 120, 177,
       182, 224
service production/co-production 20,
       38, 51–2, 118, 137
service quality 88, 118, 207–10, 217
   control 139, 175, 184, 197–8
   design of 81, 129–30, 139, 197,
       199–200, 202, 205–7, 224
   program 206–7, 211–13
   quality circles 206
   reasons for failure 210–11
service society 1, 3
Service Master 35, 93
services
   characteristics of service
       organisations 18–20
   industrialization of services 11–13
Sheehy, G. 94

Simon, H.A. 213
'small is beautiful on a large scale' 57,
       219–220
SMG 10, 35
social innovation 26, 173, 180, 198, 208,
       218
   client participation 28
   new linkages 27, 52–4, 83
   new sources of human energy 27, 30,
       32, 92
   role sets 27, 29, 32
status, service industry 14–16
strategies 43, 211
   of change and growth 89, 90, 181
   pricing 164, 166, 168
   reproduction formula 162, 172, 174
Sweden 3, 6, 10, 17, 96, 193
Swissair 97
synergy 183, 185

technical innovation 26, 27, 44
technology
   introducing new 147–8
   transforming 136
time, use of, in services 7, 11
Toffler, A. 8, 115
transportation industry 10–11
Treaty of Rome 17
Troisgros 46, 49–51, 51, 55, 77, 97, 118,
       133, 173, 202

USA 6, 17

value creation 10, 14, 24, 33, 35, 37, 40,
       162
Varela, F.J. 149
Volvo 9, 35

Waterman 220
Weight Watchers 26, 85, 180
West Germany 6–7
Wilson, A. 126, 168
Wyckoff, D.D. 18, 79

Xerox 123, 146

Young, R.F. 116, 117, 124

Zeleny, M. 115